THE REFERENCE SHELF   VOLUME 38 NUMBER 2

THE
RUSSIAN-CHINESE
RIFT

ITS IMPACT ON WORLD AFFAIRS

EDITED BY
IRWIN ISENBERG
Senior Editor, Foreign Policy Association

THE H. W. WILSON COMPANY
NEW YORK   **1966**

THE REFERENCE SHELF

The books in this series contain reprints of articles, excerpts from books, and addresses on current issues and social trends in the United States and other countries. There are six separately bound numbers in each volume, all of which are generally published in the same calendar year. One number is a collection of recent speeches; each of the others is devoted to a single subject and gives background information and discussion from various points of view, concluding with a comprehensive bibliography.

Subscribers to the current volume receive the books as issued. The subscription rate is $12 ($15 foreign) for a volume of six numbers. Single numbers are $3 each.

PREFACE

Of all the events which have shaken the Communist world since the death of Stalin in March 1953, none has had a greater impact on the course of international relations than the growth of the rift between the Soviet Union and China. Dissent, however muted, has always been present in the Communist world. Mao Tse-tung and Stalin had differences over strategy in the years when the Chinese Communists were waging their civil war against the Nationalist army of Chiang Kai-shek. In 1948, Yugoslavia refused to accept Soviet domination and was expelled from the Communist camp in a hail of bitter invective. But it was not until Stalin disappeared from the scene that the Communist monolith began to show serious signs of cracking.

The East Berliners rebelled briefly in June 1953. Khrushchev made his secret speech denouncing Stalin in February 1956. Some eight months later the Polish government demanded—and received—a greater degree of freedom from Soviet control. Several days after Poland's "victory" Hungary erupted in revolt against Communist rule and was bloodily suppressed.

As these events occurred, Chinese confidence in the wisdom of Soviet leadership was severely shaken. These doubts burst into headlines in the late 1950's and early 1960's when Peking launched an attack upon a broad range of Moscow's doctrinal stands. But the schism did not spring simply from ideological carpings. It was also based on a deep conflict of interests and aspirations between Peking and Moscow.

As a mighty industrial power with a rising standard of living, the Soviet Union has a vested interest in avoiding a major conflict, which could jeopardize all Moscow has gained over so many years of backbreaking effort. China, in the first stages of economic development and with major territorial ambitions beyond its borders, is more willing to follow a belligerent foreign policy. Even if Moscow and Peking agree on the ultimate goal—which is to see communism triumphant everywhere—they are in basic disagreement on the most desirable path toward that end.

These differences have produced a new climate in international relations. Moscow and Peking have been competing for influence throughout the world. The competition has been particularly sharp in the underdeveloped countries. The rift has also affected almost every Communist party, with most of them having their pro-Soviet and pro-Chinese factions.

Partly as a result of the rift, the smaller Communist countries have had an opportunity for maneuver and a chance to play off Moscow against Peking. Albania, for instance, jumped into the Chinese camp because it feared that Soviet offers of friendship with Yugoslavia might result in a deal whereby the Yugoslavs, with Moscow's approval, would encroach upon Albanian territory. Rumania rejected Soviet plans for the integration of the East European economies and Moscow apparently chose not to apply all the pressure it could have, perhaps because it feared that this might cost it Rumanian support in the split. As it was, Rumania showed more sympathy for the Chinese position than the Soviet Union would have liked.

The rift has not only given a new look to the Communist world. It has provoked new directions in Western policy. While Chinese hostility toward the United States has, if anything, increased, Washingon and Moscow have been flirting with various methods of relaxing tension. There are those who even foresee an eventual link between the Soviet Union and the United States directed against China.

The articles in this book trace the development of the rift, consider what its impact on world affairs has been, and discuss possible Western policy responses. The editor wishes to thank the authors and publishers who have granted their permission for the use of the materials presented in this volume.

IRWIN ISENBERG

April 1966

A Note to the Reader

For material on how the split has affected the Communist states of Eastern Europe, the reader should consult *Ferment in Eastern Europe,* published in 1965 (The Reference Shelf, Volume 37, Number 1).

CONTENTS

Communist states that support Russia **Communist state neutral in issue**

NORWAY
FINLAND
North Sea
SWEDEN
DENMARK
Baltic Sea
Moscow
NETH.
EAST GERMANY
POLAND
SOVIET UNION
BEL
WEST GERMANY
CZECH.
SWITZ.
AUSTRIA
HUNGARY
RUMANIA
YUGOSLAVIA
Black Sea
ITALY
BULGARIA
ALBANIA
GREECE
TURKEY
Mediterranean Sea
TUNISIA
0   500 Mi.

From "Communist Split: as Both Sides See It," by Harry Schwartz. New York Times. p E5. Mr. 14, '65. © 1965 by The New York Times Company. Reprinted by permission.

THE SPLIT IN COMMUNISM

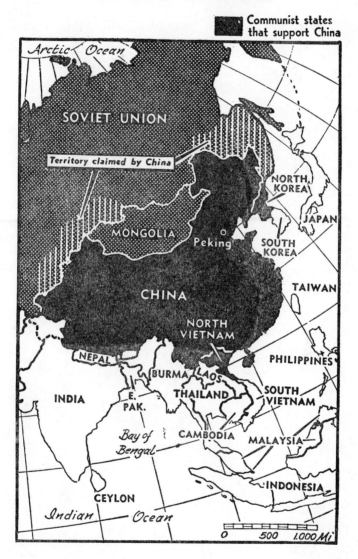

I. RISE AND FALL OF THE MONOLITH

EDITOR'S INTRODUCTION

For several years many Westerners suspected that the Sino-Soviet rift was a dangerous and deceptive maneuver designed to induce the anti-Communist world to relax its guard. These suspicions stemmed from the belief that Marxists, subscribing to a common creed, could not be split by ideological or other differences.

This fallacy has now been laid to rest. The split has not necessarily made the Communist world any less menacing. But it has shown that the Communist alliance has been unable to withstand the pressures and strains rising from the conflicting interests of its member states. This is saying no more than the Communist alliance has experienced that which all alliances experience—the erosion brought on by changing times.

This section surveys the course of the rift in the Communist world. The first article offers a brief view of communism's disarray. The author makes the point that the imposition of monolithic uniformity under Soviet control proved to be incompatible with the needs and problems of the various countries which came under Communist control after World War II.

The next article reviews the military, political, and economic links which Moscow and Peking formed after 1949, when the Chinese Communists won control of China, and then recalls the origins of the Sino-Soviet rift. The following piece, by W. E. Griffith, offers a detailed account of the development of the schism and an authoritative analysis of the behind-the-scenes activities which took place among the Communist parties. Malcolm Mackintosh discusses the military aspects of the dispute, giving special attention to the role of the atomic bomb in the rift. He speculates on the possibility of war between the Soviet Union and China. Finally, Richard Lowenthal probes the factors of unity and conflict in Sino-Soviet relations. He stresses that the basic interests of the two countries tend to be in opposition.

Whatever the future course of the rift, the articles in this section would seem to indicate that the days of Stalinist uniformity are unlikely to be seen again. In fact, China's refusal to attend the twenty-third Soviet party congress in the spring of 1966 moved Peking and Moscow closer to an open break than ever before. What this could mean in terms of Western policy options is a subject to be discussed in succeeding sections.

A WORLD IN DISARRAY [1]

For almost a quarter century, from 1929 until 1953, international communism was characterized first and foremost by monolithic unity. All the Communist parties of the world (with the exception, since 1948, of the Yugoslav one) were subordinated to Stalin's leadership in Moscow. Every political shift of the Kremlin was obeyed by Communist parties from Germany to Indonesia. One nod from Moscow was all that was needed to remove a displeasing leader and to appoint a desirable one; one phrase in a Soviet article was enough to alter overnight the line of any party. The uniform monotony went so far that Communist party resolutions of Sweden, Ceylon, or Venezuela could hardly be distinguished one from the other. To be sure, during this period there existed, probably more than has been generally assumed until now, serious opposition to Soviet domination, criticism of the line handed down from Moscow, oppositionist currents and different concepts and controversies, but these could not be aired openly in the conditions prevailing at that time. In that quarter century the international Communist movement seemed—not only to the outside world, but even to many of its own members—like an instrument uniformly directed and led from Moscow, without any independence whatsoever.

[1] From article by Wolfgang Leonhard, a German authority on Communist affairs. *Problems of Communism* (a publication of the United States Information Agency). 13: 16-26. Mr.-Ap. '64.

All this now belongs to the past. Within a few years the Communist world movement has departed from its earlier monolithic structure to an astonishing extent and with startling swiftness. This development has led to the formation within the international Communist movement of several political groupings which take entirely different attitudes toward decisive political questions; it has led to open controversies between the different groupings and, consequently, to new relations within the movement as a whole. . . .

The basic causes for the "decentralization" of world communism lie chiefly . . . in the fact that the function and type of organization of the movement as created and fashioned by Stalin had increasingly come into conflict with changing realities. Just as internal changes in the Soviet Union became necessary because many characteristics and methods of the Stalinist system proved unsuitable to the conditions of a rising, modern industrial society, so in the international sphere the imposition of monolithic uniformity under Moscow's leadership proved incompatible with the development of Communist countries which had been formed under different conditions, and which faced different social, economic, and political problems. The dogmatic ideology of Stalinism could no longer serve as an exclusive model, nor could the Soviet system serve as the only blueprint for countries and parties undergoing a transformation. Once this process of change was set in motion, it could no longer be halted; one controversy led logically to another.

The Moscow-Peking conflict would hardly have produced such a great impact on the Communist world movement if the ground had not already been prepared for it by other events. April 12, 1948, can be designated with some justification as the starting-point for the crumbling of the monolithic structure; this was the day on which the Yugoslav Central Committee, meeting at the library of the former castle of King Alexander in Belgrade's suburb of Dedinje, passed a resolution rejecting the Soviet accusations against its party. Not only was this proof that a Communist party could resist the seemingly omnipotent leadership of Stalin, but it also laid the cornerstone for the evolution of communism in

Yugoslavia. The independence achieved by the Yugoslav Communists may thus be said to have been the first chapter of de-Stalinization—a chapter that began to unfold, of course, while Stalin was still alive. For the first time Stalin's policy was challenged successfully by different alternatives coming from *within* the Communist movement.

To be sure, in 1948-1949 Stalin was still powerful enough to prevent an alliance of other Communist parties with the "renegades in Belgrade," but undoubtedly the independent policy of the Yugoslav Communists and their open Marxist polemics against Stalinism had a lasting influence on many oppositionist circles in other Communist parties. . . .

From that time on, reform-Communist ("revisionist") tendencies, which heretofore had been limited to Yugoslavia, began to play an increasingly important role in the entire world movement. The "revisionist" groups did not want to confine themselves merely to condemning a few "errors" of Stalin: their purpose was, and still is, to eradicate Stalinism as an ideology and as a system. Any central control of the world Communist movement is to be rejected. Communist parties of all countries should operate independently of one another; their collaboration is to be secured on a bilateral basis, by an exchange of practical knowledge, without restrictions on individual autonomy. The path to socialism depends on the conditions and potentialities of one's own country. Every Communist party should therefore develop its policy in conformity with the historical traditions and the political, economic and cultural peculiarities of its country. In case of victory, the transition to communism should be effected in the most humane ways possible. Once power is secured, the Communist parties should not interfere in everything, but offer guidance and leadership only in crucial areas. In the economic sphere, they should strive for industrial self-management instead of a centralized, state-planned structure; in agriculture, rather than collectivize by force, they should initiate a long-term evolutionary cooperative development; and cultural and scientific development should not be constrained and hindered under the pretext of *partiinost* (party-mindedness) and "socialist realism." . . .

The Soviet concept (insofar as it concerns the Communist world movement) places the socialist countries in the center. It envisions a long period of coexistence (in the diplomatic but not in the ideological sphere), which Communist countries should utilize for the purpose of achieving economic superiority over the West, and eventually, of course, political domination as well.

Communist parties of capitalist countries should support this process, strengthen their political power and influence, and make use of all revolutionary opportunities, whenever possible, to seize power in a peaceful and "parliamentary" manner. Although the seizure of power by force and violence is by no means eschewed, Soviet theoreticians have emphasized the desirability of strengthening political influence, as a method which carries with it lesser risks. The struggle for "peace"—in other words, the support of Soviet policies—takes precedence over revolutionary experiments. Similarly, Communists in the emerging countries should not, as a rule, assume power hastily, but instead they should try to influence the dominant political forces of their countries, and to exert pressure in the direction of a "non-capitalist path."

The Peking thesis, on the other hand—if we confine ourselves here . . . to outlining the basic guidelines for the Communist world movement—proceeds from the assumption that the revolutionary center of the world has shifted to the emerging countries. The main task of the Communist countries must be to further the revolutionary movement in the underdeveloped countries and to support it by an uncompromising attitude toward the West ("imperialism"). The "mass organizations" (peace movement, trade unions, women and youth organizations) should become firmly integrated into the revolutionary struggle; the Communist parties in Western countries should prepare themselves for the imminent revolutionary struggles. Coexistence, economic competition, disarmament and the peaceful path to socialism are either to be rejected as "revisionist" or can at best be used as tactical slogans.

ALLIANCE AND MISALLIANCE [2]

The Chinese Communists formally established their government in Peking on October 1, 1949. The U.S.S.R. recognized it a day later. In December Mao Tse-tung visited Moscow. There he signed a number of agreements with Stalin which cemented official relations between the two countries. A balance sheet of the pattern of cooperation that shaped the Sino-Soviet alliance over the next six years would list the following prominent items:

1. *Political.* Russia and Red China sign a thirty-year treaty of friendship, alliance and mutual assistance (February 1950). Under its terms each nation promises to come to the other's aid against an attack from Japan or from an ally of Japan (presumably the United States). China agrees to a number of Soviet "special rights" on its territory, among them, the joint operation of the principal Manchurian railways and joint use of the Port Arthur naval base. Moscow later surrenders all such special rights. The U.S.S.R. supports Red China's claims to United Nations membership and to Taiwan. The Communist allies agree on programs covering the development of atomic energy for peaceful purposes; joint investigation and development of the Amur River valley; the mutual use of waterways along their borders; joint construction of two new railways linking their countries via Sinkiang and Mongolia.

2. *Military.* Red China and the Soviet Union cooperate closely in waging the Korean War. They help Ho Chi Minh conquer North Vietnam from France. Moscow sends an estimated 10,000-15,000 Soviet military advisers to assist in the training and modernization of China's armies, whose pattern of organization follows the Soviet model. It provides Peking with large amounts of heavy military equipment, furnishes the Chinese air force with modern planes, and assists in training Chinese pilots and paratroops. It helps the Chinese construct air fields and contributes naval vessels and submarines to Red China's navy.

[2] From *Great Decisions 1963*. (Fact Sheet no. 2. Red China and the U.S.S.R.— How Firm an Alliance?) Foreign Policy Association. 345 E. 46th St. New York 10017. '63. p 2-5. Reprinted by permission.

3. *Economic.* Russia lends Communist China $430 million in the period from 1950 to 1954. Through 1956, it promises equipment and supplies valued at $2 billion for 211 major projects that constitute the core of Peking's industrialization program. China pledges repayment in goods and commodities. Some seven thousand Chinese students are given technical training in the Soviet Union. Moscow sends over ten thousand advisers to supervise the construction of key industrial plants and to help Red China develop its management systems, labor organizations and educational programs. A Sino-Soviet technical commission gives China six hundred kinds of blueprints to help construct factories and 1,700 working drawings for the production and installation of machines.

4. *Cultural.* The two allies embark on intensive programs to promote friendship between their peoples at the grass-roots level and up. They exchange movies and exhibitions, as well as theatrical and art delegations. An estimated 2,760,000 Chinese visit the Exhibition on Economic and Cultural Achievements of the Soviet Union held in Peking toward the end of 1954. Sino-Soviet friendship societies are established along parallel lines in China and Russia. They publish magazines, organize lectures, sponsor a variety of activities designed to strengthen Chinese-Soviet friendship.

The Alliance After Stalin

The death of Stalin early in 1953 ushered in a period of change and uncertainty for the Soviet Union but had no apparent effects on the Sino-Soviet alliance. If anything, relations between the two allies seemed to grow more cordial. At Stalin's funeral, Chou En-lai represented China and marched in a place of honor alongside top Soviet leaders. In 1954, Khrushchev and Bulganin paid the first top-level visit Soviet leaders had ever made to China. In agreements resulting from this visit, they cancelled the remaining Soviet special rights in China which Stalin had negotiated in 1950.

Khrushchev lavishly praised the Chinese Communist leaders for having "creatively applied" Marxism-Leninism. He called

Red China a "great power" and declared that "the Soviet Union and the People's Republic of China are the invulnerable bastion of the camp of peace, democracy, and socialism."

In the two years after Khrushchev's visit to Peking, Sino-Soviet relations continued to flow smoothly. Communist propaganda continually celebrated the alliance of the two Communist powers as indestructible. On the surface, the term seemed appropriate. If there were any cracks below the surface, they were well-hidden.

Most experts trace the first open signs of the Sino-Soviet rift to the twentieth Soviet party congress held in Moscow in 1956. In a secret speech delivered at the congress (later published in the U.S. press) Premier Khrushchev launched his policy of de-Staliniization. He denounced Stalin for a long list of crimes and demanded the abolition of the "cult of personality" which had deified Stalin when he was alive and, to a lesser extent, continued to adulate him in death.

Khrushchev's attack on Stalin, as experts interpret it, had two main purposes: to strengthen his personal position by associating party opponents with responsibility for Stalin's crimes; and to spur the Soviet economy to greater growth by a policy of "liberalization" which would end the worst practices of Stalinist terrorism.

The Soviet premier's unexpected indictment of Stalin as a bloody tyrant stunned and demoralized much of the Communist world. Around this time the differences between Red China and the Soviet Union began to emerge. Subsequently they hardened and deepened. . . .

De-Stalinization

Khrushchev's demolition of the Stalin myth and his attack on the cult of personality caught the Chinese Communists embarrassingly short. In their rise to power, they had had serious differences with Stalin, but they had never given any public indication of this. Their own propaganda had always extolled Stalin.

Reportedly they complained that Khrushchev should have consulted them before he embarked on his anti-Stalin campaign. For the discredit cast on Stalin affected the international Communist movement, not only the Soviet party. It also seemed to reflect adversely upon Mao, who was surrounded by a Stalin-like cult of personality in China. Khrushchev had thus not only ignored his junior partner on a matter of the greatest mutual importance but indirectly appeared to be striking at Mao's prestige.

Peking's reaction to de-Stalinization was cool. For two months after Khrushchev's twentieth congress speech, Chinese Communist communications media virtually ignored the problem, although it was being hotly discussed everywhere else in the Communist world. And when the Peking regime finally did bring the matter into the open, its treatment was markedly restrained. It took obvious pains to protect Mao from the charge that he was following in Stalin's footsteps, and was much less severe than Moscow in its condemnation of Stalin.

10874

Is World War Inevitable?

Classical Communist doctrine says yes. It claims: (1) war springs from the "contradictions" of capitalism; (2) war is inevitable so long as capitalism exists; (3) war will be the midwife of ultimate Communist triumph. . . .

[After] the twentieth party congress, Soviet Premier Khrushchev appears to have departed from these doctrines. He . . . proclaimed "peaceful coexistence" the basic principle of Soviet foreign policy and . . . [asserted] communism will win the world through means short of all-out war.

The Soviet premier . . . [distinguished] three types of war: world war, local war, and colonial wars of liberation. He . . . declared that world war is no longer a "fatalistic inevitability" and that there is a "real possibility of excluding world war from the life of society" even though capitalism still exists in parts of the world. Local wars, he . . . [argued], can also—and should be—avoided since they may lead to world war. Only colonial wars . . . [were] left uncovered by Khrushchev's umbrella of peaceful coexistence. Communists support colonial wars of liberation, for they consider them to be just. But Khrushchev . . . [advised] caution here too, because of the risk that colonial wars may escalate into wider conflicts. . . .

To Peking, Khrushchev's views on war conflict with Marxism-Leninism in theory and are overcautious in practice. The Chinese Communists grudgingly concede the possibility of avoiding world war only because they feel the West fears the strength of the Communist world. But they view local and colonial wars as inevitable and urge Communists to support them regardless of the risks of escalation.

In 1957, after the Soviet Union launched its sputnik and claimed superiority over the United States in nuclear missiles, Mao declared the world balance of power had altered in favor of world communism. Accordingly Peking pressed Moscow to adopt a more aggressive policy toward the United States. It manifested sharp disappointment with what it regarded as Moscow's weak response to the landing of American Marines in Lebanon in 1958. It was consistently hostile to Khrushchev's efforts to promote summit diplomacy.

Sino-Soviet differences over the role of war in promoting the advance of communism undoubtedly reflect the fact that Russia is a nuclear power and China is not. [In 1964 Peking exploded a nuclear device.—Ed.] On a number of occasions, Premier Khrushchev . . . [spoke] of the destruction a nuclear war would visit upon the world. Red China's leaders, on the other hand, have suggested that Soviet fears of all-out war are instilling too much caution in Soviet diplomacy and preventing it from exploiting opportunities to expand communism. Peking has not been noticeably apprehensive about the consequences of major war. Chou En-lai is reported to have said that after the next world war, there will be "twenty million Americans, five million Englishmen, fifty million Russians, and three hundred million Chinese left."

The Communes: Short Cut or Dead End?

In August 1958, Red China announced a drastic reorganization of its rural economy. Farm collectives were to be consolidated into communes, huge self-contained administrative units under virtual military discipline. The purpose of the move? To speed China's transition into full communism by a great leap forward.

"The attainment of communism in China is no longer a remote future event," boasted the official resolution on the communes. The regime's propagandists declared the communes would advance China toward communism faster than more gradual Soviet methods and even suggested that the commune experiment offered a model suitable to all underdeveloped countries.

Moscow greeted Peking's claims for the communes with an evident lack of enthusiasm. At the twenty-first party congress [in 1959] Khrushchev said that the transition to communism had to take place by gradual stages; there were no short cuts. [The then] United States Senator Hubert Humphrey reported that during an interview the Soviet premier told him the Russians had experimented with communes after the Bolshevik revolution, and they did not work because "you can't get production without incentive."

In 1959 amid signs of a developing economic crisis, Red China abandoned the communes. The failure confirmed Khrushchev's misgivings. Observers believe that if Mao had embarked on the experiment without so much fanfare, it would have had little impact on Sino-Soviet relations. But Moscow resented Peking's exaggerated claims for the communes. It apparently saw them as a challenge to its role as pacesetter for the Communist world.

Communism and Nationalism

Moscow and Peking agree that the underdeveloped countries of the world offer rich opportunities for extending Communist influence. They disagree on how to exploit these opportunities most effectively.

Moscow has been willing and eager to do business with nationalist leaders . . . even though they are avowedly non-Communist. . . . At the twentieth congress, Khrushchev even suggested that ex-colonial countries might make social progress through parliamentary means—in effect, downgrading the necessity of revolution as the exclusive method for communism's road to power.

Peking considers the Soviet approach "soft" and "opportunist." It distrusts "bourgeois nationalists.". . . The effect of Soviet diplomacy in many underdeveloped countries, in its view, is to hamper the efforts of local Communists to take power. Peking is less apprehensive than Moscow that Communist-inspired violence will lead to conflict with the West and is prepared to accept the risk. It has competed against Moscow for leadership of the Communist parties in a number of underdeveloped countries and its propagandists have implied that Red China is better qualified than Moscow to lead the underdeveloped world to communism.

COMMUNISM DIVIDED [3]

Some students of the long history of relations between the Russian and Chinese empires always doubted that the Sino-Soviet alliance could indefinitely continue to be genuinely friendly. Why? In the first place ours is an age of nationalism, even more so perhaps than was the nineteenth century. Both the Soviet Union and Communist China are still in the stages of rapid industrial development and of recovery from invasion or near-conquest by foreign powers. As is normal in these stages in the life of nations, they are also passing through a period of strong nationalism. The element of racial antagonism, as the Chinese are increasingly making clear, has added another and even more embittering dimension to Sino-Soviet relations. The Chinese are clearly trying to profit from the worldwide emancipation from colonialism of that three quarters of the world's population which is not white.

The historic relationship between the Russian and the Chinese empires was itself in some respects one of the conqueror and the conquered. In the seventeenth century the initial contact between the Cossack adventurers sweeping eastward from the Urals to the Pacific and the Chinese border posts in what is now Soviet Central Asia and the Soviet Far Eastern Maritime Territories led to a series of Russo-Chinese conflicts, which resulted in a standoff between the two empires.

But not only did the czarist empire continue to expand thereafter; . . . by the beginning of the nineteenth century the Man-

[3]From *World Communism Divided,* pamphlet by W. E. Griffith, director of the International Communism Project at the Massachusetts Institute of Technology and author of *The Sino-Soviet Rift.* (Headline Series. no 166) Foreign Policy Association. 345 E. 46th St. New York 10017. Ag. '64. p 6-34. Reprinted by permission.

chu empire had clearly passed into a stage of decline. During the nineteenth century the European maritime powers forced China to make one series of humiliating concessions after another along its coast and rivers. Meanwhile the czarist empire, which bordered on China for thousands of miles, extracted a series of concessions from the imperial court in Peking. One of them permitted Russia to build and own the Chinese Eastern Railway (the short route from Siberia to the Pacific through Manchuria). During the eighteenth and nineteenth centuries, moreover, Russia annexed large portions of Chinese territory: the entire Soviet Far Eastern Maritime Territory with its capital at Vladivostok, plus a considerable portion of what is now Soviet Central Asia.

Nor did Russian pressure on China cease with the coming to power of the Bolsheviks; on the contrary, it was only briefly interrupted. Stalin established effective control over the ostensibly independent first Soviet satellite, Outer Mongolia, which had been a "special territory" of the Chinese empire, by successfully detaching it from the sovereignty as well as the control of Peking. Furthermore, during the period 1933-1944 the westernmost province of China, Sinkiang, was under Soviet influence; only after his coming to power did Mao reestablish Chinese control over it.

Party Relationships

Thus Communist China . . . has historic territorial claims against the Soviets. But the causes of Sino-Soviet antagonism are not only due to the long-standing hostility between the czarist and Chinese empires. They are also deeply rooted in the history of relations between Stalin and the Chinese Communist party during the 1920's and 1930's. Mainly for reasons of internal policy, such as his struggle with Trotsky, but also because of his errors of political and military calculation, Stalin in 1926-1927 forced the Chinese Communist party leadership to blunder into a series of premature uprisings which were crushed by Chiang Kai-shek. For decades, as a result, communism in China had no urban base. Only after Stalin had subsequently appointed and removed several heads of the Chinese Communist party did Mao Tse-tung succeed in the early 1930's in taking over its leadership and shifting its emphasis to guerrilla war in rural border areas of China. True, Mao continued during the 1930's and 1940's to give public support to Soviet policy, but there is considerable evidence that the scars inflicted by Stalin were long-lasting, and that Mao found additional cause for grievance in the arrangements made by Roosevelt, Churchill, and Stalin at Yalta in 1945 regarding postwar China and in some of the terms of the Sino-Soviet 1950 friendship treaty. Even before Mao came to power, some Chinese Communist statements indicate that his ambitions included not only the reestablishment of a strong central regime but also the recovery of China's historical boundaries and its even larger historic sphere of influence in Asia. In the early 1950's Moscow gave China large-scale economic aid, and Chinese Communist leaders were profuse in their reiterated assertions of undying loyalty to the Soviet Union. But even then, certain obscure indications, which have now acquired much more significance, showed that the Chinese Communist ideological position, and, therefore, presumably its policy as well, was far from totally identical with Moscow's. . . .

After Stalin

In Poland and Hungary the death of Stalin not only caused serious difficulties for the new Soviet leadership but also led to sharp disagreements with the Chinese. Peking now maintains (and one must assume that there is considerable truth in what it says) that shortly after the twentieth party congress of February 1956, during which Khrushchev delivered his famous speech denouncing Stalin, Chinese leaders took serious exception to his de-Stalinization policy, to his emphasis on a peaceful and parliamentary, rather than revolutionary, strategy by Communist parties and to his policy of "peaceful coexistence," that is, his desire for a détente with the United States. They further objected to his active policy of aid to and acquisition of influence in the underdeveloped areas, and in particular to Soviet aid to India, which, with some reason, they viewed not only as one cause of decreased Soviet economic aid to China but also as the expression of a Soviet desire to build up a potential ally against China. They also objected to Khrushchev's having done all these things without consulting Mao, who, after the death of Stalin, considered himself the senior living Marxist-Leninist theoretician.

In 1956 unrest in Poland and a revolution in Hungary enabled the Chinese to play a role on the Eastern European political scene. Their influence was probably only peripheral. One may doubt that, as the Chinese now maintain, their advice was the decisive element in Moscow's decision to accept Wladyslaw Gomulka in Poland and crush Imre Nagy in Hungary; but certainly the influence they wielded gave them a taste for more.

The Chinese differences with the Russians became much more serious in the following year, 1957. This was the year in which the Soviet Union achieved a strategic guided missile capability and launched its first sputnik—developments which produced not only apprehension in the United States but also great optimism in China. Mao, it appears, felt that Soviet military strength had now become so great that Moscow could, and therefore should, take much higher risks vis-à-vis the United States in helping Communist China to obtain its objectives in the Far East, specifically to conquer Taiwan and the offshore islands of Quemoy, Matsu, and the Pescadores. . . .

In the fall of 1957, concerned with his continuing difficulties in Eastern Europe, hoping he need not abandon his rapprochement with Yugoslavia, and anxious to avoid if possible a split with China, Khrushchev did make certain concessions to the Chinese. In particular, on October 15, 1957, he promised to provide China with a sample A-bomb and technical data concerning the manufacture of atomic bombs. Even so, the November 1957 Moscow meeting of the twelve ruling Communist parties was, as the Chinese have now revealed, the first major instance of direct Sino-Soviet verbal confrontation. Probably only Khrushchev's sacrifice of his policy toward Yugoslavia plus concessions to China on the atomic issue enabled any agreement with Mao to be reached at all.

The 1957 Sino-Soviet agreement, which endorsed Soviet leadership of the Communist world, however, was more apparent than real and soon gave way to renewed deterioration of relations. The Chinese continued to urge on the Soviets a more radical and risky anti-American strategy, but [during 1957 and 1958] Khrushchev made increasingly clear his intention to work toward a détente with the United States. . . .

In retrospect 1959 was probably the year of no return in Sino-Soviet relations. Before that year both Khrushchev and Mao doubtless thought that at least a temporary and partial reconciliation was not only desirable but probable, and that therefore both should and would make significant concessions in order to avoid a rupture. Thereafter, in the writer's view, neither Khrushchev nor Mao felt reconciliation was likely; rather, both must have calculated that total rupture could not be prevented. Each concentrated upon maneuvering to lay the blame for it on the other, to gain influence in other Communist parties, and to deprive the other of influence.

By 1959, then, Khrushchev was determined to force the Chinese to conform with Soviet policies. He was the more anxious to do so because the Chinese were showing increasing signs of preparing to use military force against the Indians on the Indian northern frontier and because he himself was planning to go to Camp David to hold discussions with President Eisenhower, looking toward a Soviet-American détente. In June 1959 . . . he formally withdrew his 1957 commitment to aid the Chinese obtain an atomic capability. In either 1959 or in the previous year there were reportedly also serious Sino-Soviet disagreements over such joint military programs as radar defense.

More serious from Mao's viewpoint, Khrushchev was at least aware of and probably supported an attempt by a minority group within the Chinese leadership, headed by the Chinese minister of defense, Marshal P'eng Teh-huai, either to force Mao to abandon his extremist and anti-Soviet course or perhaps even, failing this, to force a change in the Chinese leadership. This attempt was crushed by Mao in August and September of 1959. In the latter month, all Soviet attempts to dissuade them having failed, the Chinese initiated their first significant border incident against the Indians in Ladakh, whereupon, over Chinese protests, the Soviet Union publicly indicated its neutrality on this issue. The Chinese then made public their disapproval of Khrushchev's Camp

David talks, and when the Soviet leader in September 1959 visited Peking, the Sino-Soviet controversy over Taiwan and the offshore islands became worse.

"Long Live Leninism"

In April 1960 the Chinese published an article entitled "Long Live Leninism," which contained in terminology clear to Communist activists, although still somewhat too esoteric for the non-Communist West, a detailed and drastic attack upon Soviet foreign policy positions. [See "Long Live Leninism," in Section III, below.]. . .

Thereupon Khrushchev decided (as, ironically enough, Stalin had in 1948 with respect to Tito) to use political and economic pressure to force Communist China's leaders to submit. In . . . June 1960, he launched a violent (but unpublicized) attack against them at the third congress of the Rumanian Communist party in Bucharest. Shortly afterward he withdrew all Soviet technical experts from China and cut off all Soviet economic aid. Obviously Moscow hoped that the resultant economic crisis would force Peking to come crawling on its knees for renewed Soviet support or at least would deter other Communists from following Mao's lead.

But crawling on their knees, as the Chinese later publicly declared, was exactly what Mao was under no circumstances prepared to do. In spite of the enormous economic and military setback which the suspension of aid represented, Mao apparently never hesitated a moment. Not only did he flatly refuse Khrushchev's terms, but he so vigorously assured Peking's actual and potential Communist supporters of his intention and ability to defy the Soviets that he soon began to pick up considerable support outside of China itself.

Albania Sides with Peking

The most immediate and striking example was . . . the small, poor, Communist state of Albania. The fundamental cause of Albania's defiance of the Soviet Union arose from its relations, not with China, but with Yugoslavia. The Albanian Communist party was established in 1941 under Yugoslav tutelage, and its present leaders, Enver Hoxha and Mehmet Shehu, were saved from Yugoslav-sponsored liquidation only by Stalin's break with Tito in 1948. After Stalin's death, when Khrushchev adopted a policy of rapprochement with Yugoslavia, Hoxha and Shehu feared they would be sacrificed by Moscow for Belgrade's favor. This time, only the Hungarian revolution and the subsequent second Soviet-Yugoslav break (in part, significantly, forced by China) saved Hoxha and Shehu from purge, if not liquidation. By 1960 the Albanian leaders could see that Khrushchev was again steering toward a rapprochement with Belgrade. To protect themselves against this, they had been improving their relations with Peking, which had by then assured them of its determination to support them politically and economically against Moscow's and Belgrade's hostility. By the time of the June 1960 Bucharest meeting Albania had had to choose sides, and, not surprisingly, it chose Peking. Most of the East Asian Communist parties also either supported Peking to a greater or lesser degree or at least took a relatively neutral position on the Sino-Soviet differences.

Behind Closed Doors

November 1960 saw the convocation in Moscow, at Chinese request, of a worldwide meeting of eighty-one Communist parties. There, for weeks, the Sino-Soviet differences were thrashed out in all their bitterness. The discussion was of course held behind closed doors, and the resultant communiqué, although in fact a meaningless compromise, for a time successfully deceived many Western observers into thinking that such differences as did exist between Moscow and Peking had been greatly diminished by the Moscow meeting. In fact, nothing was further from the truth. . . .

To the non-Communist world, however, until October 1961, when Khrushchev publicly denounced the Albanians at the twenty-second party congress (he broke off diplomatic relations with them in November), it seemed that Sino-Soviet relations had improved. It was clear to all present at the Moscow meeting, however, that this was only so on paper; and in fact they continued to worsen thereafter . . . .

Only those few Western observers who focused their vision on the ideological declarations of the Albanians realized that the period from December 1960 until October 1961 marked a continuing worsening of Sino-Soviet and of Soviet-Albanian relations. Moscow brought increasing economic and political pressure to bear on Albania, but, like their Chinese senior partners, the Albanians continued to defy it. Once again the Stalinist tactics of economic boycott and threat of military subversion (which Khrushchev had unsuccessfully tried in the summer of 1960 against the Albanian leadership) proved as ineffective as they had against Tito in 1948. This was not surprising; like Tito, Mao, and Ho Chi Minh, Hoxha had come to power at the head of a guerrilla army; unlike other Eastern European Communist leaders, he did not depend for his acquiring or maintaining of power upon Soviet army tanks.

Worsening of Relations

At the twenty-second Soviet party congress, Chou En-lai criticized Khrushchev for publicly attacking the Albanians. He ostentatiously laid a wreath on Stalin's grave and then precipitously departed for Peking. . . . On the level of esoteric ideological communication, the Chinese attack against the Soviets continued unabated. Furthermore, the Soviets rapidly intensified their political, economic, and ideological rapprochement with Yugoslavia. This indicated to the Chinese and to the rest of the Communist world that they and their adversaries refused either to accept the status quo or to work toward a compromise. There also occurred in the spring of 1962 a development about which the West learned only months later: a serious anti-Chinese revolt in western Sinkiang by Turkic nomad tribesmen, who, crushed by superior force, fled across the border into Soviet Central Asia. These tribesmen, Uighurs and Kazakhs, had always been restive under Chinese rule and resented Chinese arrogance toward minority nationalities, a policy which Peking had intensified subsequent to the 1958 great leap forward. The tribesmen had hundreds of thousands of kinsmen in Soviet Central Asia, and the vast barren border made communication easy. Moscow agreed to give these tribesmen asylum, thus at once symbolizing the worsening of Sino-Soviet relations and providing an additional cause for further deterioration.

Both the Chinese attack on India's northern border on October 20, 1962 and the Soviet retreat which ended the Cuban missile crisis later that month further aggravated the rift. Ever since 1959 the Indians had been trying to outflank and force the retreat of Chinese troops established in Ladakh in 1955, territory claimed by India. During 1962 the Chinese publicly warned the Indians that they would not long tolerate Indian pressure; yet [Indian Prime Minister] Nehru made no effective military preparations to meet the impending attack; and when it came on October 20 (after vain Soviet attempts to prevent it), the Indian forces in Ladakh and in the North East Frontier Agency area were badly defeated. China gained its immediate objectives: India's image of strength was shattered and most of the East Asian neutralists hastened to make up with Peking. . . .

The emplacement of missiles in Cuba was primarily a Soviet attempt to catch up cheaply, rapidly, and with maximum political effect to the increasing American lead in strategic weapons, particularly in invulnerable second-strike deterrents. If the Soviet-installed intermediate range ballistic missiles (IRBM's) had become operational, much of the United States Strategic Air Command would have become vulnerable; and the ensuing psychological and political defeat suffered by the United States would have enabled the Soviet Union, Khrushchev must have calculated, to move effectively against the Western position in Berlin.

But President Kennedy's firm stand forced Khrushchev to withdraw the missiles. Thereupon, the Chinese, who had initially endorsed the Soviet move, unleashed a major wave of denunciations. They declared that Khrushchev had committed the sin of adventurism by putting the missiles into Cuba and that of "capitulationism" by taking them out. Furthermore, the Chinese utilized this Soviet retreat to reinforce Castro's anger with Moscow for what he regarded as the Soviet abandonment of Cuban interests, and, as a result, Soviet-Cuban relations cooled for a time. . . .

By . . . [1963] the Chinese challenge had had sufficiently serious results to give the Soviets the gravest concern. The Chinese were beginning to establish parallel front organizations in Africa and Asia which they used as a vehicle both to subvert Soviet influence within the existing ones and to emphasize the racist aspects of Chinese propaganda. Furthermore, they were intensifying their efforts to replace Soviet influence in Communist parties throughout the world. As a first step toward this goal, they tried to organize splits within these parties and to set up and support new Communist parties which then excommunicated the former "revisionist" leadership and proclaimed to the world that they were the only true "revolutionary Marxist-Leninists." In December 1963 Chou En-lai visited Africa for a seven-week trip as the Chinese stepped up their efforts to influence and attract radical nationalists in Africa, Asia, and Latin America. [See "Sino-Soviet Competition in Africa," in Section II, below.]

Just before the July 1963 Sino-Soviet meeting, Khrushchev suddenly indicated his willingness to sign a partial test ban treaty with the United States and Britain, a move which the Chinese made clear they regarded as treason to the Socialist camp. In mid-June Peking published a twenty-five-point letter to the Soviet Union, which amounted to an ideological platform for a split in the international Communist movement. In it, for the first time, the Chinese publicly indicated their differences with Khrushchev's domestic de-Stalinization program, which they termed clear treason to Marxism-Leninism. The test ban treaty negotiations came to a successful conclusion, while the Sino-Soviet talks collapsed in late July.

Bitter Exchanges

There followed, for the first time in the history of the Sino-Soviet dispute, a series of overt, all-out polemics initiated by Peking and replied to in kind by Moscow. Each side accused the other, in so many words, of a series of the gravest crimes against Marxist-Leninist orthodoxy. The Chinese remained on the offensive. Not only did they attack Khrushchev by name with all the weapons of personal accusation, satire, and ridicule at their disposal, but they also now brought out into the open the atomic issue, the border issue, and their own long version of the whole previous course of the dispute. They made it quite clear that they regarded Khrushchev as a conspirator with "American imperialism" against both Marxism-Leninism and the national and ideological interests of the Chinese People's Republic. The Soviets replied with equal fury. They denounced the Chinese as warmongers who were only interested in splitting the international Communist movement and conspiring with all and sundry against them. . . .

The end of 1963 and early 1964 were characterized by relative Soviet quiescence and by a series of Chinese attacks on Moscow. In December 1963 and February 1964 Peking formally proclaimed the existence of a Soviet plot to split the international Communist movement and stressed the necessity for all true "revolutionary Marxist-Leninists" to foil it by splitting or taking over control of Communist parties and front organizations. In late March Peking openly called for the removal of the "greatest revisionist of all time"—Khrushchev. Meanwhile, in mid-February 1964 the Soviets had decided . . . to call an international Communist conference to excommunicate the Chinese. They were, however, persuaded . . . by the Rumanians to postpone the resumption of public controversy. The Bucharest leadership then tried to mediate between Moscow and Peking, but with little success. The Chinese remained defiant, and, as an extensive exchange of letters between Moscow and Peking indicated, neither side was prepared to make significant concessions, and both anticipated rupture. . . .

Differing World Views

Both the Russians and the Chinese maintain that the most important issue dividing them is their differing conceptions of "the fundamental nature of the present epoch," that is, What is the world situation and what are the best revolutionary strategy and tactics for bringing about the victory of communism? Moscow maintains that the threat of thermonuclear war is so great that the struggle for peace and disarmament must be given absolute priority, both in general and with respect to the "national liberation struggle" in Asia, Africa, and Latin America. Peking, on the other hand, insists that absolute priority must be given to the "national liberation struggle," which, it maintains, in no way involves the threat of thermonuclear war and which can and must, where necessary, be won by violent means. The differing Soviet and Chinese attitudes toward the partial test ban treaty have most recently made this difference clear.

To phrase the Sino-Soviet difference on this point in specific foreign policy terms: According to Moscow, the risk that even limited war with the United States would escalate into general and therefore thermonuclear war is sufficiently great that safeguards against it must be found. Communist powers, for example, must not and the Soviet Union will not support the national liberation struggle when there is a serious danger of major United States intervention.

This is the strategic reality behind the ostensible Soviet and Chinese differences on such ideologically formulated issues as "peaceful coexistence" and the "inevitability" or "noninevitability" of war. One caution, however, should be added: It is not true, as the Soviets and all too many people in the West maintain, that the Chinese, in fact, favor a high-risk policy vis-à-vis the United States, that is, that they are much more willing than is the Soviet Union to incur the danger of major war with the West. On the contrary, available evidence indicates that the Chinese have a sober realization of their own military weakness and of American military strength, and that they will be careful to avoid precipitating the use of American strategic power against them. What they do maintain is that (a) limited or guerrilla war does not, as Moscow asserts, carry with it the risk of escalation to general and thermonuclear war, since America, a "paper tiger," cannot win in guerrilla warfare and will not dare to escalate a limited war, and that (b) through limited or guerrilla war "colonialism and neocolonialism" can be defeated, Western influence can be destroyed, and Communist predominance established in Asia, Africa, and Latin America.

Charge and Countercharge

With regard to the clash of state interests, China believes that the Soviet Union has refused to run sufficient risks to support Chinese interests against the United States, specifically with respect to Taiwan and the offshore islands. On the contrary, the Chinese maintain, . . . [the Soviet Union] so eagerly desires a détente with the United States that to achieve it . . . [the U.S.S.R.] is sacrificing the legitimate interests of China and, what is worse, betraying Marxism-Leninism and the interests of the international Communist movement by allying Russia with the United States against the Chinese. Furthermore, the Chinese declare that Moscow, after first agreeing to do so, refused to aid them obtain an atomic weapons capability. Khrushchev, the Chinese continue, . . . supported such pro-American and anti-Chinese states as India. Finally, the Chinese claim that the Soviets hold territory in Central Asia and in the Maritime Territory in the Far East which rightfully belongs to China.

The Russians deny most of these charges. They declare that the Chinese have violated the Soviet boundary, that the Chinese claims to Soviet territory are completely chauvinistic, and that Soviet policy toward Taiwan and toward the United States is simply the logical and proper implementation of the policy of peaceful coexistence. Moscow contests the truth of the charge that it did not give Peking enough economic aid and asserts that the Chinese wrongly stress the economic self-sufficiency of each Communist state.

In theory Moscow tends to emphasize support of non-Communist nationalist regimes in the underdeveloped areas, while China until recently placed more emphasis on the necessity of supporting Communist movements in these areas. But the increasing bitterness of the rift has made both Moscow and Peking take a very practical attitude on this issue; both will deal with kings as well as with Communists, and Peking has declared that socialism can be built without the leadership of a Communist party.

Summing up, the Chinese emphasize the necessity of violent revolutionary struggle for the victory of communism; the Soviets prefer peaceful economic competition and a peaceful, evolutionary "road to socialism." The Soviets emphasize the importance of communism in Europe; the Chinese declare that the center of the world revolutionary struggle is in Asia, Africa, and Latin America, and they combine with this a strongly racist note in their propaganda and policies. The Chinese denounce the whole of Khrushchev's de-Stalinization policies as a betrayal of true Marxism-Leninism; the Soviets reply that the Chinese are Stalinist and Trotskyite. Finally, and perhaps most seriously, the Chinese are attempting to destroy Soviet primacy in the international Communist movement and eventually to replace it by Chinese leadership, while the Soviets insist on retaining the primacy which they have held since 1917. . . .

The Current Lineup

Serious tension between the two leading members of a multination alliance normally enables its other members to gain increased influence and freedom of maneuver by supporting or playing off one against the other. Not surprisingly, therefore, against the background of the deepening rift, a polycentric Communist world system (one no longer subject to tight Soviet control and with a number of relatively independent centers of decision and action) has developed, and the bargaining power of the smaller Communist nations vis-à-vis Moscow and Peking has increased.

The present relationship of Communist parties to the Sino-Soviet dispute can perhaps be best understood if one classifies them by categories. There are first the unconditional supporters of Moscow. These may be, for example, genuinely pro-Soviet for policy reasons or they may be, in spite of some possible inclinations toward the Chinese, unconditionally pro-Soviet because they have no alternative. Among ruling parties, the East German, the Czechoslovak, Bulgarian, and Outer Mongolian appear to be unconditionally pro-Soviet; among nonruling ones, so is the French.

Then there are the conditionally or moderately pro-Soviet parties, those which are genuinely aligned with Moscow on policy issues, but which wish to retain the greater degree of maneuverability they have gained as a result of the dispute. In addition, some of their leaders are also opposed to a split for reasons of a genuine ideological commitment to "proletarian internationalism." These parties, therefore, are opposed to a total public Sino-Soviet rupture; they include the Rumanian, the Polish, and the Italian. So, in a somewhat different respect, are the Yugoslav Communists, who favor a split only if there is any danger of a Sino-Soviet reconciliation, which would deprive them of their now regained possibilities of maneuver and influence within the international Communist movement. However, if, as now, a reconciliation is not in prospect, they are opposed to a rupture, both to keep their ties with other parties that also oppose it and because they fear, as do the Poles, the Italians, and the Rumanians, that a total rupture might cause . . . [the Soviet leaders] (like Stalin after his 1948 break with Tito) to attempt to reestablish conformity by greatly increased Soviet pressure upon other Communist parties.

Pro-Chinese Parties

In the Chinese camp one can make the same classification. The unconditionally pro-Chinese parties are the Albanian, New Zealand, Burmese, Thai, and Malayan. The North Koreans are pro-Chinese, but not unconditionally so: they have not yet explicitly denounced the Soviet Union. The North Vietnamese from 1960 to May 1963 were formally "neutralists"—that is, they tried to mediate between Moscow and Peking. This was understandable; they needed Soviet support to prevent total Chinese domination, and they needed both Soviet and Chinese support in order to carry on their guerrilla war in South Vietnam. By May 1963, however, Ho Chi Minh abandoned his neutrality for a conditionally pro-Chinese position, one which he shares with the Japanese . . . Communists; a pro-Soviet minority apparently remains, however, in the North Vietnamese leadership. . . .

The Japanese Communist party, torn by factional strife, is also only conditionally pro-Chinese. Elsewhere, the Australian party, which was first pro-Chinese, has been recaptured by pro-Soviet elements, and a pro-Chinese Australian group has formed a new party there. The Ceylonese party, which was pro-Soviet, has now split, with a minority group, including the radical trade union leadership, forming a new pro-Chinese party. The Indian Communist party was badly divided by the impact of the Chinese attack on India in 1962. In spite of this, however, the pro-Chinese group has been steadily gaining influence, and a complete split is now developing. [The pro-Chinese Indonesian Communist party was decimated after an attempted coup in 1965.—Ed.]

Middle East and Latin America

The Middle Eastern Communist parties are small; they remain pro-Soviet. The few Communist parties and groups in Africa seem to remain largely pro-Soviet, but the Chinese are intensifying their activity there, and the developing struggle by African nationalists against the Republic of South Africa offers them great opportunities.

In Latin America the situation is complicated by the influence of Castro, who sympathizes with the Chinese on most policy issues, but who needs Soviet economic support. He has, therefore, taken a relatively pro-Soviet position, which, however, he never seems to maintain consistently or totally. [In recent months Castro has accused the Chinese of interference in Cuban affairs and has launched bitter broadsides against Peking.—Ed.] The struggle for control of the Communist parties of Latin America is a tripartite one. The Castroites normally cooperate with the Chinese against the Soviets. This struggle has already led to splits in several Latin American Communist parties. The Panamanian party is pro-Soviet; that of Venezuela appears to be under Castroite influence. In Peru the party has split, and there are now rival pro-Soviet and pro-Chinese parties. There are two Communist parties in Brazil, the smaller being pro-Chinese, plus a third group of pro-Castro non-Communist peasant radicals led by Francisco Juliao. In Chile there is a small pro-Chinese group in the Communist party. The Chilean Socialist party, which has been aligned with the Communists, has been seriously influenced by Chinese and Castroite ideas.

It can thus be seen that the result of the Sino-Soviet split has by no means been solely a bipolarization of the Communist world; on the contrary, that polycentrism which Italian Communist chief Palmiro Togliatti prematurely advocated in 1956 characterizes the international Communist scene. World communism is thus in the process of becoming much more regional in character. Clearly the Soviets will continue to dominate most of the East European Communist parties, although to a lesser degree than before the Sino-Soviet split. Rumanian defiance of Moscow, as well as the Albanian revolt in 1960, shows how limited Soviet influence can become. Only in a country such as East Germany, where twenty Soviet army divisions are present, or in Bulgaria, where all elements of the leadership not totally pro-Soviet have been purged, does Soviet control appear to remain fully in force. Khrushchev's readmission of Yugoslavia to the Soviet camp not only was possible because of this looser system of control, but also furthered it.

Soviet Influence Declining

In Western Europe and elsewhere Soviet influence is declining. For example, there appears to be in the process of formation, under the leadership of the Italian Communist party, a regional grouping of Western European Communist parties which will adjust more closely to the political, economic, and social realities of Western Europe than has been possible up to now. Latin American communism is split and appears likely to become more so as long as the Chinese and the Cubans continue their subversive activities on that continent. The Chinese are clearly the dominating influence in East Asian communism.

In Africa, Latin America, and other underdeveloped areas it would probably be more accurate not to discuss individuals and groupings in the traditional categories of Communist or non-Communist. Rather, one should distinguish between orthodox Communists and radical populist nationalists. Castro, for example, was a radical and anti-American Cuban populist nationalist before he became a Communist, and in part he became a Communist for reasons of expediency, in order to cement his alliance with and his aid from the Soviet Union. In Africa, to take another example, there are few orthodox Communists, but many radical nationalists who seek to exploit Soviet and Chinese aid. These men may seem less dangerous than orthodox Communists to the West, but in some aspects they are more so. Ideologically, each adversary (the Chinese even more than the Russians) is primarily committed to support Communists in these areas. However, the violence of their competition and the general erosion of ideology brought about by the split have tended to make both Moscow and Peking work pragmatically with whatever radical anti-Western nationalists they can find. In Africa and Latin America the rift will probably bring about in the near future an intensification rather than a decline of Soviet and Chinese activity.

MILITARY ASPECTS OF THE DISPUTE [4]

The dispute between the Soviet Union and Communist China has been an accepted fact of the international scene for some years now. At first it was believed to be mainly an ideological difference of opinion between the world's two largest Communist parties whose history and development had taken different courses; and it was assumed that, as established Communist nation-states, a dispute on the interpretation of Marx-Leninism would not prevent the two governments from standing together as allied powers in matters of defense. The elements which draw the Soviet Union and Communist China together, it was felt, were much stronger than those which divided them, and each was firmly committed to defend the other under the terms of their treaty of alliance of February 14, 1950.

Information which has become available during the last few years, particularly since 1963 when the Chinese Communists and the Russians revealed something of the exchanges between them and, indeed, of the true nature of the dispute, has thrown a great deal of doubt on this interpretation. Historical work by American

[4] From article by Malcolm Mackintosh, consultant to the Institute for Strategic Studies on Soviet Affairs in London. *Bulletin of the Atomic Scientists.* 21:14-17. O. '65. "Military Aspects of the Sino-Soviet Dispute" by Malcolm Mackintosh is reprinted with permission from the October 1965 issue of the *Bulletin of the Atomic Scientists.* Copyright 1965 by the Educational Foundation for Nuclear Science.

scholars has shown that even before the Chinese Communist party came to power in 1949, disagreements on policy and tactics existed between Moscow and the Chinese party. Stalin's recommendation in 1945 that the party should form a coalition with the Nationalists was ultimately rejected by Mao Tse-tung, who proceeded to win a civil war against the Nationalists which Stalin thought an impossible task. Moreover there is evidence that some Chinese Communist leaders bitterly resented the Soviet looting of Manchuria in 1945, and one, General Lung Yun, was disciplined for saying so in public, though he was later rehabilitated when the Sino-Soviet dispute came out into the open. . . .

Although no direct criticism of the Soviet decision to launch the Korean war has so far emerged from China, the fact that Stalin obviously miscalculated American and UN readiness to halt the aggression by force, and then committed the Chinese regular army to participate in a war which may have cost it 400,000 casualties at a time when China was exhausted after five years of civil and eight years of national war, probably raised doubts in Peking even then on Russia's fitness to dominate the Communist camp's foreign policy as her right. Stalin furthermore insisted in 1952 on extending the Soviet military occupation of Port Arthur to all intents and purposes indefinitely, and although Stalin is today hailed in China as the mastermind of Communist strategy, the memory of his treatment of the Chinese Communists can hardly be a happy one in Peking.

After Stalin's death in March 1953 and until about 1958, it seems that the Soviet Union, first under Malenkov and then under Khrushchev, made some attempt to put Sino-Soviet military relations on a new footing. In October 1954 the Soviet government undertook to withdraw from Port Arthur within six months, and the base and all its installations were handed over to China in May 1955. China was invited to be present at the founding ceremony of the Warsaw Pact, and from 1955 onward Soviet and Chinese governmental and military delegations visited each other's capitals with all the appearances of a busy and intensive exchange of military liaison. . . . It is clear that the Soviet Union stepped up its military aid to China after 1955, both in operational weapons systems and in armaments plants. The Soviet Union also supplied China with an atomic reactor which became operational in 1958, and accepted Chinese physicists for training at the Soviet atomic center of Dubna, near Moscow. With the successful Soviet firing of an ICBM in August 1957 and the subsequent launches of the first two sputniks, Chinese comment on Soviet weapons development became enthusiastic, and much emphasis was put on the value of Soviet military aid in the Chinese press. It was against this background that a major Sino-Soviet defense conference opened in Moscow in October 1957, which was to prove decisive in the development of Sino-Soviet military relations.

No one can say with certainty what exactly happened at this conference. The Chinese revealed in 1963 that on October 15, 1957, the Soviet government signed an agreement with the Chinese on "new defense technology," and promised to supply China with a sample atomic bomb and data on its manufacture. The Russians have not denied this directly, but have said that the Chinese version is "distorted," and attempted to blur the issue by accusing China of revealing the defense secrets of the Soviet bloc. Yet in spite of what appears to have been a successful defense conference, six months later the Chinese convened their own conference on military affairs in Peking, and Chinese spokesmen began to talk about the need for China to develop her own atomic weapons, without outside help. Chinese press treatment of the military conference in Peking, which lasted from May to July 1958, suggested that snags had developed in Soviet aid to China, and emphasis was laid firmly on a defense policy based on Chinese efforts and Chinese resources.

The sudden change in Chinese press treatment of the value of Soviet aid and advice in 1958 suggests that at some point in time early in that year the Soviet Union placed conditions or restrictions on part, at least, of its military aid program to China which the Chinese Communists were unable to accept, probably on purely nationalist grounds. Most likely this concerned the control of atomic bombs and warheads for future Chinese missiles, since the Chinese claimed that the Russians "tore up" their agreement on the supply of a sample of an atomic bomb on June 20, 1959. Although this date was a year after the military conference in Peking at which China's need to have her own atomic weapons was first mentioned, it is possible that the intervening twelve months was spent in hard bargaining between Moscow and Peking on the Soviet "strings" to the proposed atomic weapons agreement. When further arguing proved fruitless, it seems likely that the Russians finally broke off the negotiations with a characteristic Khrushchevian abruptness which left considerable resentment in Peking.

This, however, is largely speculative. But in view of the Chinese allegations that the Russians tried to enslave China militarily, and that one attempt at this was a Soviet proposal for a joint Sino-Soviet fleet in the Pacific, it is also possible that Khrushchev had the idea of refashioning the Sino-Soviet defense alliance in the form of a Far Eastern counterpart to the Warsaw Pact. This would have allowed the Soviet Union to use Chinese territory for air warning installations, airfield landing rights, and bases of different kinds, including missile and submarine, and would have given Russia a high degree of military control over China's use of her armed forces. In return, China would have been offered reciprocal rights on Soviet territory (a rather meaningless concession in the circumstances) and good supplies of advanced weapons: submarines, missiles, an air defense system, aircraft of all kinds—and atomic bombs and warheads under the same Soviet controls as are operative within the Warsaw Pact. It is probable that it was this kind of offer which the Chinese rejected, possibly against the advice of their own Minister of Defense, Marshal P'eng Teh-huai, who was dismissed in disgrace in September 1959.

While this presumed debate was going on between Moscow and Peking, the crisis in the Taiwan Straits from August to October 1958 confronted the Soviet government with the possibility that China might invoke the defense treaty against the United States. On August 23, China began the artillery bombardment of the offshore island of Quemoy, whose garrison was supplied by Nationalist Chinese ships escorted into what Peking claimed as its territorial waters by American naval vessels. Widespread air operations were also carried out over the Straits and the mainland by Nationalist and Communist aircraft, the former using sidewinder air-to-air missiles in the later stages of the crisis. At the height of the crisis, Soviet comment was restrained, Khrushchev even declaring that he saw no war clouds on the horizon. When the crisis moved into its second and less tense phase, Khrushchev twice wrote to President Eisenhower emphasizing that an American attack on mainland China would lead to Soviet support for Peking, including the use of nuclear weapons if necessary. But the Soviet leader stressed that he had no intention of backing up the Chinese "civil war" against Taiwan. It was probably this qualification which led the Chinese to complain in 1963 that the Soviet Union offered to come to China's support in 1958 with nuclear weapons only at a time when there was no danger of nuclear war.

Sino-Soviet relations deteriorated rapidly after the Taiwan Straits crisis, until in July 1960 the Soviet government suddenly withdrew all its military and most of its civilian technicians and advisers in a way which particularly angered the Chinese, and while petroleum shipments from Russia to China have continued at a reduced level, there is no evidence that the supply of weapons has been resumed since then. The Chinese Air Force, for example, according to the New York *Herald Tribune* of April 22, 1965, contains ten to fourteen TU-4 long-range piston bombers (originally copied by the Russians from the B-29 bomber), ten TU-16 jet bombers, 275 IL-28 light bombers of 1955 vintage, 75 MIG-19 fighters, with the remaining 2,000 planes made up of older MIG-15, MIG-17, and transport aircraft. The Soviet Union has refused to give China any MIG-21's (which she has supplied to Egypt, Cuba, and Indonesia) and has supplied no spare parts for existing planes of Soviet origin. On the ground, artillery and armor are in such short supply that nearly half of the 110 to 115 infantry divisions are thought to lack their organic artillery regiment, and only four divisions are known to be armored—a smaller number of such divisions than the Soviet Army has in the Far East and central Asia alone. The Chinese Navy is believed to have twenty to twenty-five submarines and four destroyers, although Hanson Baldwin, in the New York *Times* of October 5, 1964, mentioned reports that the Chinese have some cruise-type missiles similar to those installed on Soviet Komar class missile destroyers. China is known to have its own missile program, which must originally have been Soviet-supported, but the results have not so far appeared in the Chinese defense inventory.

While Soviet military aid to China halted in this way in 1960, there were unmistakable signs that the Soviet Union began to warn China that its defense commitment to come to Peking's aid might be invalidated by China's hostility to the Soviet Union in Communist party and foreign affairs. In August 1960 a Soviet writer warned China that her policy might isolate her from the rest of the bloc in the event of war, and in January 1962 the Soviet Defense Minister, Marshal Malinovski, pointedly declared that Soviet military might was available to defend "members of the Socialist camp who are friendly to us." The Soviet note to China of September 21, 1963, accused the Chinese of following a course which could not be supported by the military forces of the rest of the bloc. Taken in conjunction with China's probable reaction to the Soviet Union's behavior during the Taiwan Straits crisis, it seems very likely that both Russia and China regard their defense treaty as valuable as a limited deterrent, but virtually invalid as far as military commitments are concerned. The only available references to it in Soviet material from 1960 to 1964 came in attempts to persuade the Chinese not to acquire their own atomic weapons, arguing that they were unnecessary since China was protected by the Soviet guarantee. But since China exploded her first atomic device in October 1964 this argument is out of date, and is no longer used.

In the Event of a Sino-American War

One part of this question, however, remains open: what would the Soviet Union do in the event of a full-scale war between Communist China and the United States, perhaps escalating from a Sino-American clash over Vietnam which first involved United

States attacks on targets in Southern China, and then spread north to cover the whole country? One thing can be ruled out from the start. There seem to be no conceivable circumstances in which the Soviet Union would launch its nuclear strike forces against North America and thus initiate a world nuclear exchange on behalf of Communist China. Nor is there any likelihood that the Soviet Union would initiate action against United States bases in the Pacific at China's request.

In the event of a Sino-American war, the Russians may merely make a show of supporting the Chinese Communists, mainly for the benefit of the rest of the Communist movement, would launch a vigorous propaganda campaign against the United States, and issue solemn warnings about military aid or volunteers for China. If the extension of the war came about as a result of an open provocation of the Americans by Peking, it is possible that the Russians would do little more than warn America publicly, while privately seeking a tactical "sphere of influence" agreement with Washington, in an attempt to keep military operations as far away as possible from Soviet territory. In this situation, the Russians might ask the Americans not to bomb Manchuria or northern China in return for no military intervention on China's behalf.

In the second case, in which the responsibility for the expansion of the war would be less easily defined, or if Soviet-American relations were severely strained, the Russians might offer to defend a limited number of Chinese cities or target areas in the north or northeast against air attack, assuming that the Chinese granted the Russians the necessary local facilities. The main purpose of this offer would be to deter the Americans from attacking targets in northern and northeastern China, but if deterrence failed, they would probably attempt to defend these targets.

The third course which the Russians might take could be applicable if American retaliation against Communist China were so overwhelming that the control of the country by the central government was endangered or on the point of collapse. China might, in these circumstances, dissolve into chaos or guerrilla warfare, and Russia might face a real threat of breakdown along her own borders. The Russians might argue that the only way to restore order and security in the frontier would be to use her own armed forces on Chinese territory, to intervene and occupy on a temporary basis areas such as Manchuria, Inner Mongolia, or Sinkiang. Once order has been restored, and depending on the general situation, the Soviet government might be tempted to recruit a Chinese Communist leadership in the areas under its control which would be more amenable than Mao Tse-tung to Soviet influence. This, however, would be a secondary or long-term objective: in the immediate crisis, the security of the Soviet frontiers is likely to be the Russians' prime consideration.

For the Future: Superpower Stalemate?

Turning from possible Soviet attitudes during a Sino-American war to the future of Sino-Soviet military relations, it seems that unless there are major changes in the governments of one or both Communist countries (greater, for example, than that which took place in Moscow in October 1964 [when Khrushchev was replaced]) the present lack of cooperation and hostility is likely to continue. Could it ever explode into open war between Russia and China? Certainly the Chinese accused the Russians officially of provoking over five thousand frontier incidents in 1962 alone, and have raised (on a long-term basis) territorial claims on Soviet Far Eastern provinces which, Peking says, were ceded to Russia in the nineteenth century under unequal treaties. The areas claimed by the Chinese included the Soviet Maritime Province north of Vladivostok, and parts of Central Asia. On their side, the Russians appear to have taken the possibility of hostilities with some degree of seriousness, because they seem to have carried out military exercises in the Far East involving the repulse of a Chinese attack on the Maritime Province. It is possible that there exist in the Soviet Union military or other chauvinists who, in view of the enormous military superiority enjoyed by Russia over China, might advocate teaching the Chinese a sharp military lesson, perhaps in the form of precision air attacks on vital Chinese targets. Perhaps there may be arrogant or bitterly resentful Chinese who plan for the day when the Soviet Union might find itself in internal or external difficulties in the hope of using Chinese manpower to recover "lost" territories from Russia. But on the whole, such people are likely to remain in the minority in both countries, and it may be concluded that in the foreseeable future, while Sino-Soviet military relations will remain as bad as Sino-Soviet political relations, the prospect of a direct clash between the two countries is an improbable one.

Nevertheless, from the Soviet point of view, a major factor in Sino-Soviet relations will be the obvious determination of the Chinese to increase their armed strength to that of a superpower, backed now by an incipient atomic capability. There seems little doubt that Communist China intends to build a stockpile of atomic, and later, thermonuclear weapons, and will also strive to create a missile delivery system, as well as improving the armament of her air force, army, and navy. This Chinese determination clearly adversely affects prospects for bringing China into discussions on arms control, disarmament, or the nuclear test ban. Much as the Soviet government would like to bring pressure on the Chinese to halt this arms race, sign the partial nuclear test ban, or enter the arms control arena, it has to recognize that it has probably little influence left in Peking. The long history of miscalculations and misunderstanding, which has marred relations between the Soviet and Chinese Communist parties and governments, coupled with decisions such as the withdrawal of the Soviet technicians from China in 1960 and the apparent refusal of the Russians to give the Chinese nuclear weapons, and the rejection by the Chinese of Soviet plans for joint defense in the Far East have combined to set in motion what amounts to an internal arms race within the Communist camp itself. China will push her arms drive as far as her backward but growing economy will allow; Russia will react with military planning which will ensure, in the eyes of her leaders, her continuing overwhelming superiority. Yet even this situation is not without its compensations. Perhaps the balance between Russia's size and military technological superiority and China's growing population and future military potential contains not only the elements of an explosion, but also the seeds of the kind of stalemate which greater nuclear power has brought to the relations between the United States and the Soviet Union. When China realizes that Russia cannot be browbeaten, swamped, or intimidated, and Russia realizes that China cannot be conquered or dominated in traditional ways, it is possible that this potentially dangerous arena of conflict may also settle down to an unfriendly but reasonably safe state of mutual deterrence.

OPPOSITION OF INTERESTS [5]

It appears highly unlikely that an alliance between Russia and a strong and united China would ever have arisen unless both states had come under Communist rule: Their "pure" national interests tend to oppose them. The interest of Russia as a great power might require a Chinese government strong enough to limit the encroachment of other powers on its territory, particularly during a period when Russia alone was not in a position to stop such encroachment, but it hardly requires a China that is a great power in its own right. The Soviets offered support to governments controlling part of China before 1927 and to a weak National government from 1936 to 1945 in order to limit the expansion of Japanese power on the Asian continent; they backed Mao Tse-tung after 1946 partly in order to limit the spread of American influence. But they did not then expect, and apparently did not desire, the creation of a strong China united under Communist rule: They maintained diplomatic relations with Chiang Kai-shek and even negotiated with him on the border provinces until the very eve of his expulsion from the mainland.

Conversely, Chinese national interest was opposed to interests of all the powers who had been exploiting Chinese weakness in a scramble for spheres of influence and privilege, including Russia, and, as British and French influence in East Asia declined, Russia came to rank second only to Japan as a danger to Chinese unity. Only the United States, because of its physical remoteness and its Open Door tradition, could appear as China's "natural" ally against the neighboring powers.

[5] From "Factors of Unity and Factors of Conflict," by Richard Lowenthal, professor of international relations at the Free University of Berlin. *Annals of the American Academy of Political and Social Science.* 349:106-16. S. '63. Reprinted by permission.

Even the Sino-Soviet alliance, created as an expression of the common "ideological" needs of two Communist regimes, did not end the role of "pure" national interest as a divisive factor. This showed itself in Stalin's attempt to maintain Russian privileges in Manchuria and Russian influence in Sinkiang, which was only dropped by his successors in 1954 in deference to Chinese pressure, and in later Chinese attempts to regain influence in the Mongolian People's Republic that were opposed by the Soviets, as well as in the recent bitter rivalry of both powers for control of the Communist regime in North Korea.

In trying to judge the importance of this factor of conflict and its trend of development, it may be said that it was acute when China was just emerging from prolonged civil war and international impotence, that it became dormant during the period when Chinese consolidation had been accepted by Russia as a fact but Chinese great-power ambitions had not yet begun seriously to manifest themselves, roughly between 1954 and 1957, and that it has since entered a new phase of virulence owing to the visible growth of these ambitions. The characteristic of that new phase is that the opposition of interests is no longer confined to the border regions from Korea to Sinkiang but has broadened into general Soviet opposition to the expansion of China as an Asian power and to its potential growth into a world power. Both the Russian policy of maintaining India as a counterpoise to China on the Asian continent and the Chinese effort to demonstrate India's impotence, while partly motivated by differences on Communist world strategy to be discussed below, are also manifestations of this direct opposition of national interests. The same applies to Moscow's evident determination to keep China out of the atomic club as long as possible. Finally, Russian opposition to the rapid growth of Chinese power is clearly one of the major factors limiting Soviet economic, military, and diplomatic aid to Communist China.

It follows that the opposition of national interests must become more acute the more the Chinese succeed in building up their independent power—unless and until they reach a point where Russia has to resign herself to a basic change in the relation of forces. The setbacks suffered by Peking in its attempts at rapid industrialization do not suggest that such a point will be reached soon, if at all, while its remarkable success in expanding its sphere of influence in Asia—among non-Communist no less than among Communist countries—indicates that the area of direct Sino-Soviet opposition may equally expand in the near future.

Common Goals and Common Enemies

The Russo-Chinese alliance, then, was originally wholly due to the ideological factor: It was concluded as a result of the conquest of power by the Chinese Communist party—a party which for reasons of principle as well as of self-preservation was determined to lean to one side in world affairs. The victorious Chinese Communists were not a satellite party—they were not led by Soviet agents, and they owed little to direct Soviet support —but their party structure and their ideas had been formed in the main on the Bolshevik model. They proposed to transform China in the Soviet image, if partly by different methods, and to cooperate with the Soviets in fostering the progress of "world revolution"—that is, in supporting the spread of Communist party rule to further countries. In struggling for this common goal, they were bound to encounter the opposition of the same enemies—the "imperialist" powers led by the United States. To this day, the common ideological goals used by both parties to legitimize their rule and the common enmities provoked by the pursuit of those goals remain the chief factors holding the alliance together.

It must be observed at once that, although the ideas and the structure of the Chinese Communist party regime were largely shaped by the Soviet model, as well as by the common Marxist-Leninist sources and the common needs of modern totalitarian power, they were never identical. Influenced possibly by the tradition of Chinese political thought with its stress on the skill and wisdom of the ruling group rather than on institutional forms, and certainly by the experience of surviving against overwhelming odds and triumphing over extreme hardships after decades of struggle, the Chinese Communists from the start put even greater emphasis than the Bolsheviks on the "subjective factor"—on the power of the revolutionary will, if combined with "correct thinking," to transform objective economic conditions and on the need to change the consciousness of the masses accordingly. The resulting differences in the style of work and the internal climate of the two ruling parties always contained a potential of ideological divergence, but they did not in fact lead to ideological conflict so long as their effects were confined to differences in the methods and pace used by either for revolutionizing their respective societies. Stalin, in contrast to his behavior in the Yugoslav case, never presumed to tell the Chinese how they should run their state, nor did Mao hint at any criticism of Soviet methods while Stalin lived. After his death, recognition of the right of each ruling Communist party to find the right institutional forms and the right pace for approaching the common goal in its particular conditions soon became part of official Soviet doctrine as laid down by Khrushchev. Hence it seems safe to say that the first Sino-Soviet ideological dispute on domestic problems—the debate on the "People's communes" and the preconditions for moving to the "higher stage" of communism at the turn of 1958-1959— would not have broken out but for previous disagreements in the international field. . . .

Different Situations in the Common Struggle

The relevant differences in the situations of the two powers concern their level of economic development, their military security, and their room for diplomatic maneuver. . . .

Economically, the Soviet Union has reached a stage of industrial development where further advance in any desired direction depends only on its own choice of priorities: It is in a position to achieve substantial improvements in its backward agriculture and in the standard of living of its people, or to continue the arms race at the desired pace, or to engage in massive development aid to its Communist allies or to uncommitted powers, though it cannot afford to do all these things at once. China is still in an early stage of her industrialization effort, which, for reasons of the lower starting level and the higher population pressure, appears considerably more difficult than even that of the Soviet Union under Stalin. A first attempt to achieve an industrial "leap forward" by original methods without massive foreign aid has collapsed; yet, because of the conflict with the West, no substantial capital aid can be expected from the advanced Western nations.

Militarily, the Soviet Union is one of the two world powers; owing to its possession of thermonuclear bombs and intercontinental means of delivery in adequate numbers, its leaders feel reasonably secure against deliberate attack from their enemies and consider that their national security could only be endangered by the unforeseen and unintended escalation of a local conflict. China has no independent deterrent and no near prospect of an effective one, as a few atomic bombs by themselves no longer fulfill this role. Without the broad basis of an all-round modern arms industry capable of steady technological advance, China may continue, as the leading regional power in Asia, to intimidate her underdeveloped neighbors but cannot become a world power capable of assuring its own security. Achievement of that status thus depends on the solution of her industrialization problem, which is uncertain in principle and certain to be slow at best.

Diplomatically, the Soviet government not only is almost universally recognized and holds a permanent seat in the Security Council of the United Nations but also is regarded by its opponents as a necessary partner for recurrent negotiations. Both the Soviet Union and the United States are aware that they have a common interest in avoiding nuclear war as well as opposite interests in the East-West conflict, and efforts to control the forms of the conflict by negotiation are the logical consequence of that awareness; they are facilitated by the fact that the areas in dispute between them, however important to one or both of them, do not form part of the national territory of either power. Communist China's government is not recognized by the United States and most of its allies and is kept out of the United Nations by their influence; moreover, its most direct dispute with the United States, concerning its protection of what the United States regards as the legitimate government of the Republic of China, is regarded by the Communists as the unlawful occupation by the United States of part of their national territory, the island of Taiwan. Hence, while, for the Soviets, diplomatic relations with the enemy are one of the natural forms of carrying on their conflict with him, they play almost no role in the Chinese arsenal.

Lopsided Dependence

The Soviet Union is, thus, the only country from which a Communist China can expect the capital aid that it desperately needs for its industrialization. It is the only country that can protect a Communist China from the supposed danger of an American or American-controlled attack or furnish it modern weapons for pushing its demands against American resistance. And it is the only great power that may be called upon to take care of the interests of Communist China in diplomatic negotiations with the enemy, particularly in the United Nations. In all these fields, the dependence is not only complete but also largely one way: Russia has no substantial need of Chinese economic cooperation; Chinese military strength makes at best an indirect contribution to Soviet security by diverting part of the enemy's energies and, above all, by preventing the establishment of a pro-American government at Russia's Far Eastern border; Chinese political influence with some Asian countries has proved at times useful, but by no means indispensable to Soviet diplomacy.

Now it will easily be seen that, while mutual dependence among allies is a powerful bond of unity, one-sided—or at least strongly lopsided—dependence of the kind here described is a factor of unity and a cause of conflict at the same time, because it tends to produce sharp disagreement about the place of the weaker power's interests on the stronger power's list of priorities. Economically, the urgency of China's need for capital aid conflicts with the Russian inclination to put the arms race first, the improvement of living standards at home second, and even the wooing of uncommitted nations ahead of aid for China, which, being Communist, tends to be taken for granted. Militarily, the Chinese demand for all-out Soviet support of the pressure against Taiwan conflicts with the Soviet sensitivity for risks of nuclear war and the consequent tactics of pursuing any local offensive only to the point where the risk of escalation appears serious. Diplomatically, the Chinese insistence on being fully consulted about any negotiations between Russia and the American enemy conflicts with the Soviet desire at certain moments of crisis to achieve a relaxation of tension quickly, without much regard for Chinese consent or prestige. The result has been a series of disappointments for China in each of these fields.

Differences of Strategic Outlook

In addition to producing a lopsided dependence of Communist China on the Soviet Union with its attendant tensions, the different situations of the two major Communist powers have led them to see the outside world from different angles, and hence to develop different strategic ideas for their common struggle. In particular, the Soviets are more concerned to keep the risk of nuclear war under control, both because they have more to lose in a material sense and because they do in fact have more control over it. The Chinese, in view of the vastness of their country and population, of its comparatively poor development, and of their lack of an independent deterrent, are more inclined both to regard the risk as bearable and to feel that it does not depend on them. Similarly, it is natural for the Soviets to seek to coordinate the use of diplomacy in relations with non-Communist powers, both hostile and neutral, with the use of revolutionary movements. The greater limitation of Chinese diplomatic possibilities leads them to regard the maneuvers of Soviet diplomacy with skepticism and suspicion and to rely primarily, though not exclusively, on the revolutionary weapon.

To the Soviets, the United States is both the leader of the enemy camp that must be broken up by a judicious mixture of nuclear blackmail, support for revolutionary movements, economic competition, and well-timed offers of negotiation and the partner in an effort to prevent the struggle from leading to a nuclear holocaust. To the Chinese Communists, the United States is also the leader of the enemy camp, but it is no partner in any diplomatic effort; instead, it is resented as the direct *national* enemy as well—the backer of the "counterrevolution" in a recent civil war, the bitterly hated opponent in the even more recent, sanguinary Korean war, the occupant of part of the national territory. In terms of Soviet demonology, the United States presents in the eyes of the Chinese Communists the interventionist powers of 1918-1920, the Nazi German invader, and the real United States of today—all rolled into one imperialist monster. As a result, the chance of obtaining anything from them by diplomacy appears as nil; the risk of provoking their military action appears as both inevitable and manageable—after all, the Peking regime has survived it before.

To the Soviets, the revolutionary movements in the colonial and semicolonial countries—the only exploitable revolutionary movements that exist in the contemporary world—are both a source of strength to be tapped and a source of risks to be controlled: They are willing and, indeed, eager to support them, but they insist on their freedom to judge the precise point beyond which they cannot go. To the Chinese, who feel militarily less secure, the multiplication of armed conflicts in distant lands appears rather to diminish their direct peril because it may force the enemy to disperse his strength. Hence, their willingness to support such movements is limited only by their technical capacity—which, outside Asia, is in striking disproportion to their verbal militancy—not by any consideration of risk.

To the Soviets, it is a desirable objective to win over some of the uncommitted nations, temporarily by the promotion of conflict between those nations and some of the Western powers or permanently by the growth of Communist influence within their governments. But, failing that, even the wooing of genuinely neutral and independent nations by economic aid appears worthwhile from a Soviet point of view, not only in order to prevent these countries from sliding into the Western embrace, but also as part of their effort to influence the policy of their opponents by the pressure of world opinion inside as well as outside the United Nations: The steady campaigning to win neutral voices and votes on specific issues of the East-West conflict is one aspect of the Russian ability to conduct diplomacy in a continuous, world-wide field where a shift in any one element influences all others. To the Chinese, aid to neutrals appears justified only to the extent that they cease to be neutrals—either by getting involved in acute conflict with some Western power, or by coming under increasing Communist control from within, or by becoming part of Communist China's dependent buffer zone owing to her regional military preponderance. Aid for genuinely independent neutral states that feel free to accept support from both East and West appears to the Chinese Communists as a wanton waste of limited resources; attempts to use the machinery of the United Nations for achieving Communist-bloc objectives with the help of neutral votes are viewed by them as futile and self-defeating. In the special case of India, whose policy is regarded by Peking as the main obstacle to the expansion of its Asian buffer zone, all Soviet credits thus appear as direct aid to China's enemy—while, to the Soviets, China's attacks seem liable to push an important neutral power needlessly into the Western camp.

Ideological Rivalry

Within an alliance, differences in the priority scales and the strategic outlook of the partners are normal; it is also normal that they are settled by repeated compromises so long as the conflict with the common enemy exceeds their importance. But, where the alliance is rooted exclusively in the common ideology of ruling totalitarian parties, the disagreements arising from their different situations naturally assume the form of different interpretations of that ideology. Once such an ideological dispute has come into the open, a pragmatic adjustment of the underlying policy differences becomes far more difficult. For, in a totalitarian-party regime, the authority of the leaders depends on general acceptance of their interpretation of the ideology; hence, any open challenge to the "correctness" of this interpretation amounts to a direct attack on that leadership and, above all, on the leader himself. It follows that, from the moment of such an open challenge, the common ideology that has united the allies becomes also a factor of serious conflict between them. . . .

The familiar debates on the possibility of the separate achievement of "full communism" by advanced countries, on the chances of "eliminating war" despite the continued existence of imperialism, on the character of imperialism as a "paper tiger" or a tiger with "real atomic teeth," on the need to subordinate national liberation movements to the "general line" of "peaceful coexistence" or to subordinate coexistence diplomacy to the "general line" of "anti-imperialist struggle," on relations with the "national bourgeoisie" in the ex-colonial countries, and on the chances of seizing power in some states by "peaceful methods" have been the result of that Chinese decision. The arguments show that, in raising their challenge, the Chinese Communists could not stop at simply translating their specific policy disagreements with the Soviets into ideological terms but had to turn them into parts of a coherent system based on their own revolutionary experience and on the structural characteristics of Chinese Communist thought derived from it. Those characteristics include the belief in the power of revolutionary determination aided by theory to overcome unfavorable material conditions, in the decisive role of people rather than arms technology in war, and in the principle of "uninterrupted revolution" both at home and abroad. . . .

The logic of the schism tends to make each side pursue increasingly independent policies and dig ever deeper foundations for their ideological opposition. In foreign policy, the Chinese have increasingly turned to creating their independent power sphere in Asia. They have secured the ideological allegiance of North Korea and North Vietnam; they have built up their buffer zone in Nepal, Cambodia, and Burma and broken effective Indian opposition to this development by military intimidation; they have appeared as active competitors with Soviet influence in Indonesia. The Soviets in turn, by continuing substantial economic aid to India at the height of the "border conflict," have given open and direct support to the enemies of their Chinese allies. Behind the differences of strategy in the common struggle against the West, which were the original cause of the ideological schism, the basic differences of "pure" national interest are thus coming to the surface once again.

II. MOSCOW VS. PEKING: THE WORLDWIDE COMPETITION

EDITOR'S INTRODUCTION

The polemics between the Soviet Union and China take place on many different levels and concern many different problems. What is the correct appraisal of the present state of world politics? What is the advantage or disadvantage of peaceful coexistence? Conversely, what is to be said for and against greater militancy in the struggle against the West? What about Vietnam? How is the underdeveloped world to be treated? What should be the relationship between national liberation movements and the Communist countries? Moscow and Peking have their own answers to each of these questions.

This section analyzes some of the answers. The first part of the section contains two articles which focus chiefly on the economic problems within China and the Soviet Union. The different stages of economic development in the two countries help explain why they take such divergent views of the outside world. The contrast between the two also explains why the Chinese frequently accuse the Russians of going soft, losing their revolutionary zeal, and even reverting to capitalism.

The next part of this section looks at China in greater detail. The Chinese position should be seen partially in terms of the revolutionary experiences which govern much of the thinking of the present leadership. Although it is sometimes convenient to believe that the Chinese are willing to ignore the risks that their belligerence entails, these articles point out that in many respects Peking's policies tend to be cautious. At the same time, the Chinese stress that their militancy is based on a careful evaluation of the world situation as well as on correct Leninist logic.

The final part of this section examines some of the areas where Sino-Soviet competition is most keen. The first two articles in this part discuss the knotty Vietnam problem from the Communist vantage point and consider the stakes involved for both Moscow and Peking. The following selections survey Communist rivalry in the underdeveloped world. The Chinese have concentrated their efforts most heavily in Africa and in neighboring Asian countries. However, as the article from *The Wall Street Journal* explains, China's foreign policy in these areas has experienced a number of serious setbacks. While Peking's loss is not necessarily Moscow's gain, the men in the Kremlin may well feel some satisfaction as they see the problems piling up for China.

1.   Inside Russia and China

THE CONTINUING REVOLUTION [1]

In its long struggle for power, the Chinese Communist party (CCP) has known the taste of victory in the face of overwhelmingly superior foes. Rising out of the chaos and misery that has characterized most of China's history in the twentieth century, the CCP early mastered the art of survival against heavy odds. Again and again it was driven to the brink of extinction; again and again it returned to fight another day—and eventually to win.

The CCP was founded in 1921, ten years after a nationalist revolution led by Dr. Sun Yat-sen had put an end to the Manchu dynasty that had ruled China since 1644. Failing to obtain material aid from the Western powers after World War I, Sun Yat-sen had turned to the newly established Communist regime in Russia. Help was forthcoming, and with it the self-proclaimed messengers of a new order in human affairs.

Holding their ultimate goal in abeyance, Chinese Communists flocked to the banner of Dr. Sun's Kuomintang (National People's party). With the use of Soviet organizational techniques, the Kuomintang was able to impose a semblance of unity throughout much of the country by 1928, though local warlords continued

[1] From *Great Decisions 1965.* (Fact Sheet no. 1. Red China—Menace or Paper Tiger?) Foreign Policy Association. 345 E. 46th St. New York 10017. '65. p 6-9. Reprinted by permission.

to pose a major problem. Meanwhile, however, Dr. Sun had died, and the leadership of the Kuomintang had fallen to a young general who had spent four months in the Soviet Union.

That general was Chiang Kai-shek, and in 1927 he took action to rid the Kuomintang of Communist influence. Soviet military advisers were sent back to Russia, and the fateful internal struggle that was to end in disaster twenty-two years later got under way. The Communists proved an elusive quarry. Driven from Shanghai and Hankow by Chiang's forces in 1927, they retreated to the countryside of south central China. There they worked hard to win over the peasants, who constituted 80-85 per cent of China's population.

Between 1930 and 1934, Chiang Kai-shek launched five successive campaigns to dislodge the "Red bandits" from their base. In the first four, however, it was the bandits who scored gains. Mastering techniques of guerrilla warfare, the Communists wrung supplies of arms and not a few defectors from each Nationalist incursion. The fifth campaign, directed by Chiang and his German military advisers, followed a new strategy of encirclement, blockade and progressive strangulation. For a time the Reds stood their ground, suffering heavy losses. Finally they were forced into one of the most spectacular retreats in the annals of warfare. With ninety thousand troops and a mass of supporting peasants, they fled six thousand miles through some of the most rugged terrain in the world to emerge one year later in northwest China, their forces cut to twenty thousand.

The Communist Triumph

Chiang's plans for a final offensive in 1937 were never put into effect. Japan, which had conquered Manchuria in 1931, now moved to renew the conflict in north China. Communists and Nationalists joined in an uneasy truce to resist the common foreign enemy. This "shotgun wedding," as it has been called, lasted despite minor skirmishing on both sides until the end of World War II. Then, after the exhausting struggle against Japan, the civil war resumed in earnest.

Much has been written about the decisive phase of the Nationalist-Communist struggle that ensued after Japan's defeat in 1945. Much more will no doubt be written, in the light of recent history, analyzing anew Soviet Russia's relatively meager support for the Communist side and challenging the long-held American view that the Nationalist defeat was a Moscow triumph. Most historians seem agreed on three points: First, that the United States quest for a Nationalist-Communist coalition government was unrealistic in view of the wide gulf separating the two sides. Second, that Russia's occupation of Manchuria, as arranged at the Yalta conference, was, in terms of hindsight, an unnecessary boon to the Communist side. And third, that a major factor in the collapse of the Kuomintang was its lack of public support, due to widespread corruption and disunity within its ranks.

On October 1, 1949 the People's Republic of China was officially proclaimed. In the years since, through a monumental feat of organization, China's Communist leaders have imposed unity and discipline on a country which had known little of either for more than a century. . . .

The Communist revolution did not end with the proclamation of the Chinese People's Republic in 1949. In many ways it was only beginning. The fighting had stopped, but the tactics of storm and stress that had served the Communists so well in the civil war were now turned against the whole of the Chinese nation. With grim determination, China's new rulers launched an immense effort to reshape the education, economy, and life of the most populous country on earth.

That effort is still going forward today. Its ultimate goal is to make China an economically advanced industrial power, the "center of world civilization," as was the Middle Kingdom in days of old. But its most immediate impact is apparent in the "political struggle," the struggle to force China's 700 million people into a single Communist mold.

Not even Russia under Stalin pressed a campaign of political indoctrination with greater militancy than the Peking leadership, or instituted totalitarian political control with greater speed. No sooner did Chinese Red army forces occupy a village than party workers were on the scene, organizing and indoctrinating the masses in Marxism-Leninism and in the "thought" of party chairman Mao Tse-tung. Old social institutions—the traditional village organizations, guilds, and secret societies—were suppressed. In their places came the new mass political organizations—for peasants, laborers, women, youth, businessmen, artists, professional people, and virtually every definable segment of Chinese society. Together with the party apparatus, these new organizations provided a means for extending Communist authority down to the level of village, family, and individual.

Drastic measures were instituted to deal with potential sources of opposition. Obvious dissidents, such as large landholders or those labeled reactionaries, were executed after mass public trials. A campaign of violent class warfare in the villages shattered the power and influence of the landlords and local leaders. Poor peasants were set against rich peasants. In the cities businessmen and intellectuals were subjected to an ideological remolding campaign so rigorous and intimidating as to break any lingering spirit of open resistance to Communist dogma or policies.

Current Measures

The style and intensity of these campaigns were unique even among Communist regimes. They strove at once to indoctrinate and convert, and to mobilize and control. . . . Declaring that "ideology is the most important element in production," party officials took steps . . . to bring economic activities under their increased control. New attacks were leveled against "rich peasants" and "spontaneous tendencies toward capitalism." Industrial workers and peasants were ordered to attend special classes in "socialist education." Under the slogan "learn from the People's Liberation Army," the population was urged to adopt the discipline and work methods of the military and to live up to Mao Tse-tung's dictum that "all people are soldiers."

New campaigns were launched to "purify" music and drama. Playwrights were warned "to propagate socialist and Communist thoughts and warmly sing the praises of new socialist persons." A "socialist singing" movement among workers, students, soldiers, and peasants had the Chinese countryside echoing with such current favorites of the party as "Obey Only the Party," "Sing a Ballad for the Party," "Commune Members Are Sunflowers," and "Hold Aloft the Great Banner of Revolution."

Food for Thought

Yet, as Soviet Premier Khrushchev so pointedly remarked . . . before his ouster: "If you feed people just with revolutionary slogans they will listen today, they will listen tomorrow, they will listen the day after tomorrow, but on the fourth day they will say: 'To hell with you!' " His remark served as a reminder to the Chinese Communists that while their organization and control might for the moment seem near perfection, their economic performance was anything but.

Currently, economic woes constitute Peking's most pressing problems. China possesses a meager industrial base with which to sustain great power ambitions. No help in the form of foreign aid is available. About 45 per cent of the regime's total foreign expenditures in recent years has been used for grain purchases. Barter deals supply some industrial imports, but Red China has little to offer the world even in the way of barter. Though half a billion Chinese are engaged in tilling the soil, agricultural problems have provided the regime with its gravest crises. Hunger has always been the greatest enemy of the Chinese people, and, propaganda aside, it continues so today. . . .

A Sobering Experience

On coming to power, Communists had argued that China could support ten times its population; impoverishment, said Peking, was the fault of past imperialist oppression. The years since have provided the regime with a sobering experience. Agricultural output, China's Achilles' heel, has barely kept pace with the population growth rate of about 2.5 per cent a year. A legacy of primitive conditions in the countryside coupled with several years of bad weather, drought, and floods account for some of the trouble. But a substantial share of the blame must be fixed on the bungling policies of the regime.

In its first few years under Communist direction, China's economy moved forward at a brisk pace. From the start, however, agriculture was neglected. Emphasis was placed on the expansion of heavy industry. With the help of Soviet technical experts and capital goods, considerable progress was made.

But problems were developing, and by 1957 it was evident that forward momentum was grinding to a halt. Soviet aid was decreasing. The lag in agriculture was critical. Like Stalin in Russia, Chinese leaders had sought to squeeze the agricultural sector in order to pay for advances in industry. At the same time they had taken only the simplest and least expensive steps to increase agricultural efficiency. The inevitable imbalance was now threatening their plans for continued growth.

The party faced a critical choice. It could seek to redress the imbalance by shifting more funds into agriculture and cutting back on industrial expansion. Or it could push full steam ahead in both areas, hoping that a spasm of superhuman effort would break through existing bottlenecks and place China firmly on the road to industrial power.

"Great Leap Forward"

What followed was both incredible and disastrous. Choosing the latter course, the party mobilized China's vast pool of manpower in a frenetic campaign to build with human hands that which China's industry and technology could not provide. It was to be one "great leap forward," clearing all those hurdles of backwardness and poverty that afflicted China. Back-yard steel furnaces sprouted everywhere, and peasants, returning from a day in the fields, smelted metal by night. More than 100 million men and women were set to work on huge water-control projects. The eight-hour day—a party pledge back in 1931—was stretched to fourteen, sixteen and even more hours.

Almost overnight hundreds of millions of peasants were herded into twenty-six thousand agricultural communes, where their consumption of food and their time spent in preparing and eating meals could be rationed by the state in communal kitchens. In a desperate effort to raise agricultural output, Peking ordered close planting of crops under the naïve impression that twice the yield would result if the distance between rows were cut by half. Even sparrows fell victim to the great leap. As grain eaters they were marked for liquidation. An estimated one billion of them were put to death by work teams who used noise and movement to keep the birds flying till they fell exhausted to the ground.

Peking is still struggling to recover from the setbacks suffered under this waste of human effort. The steel produced by the backyard furnaces was useless. The close cropping and other agricultural innovations proved severely damaging. Output went down rather than up. Revolutionary fervor failed to provide the peasant with sufficient incentive in his work on the new communes. Even the slaughter of the sparrows came back to haunt the regime, as insects (the sparrows ate those, too) ravaged the countryside.

Soviet Withdrawal

Other blows fell hard in the wake of the "great leap" disaster. Refusing to kowtow or compromise in its ideological dispute with Moscow, Peking found the flow of Soviet aid, technical assistance, and capital goods virtually cut off in 1960. The economy was hit hard by the loss of Soviet blueprints, processing materials, replacement units, and spare parts—a setback that prompted one Peking official to accuse Moscow of trying to "strangle" China economically.

Peking leaders reportedly admit that it will now take them more than fifty years to catch up with the countries of Western Europe, assuming that large-scale Soviet aid is not resumed. Nonetheless, Peking is dogmatically sticking to the commune system—even extending it to urban factories—with some concessions to peasant incentive in the form of small private plots. It has been struggling to reorient trade toward Western Europe and Japan, but the long-term credits it needs are not being offered. The potential of industrial power is present, but it will be a long time in developing.

The Cult of Mao

Some party figures have apparently grown restless under these stringent policies. . . . There were ominous signs that a purge of such dissidents might be in the making. Yang Hsien-chen, a Central Committee ideologue who until 1961 was head of the Higher Party School, was lambasted for harboring pro-Moscow sympathies. Party journals warned repeatedly that U.S. imperialists "count on the third or fourth generation in China to bring about a so-called 'peaceful evolution' in our country—back to capitalism," in which direction Khrushchev was accused of leading Russia. They praised the ruthless purges of old-line Bolsheviks carried out by Stalin in the 1930's.

The strict orthodoxy being demanded by the party is posing problems for and perhaps tensions within the regime. In view of China's economic plight, there will always be strong pressures for a coming to terms either with the Soviet Union or with the West. And although the party is irritated by "spontaneous capitalism" among the peasantry and anxious to stamp it out, bitter experience has taught that some capitalist incentives remain essential to boost agricultural output at this stage.

Yet "orthodoxy at any price" appears to be the watchword as long as Mao Tse-tung and the old-line militant revolutionaries who surround him hold power. Mao's own prestige and authority within the party are unchallenged and compare with that of Stalin in his heyday. He is revered by Chinese propagandists as a "genius-philosopher," a near-deity who can do no wrong. The "sun, lighthouse, food, grain, weapons and compass" of the Chinese people, rhapsodized one speaker at a Communist Youth Congress. . . . Though he is aging and recent pictures show him looking frail, the CCP's chairman and his fundamentalist brand of communism—popularly known as Maoism—hold a tight grip on the masses.

In general, Maoism is a more primitive rendering of Marxism than that being followed in the Soviet Union. It is officially regarded as Marxism-Leninism adjusted to Chinese conditions. Thus it stresses what might be called the "supercollective" aspects of communism—communal living, for example—which are within China's reach. It also lays great stress on the "spiritual" side of communism—equality, sacrifice for the state, the class struggle, etc.

Khrushchev once characterized Maoism in these terms: "Communism cannot be depicted as a table laid with empty plates and occupied by highly conscious and completely equal people. To invite people to such communism is tantamount to inviting people to eat soup with a fork. This would be a caricature of communism."

China and "The Bomb"

Just as in the days of the great leap forward, human numbers rather than technology were to provide the economic breakthrough Peking desired, so in Maoist military strategy men rather than weapons have been held the most important factor in war. According to Peking, it is the fighting spirit of the soldier which, above all else, determines victory or defeat. This concept served the Communists well in their years of guerrilla warfare. It also nicely fits the over-all military posture of Red China today— namely, a superabundance of manpower but a critical lack of modern weaponry.

The People's Liberation Army—estimated at 2 to 2.5 million strong—is the biggest land force in the world. It is well equipped with Chinese-made small arms, howitzers, mortars, and tanks— all patterned on Soviet models. According to one observer, as of 1960 it resembled the powerful and complex World War II armies of the Western powers.

The Red Chinese air force and navy are poorly equipped and provide wholly inadequate support for the massive army, severely limiting Peking's offensive capabilities. The air force consists of 2,400 aircraft, mostly outdated MIG 15's and 17's, and a very few bombers. The Russians have cut off aircraft deliveries, and reports out of Hong Kong indicate the Chinese may have begun to cannibalize their aircraft to obtain needed spare parts. The Chinese were incensed by Khrushchev's offer to provide India with up-to-date MIG 21's, while they, a formal ally of the U.S.S.R., had to scrounge for parts. The navy is limited to a few submarines and coastal defense vessels and is not even on a par with the Nationalist navy on Taiwan.

Red China's detonation of a nuclear device [in 1964] is not expected to alter—for the present—its basically weak military posture vis-à-vis the United States and the Soviet Union. Peking lacks not only a sizeable and varied nuclear stockpile, but the means necessary for its delivery as well. Its industrial and technological facilities will face enormous strain if these means are to be provided within the near future. For these reasons, some observers expect Peking to shy away from any direct confrontation with a great power in the years ahead, promoting instead guerrilla and local wars.

But other analysts warn of the dangers of underestimating Chinese strength and resourcefulness. Peking's nuclear explosion, they say, was a comparatively sophisticated first try. (Some predict that an advanced thermonuclear device will follow within about five years.) And while China will be unable to match the United States in a blow-for-blow nuclear exchange for many decades, it nonetheless may within a few short years be capable of menacing all of the nations on its periphery and many off its shores. It has been in precisely these areas, in fact, that the Chinese nuclear breakthrough has had its greatest psychological impact.

MARXISM—WITH A DASH OF PROFITS [2]

The Soviet Union has lived in a state of virtual economic siege for most of its existence. In Lenin's time the economy had broken down to such an extent that he had to rely temporarily on a semicapitalistic system to keep the country going. In the thirty years of his reign, Stalin rammed through a program of industrialization and collectivization at frightful human cost. Khrushchev's de-Stalinization program tipped the balance somewhat in favor of the consumer, but the Soviet economy still has not been particularly generous to the people. There may be a few more cars on the roads and many more refrigerators in the kitchens, but

[2] From *Great Decisions 1966.* (Fact Sheet no. 5. Russia After Khrushchev—Does Coexistence Have a Future?) Foreign Policy Association. 345 E. 46th St. New York 10017. '66. p 53-6. Reprinted by permission.

an automobile is beyond the pocketbook of the average man, and there is liable to be a frustratingly long wait for new housing, even in the form of two-room apartments.

On the Farm

Agriculture remains the perennial Achilles' heel of the Communist system. In a sense, Soviet agriculture has never completely recovered from the impact of collectivization decreed by Stalin in the late 1920's in an effort to ensure the cities an adequate supply of food. "There is simply not enough meat in the Soviet Union," Khrushchev admitted in 1962. Prices had to be increased sharply in order to slash demand. A disastrous grain harvest in 1963, which forced Moscow to buy twelve million tons of grain from abroad, further dramatized the shortcomings of Soviet agriculture. In 1964 a bountiful harvest put unexpectedly large quantities of food on the market. In 1965, however, another small harvest forced the Soviet Union to import large quantities of grain from Canada, Argentina, and France. Soviet leaders said that in some respects Soviet agriculture was worse off than before World War II, when there were forty million less mouths to feed.

Though food supplies today are generally adequate, frequent scarcities develop and prices are likely to be high. Furthermore, increases in food production have fallen far short of expectation, and Soviet boasts about catching up with the West by 1965 in the per capita production of wheat, butter, and meat have been quietly buried.

The collective farm itself most clearly exposes the deficiencies of Soviet agriculture. There exist model farms, with modern equipment, well-kept buildings, and an apparently industrious and relatively well-paid (by Soviet standards) group of farmers. These are the farms the tourist sees. Most collectivized farms, however, are dreary places. In his book, *One Day in the New Life*, Soviet novelist Fyodor Abramov tells a depressing story of farm existence. The new life turns out to be a bitter joke. Mechanized equipment is in short supply and often ends up prematurely for a long stay in the repair shop—where spare parts are not available. The farm villages are shabby. Perhaps, aside from more plumbing and electricity, they are not too much different from czarist times. Wages, based on the number of workday units earned by the collective farm member, are low. The farmers are often indifferent and careless, causing waste and low yield. As a result of these and other factors, the Soviet farmer raises enough to feed only 6.5 people, including himself, while a typical U.S. farmer raises enough to feed a total of 26 people.

One of the biggest problems of the farm manager, who usually is a member of the party, is how to spur interest and incentive in a system where the farmers do not own the land or its produce. Two Communist countries, Poland and Yugoslavia, have by and large rejected the collective system and operate chiefly with private farming.

Collectivized farming is not going to be discarded in the Soviet Union. In a concession to free enterprise, however, each farm family is allowed to cultivate a small private plot, averaging less than an acre, and to keep a small amount of livestock. A farmer is likely to give far better care to his private plot, the produce of which he uses in his own home or sells in the open market, than he gives to the collectivized acres. When they can get away with it, the farmers are not above pilfering a little collectivized fodder for private use or encroaching a bit on collectivized land. Though private plots cover less than 5 per cent of the total cultivated area in the Soviet Union, they account for about half the meat, dairy products, and vegetables, and more than two thirds of the nation's potatoes produced each year.

The long-lasting ills in agriculture have spawned a number of remedies, none of which have been able to cure the patient completely.

After 1950, collective farms were merged into larger units so that mechanized machinery could be used to better advantage. Various financial incentives have been offered through the years. Khrushchev tried to increase efficiency by making one wing of the Communist party specifically responsible for agriculture (and the other wing responsible for industry). He concentrated on intensive planting of corn, then stressed fertilizer production. In addition, beginning in 1954, he spent enormous sums in putting tens of millions of virgin acres in the Urals, Siberia, and Central Asia under cultivation. Initially, crops in the virgin lands were good, but because the region suffers from a scarcity of rainfall, later results were sharply disappointing.

The Brezhnev-Kosygin team initiated a new series of measures. More than $2 billion in collective farm debts to the state were canceled. Collective farmers were included under the state's pension plan for the first time. New stress has been put upon modern methods of cultivation. Prices received by the farms for their products have been increased and compulsory delivery quotas cut. Wider latitude has been given to those farmers wishing to sell their goods on the open market. Some $78 billion is to be spent from 1966 through 1970 on farm machinery, chemical fertilizers, irrigation, drainage, and other essentials. This is about double the investment figure for the 1961-1965 period. While this new effort will undoubtedly bring improvements, it remains to be seen whether it will solve the deep-rooted problems of Soviet agriculture. The farm crisis can be expected to remain a Soviet headache for some time to come.

In the Factory

Unlike agriculture, industry is a relatively bright star in the Soviet economy. Under Stalin, the Soviet Union embarked upon a program of frenzied industrialization; under his successors, it has emerged as the world's second largest industrial power, with a large steel-producing capacity, a machine-tool industry, space apparatus, and the most sophisticated military hardware.

Despite a recent slowdown in its rate of industrial growth, the Soviet Union continues to move ahead industrially. Soviet figures (which tend to be exaggerated) indicated 1965 industrial output would be 84 per cent higher than that of 1958, with heavy industry producing 95 per cent more than in 1958. Consumer goods production would be, according to Soviet sources, 63 per cent higher than in 1958. All this has been accomplished under a system of centralized state planning so rigid that it specifies everything down to the placement of the last bolt in the smallest machine.

Imagine tens of thousands of government employees sitting before an enormous console wired to the Soviet economy. The console records millions of pieces of separate information on the Soviet economy. It also specifies what the master economic blueprint as detailed in the current Five- or Seven-Year plan, requires. The planners then calculate how to use the resources of the country to achieve the goals set by the leadership.

State economic planners decide how large the labor force in each factory should be, how many units of each product should be turned out, what the per unit cost should be, where and at what cost raw materials are to be procured. No item, no matter how insignificant, escapes the attention of the planners.

This system has given birth to a monstrous bureaucracy almost without parallel. The state plan for the construction of a steel mill is reported to have filled seventy thousand pages, with careful attention devoted to the placement of the wash basins and, so it is said, little consideration given to the over-all impact of the enterprise in the specified location.

Factory managers are continually bombarded with reams of instructions, and the instructions often conflict, since they come from a dozen different government ministries. To resolve such problems, to effect a change in plan because of some local difficulty, to amend instructions or to adapt to changing situations is a frustrating exercise because of bureaucratic red tape.

Yet, as long as the economy was relatively unsophisticated, and heavy industry, which lends itself to government planning, received primary attention, centralized state control, for all its inefficiency, worked. Soviet industrial progress is evidence of that fact.

But as the economy has become more complex, the men at the imaginary console have found themselves inundated by a flood of new complicating factors. For example, in an economy of scarcity, the consumer buys whatever is on the shelves, no matter how poorly styled or made. He has no other choice. But as some of the basic consumer demands were slowly filled in the last decade, the Soviet buyer found he could be more selective. Since he already had a pair of usable shoes, he did not have to purchase another pair if it did not meet his tastes. Billions of dollars worth of unsalable items piled up in the stores. Like a surrealistic nightmare, however, the factories had to keep turning out more of the goods which would not sell because the state plan called for them to do so. The plan was everything; the quality of the output was of lesser consequence.

The measure of a factory's success was not, as in the United States, profits—which reflect consumer satisfaction—but fulfillment or overfulfillment of its quota in the over-all countrywide plan. Factory managers were tempted to use every trick to have their target figures set as low as possible. Once the target was set, the manager would use every expedient to meet the quota. If his output was measured by the number of units produced, he would concentrate on smaller units, since they could be made more quickly. If output was measured by weight, the plant manager made his product as heavy as possible, with consequent waste of raw materials. Few people were interested in quality, because the strict enforcement of quality control was time consuming and might impede the race to meet the target figure. (These problems applied particularly to consumer-oriented industries, but they also affected such enterprises as tractor or tire plants, which are more closely related to critical elements in the economy.)

The Great Debate

Some Soviet planners believed that the answer to the problem of running an increasingly complex economy lay in more efficient, tighter central control and in a greater use of computers. Other experts, however, suggested that certain fundamental modifications in the planning system itself be considered. Let the state retain the main levers of control, they said, but leave the detailed operations in some factories to the plant managers.

This may not sound quite like a revolutionary proposal, but it occasioned a long and stormy debate in Soviet political and economic circles. For instance, it was argued that if the government abandoned the levers of control, it would be abandoning Marxism and the Communist party might eventually lose its role as the key directing element in the Soviet Union.

Those who favored some decentralization, however, countered that they were not out to undermine communism, but to improve efficiency. One economist, Yevsey Liberman, argued that the best way to improve efficiency was not only to decentralize but also to make profits and sales rather than plan fulfillment the criterion of success in certain industries. Although Liberman first broached his proposals in the late 1950's, it was not until the 1960's that his ideas began to be tested.

According to what is known as Libermanism (though many Soviet economists have now taken similar views), the central planning authority would continue to set over-all targets. But in selected industries the size of the work force, the salary and bonus rate, the reinvestment schedule and other basic matters would be left up to the factory manager and his immediate associates. A successful factory would be one which showed a profit at the end of the fiscal year—and the profits would be shared by the state, the managers and the workers. Efficiency would thus be recognized and incentive spurred.

The Little Switch

In 1964 a men's clothing factory in Moscow and a women's garment factory in the city of Gorki were converted with great fanfare to the profit system. The factories set their production schedules on the basis of orders received from retail stores rather than on the basis of figures laid down by the government. At the same time the factories kept in touch with the retail stores to see what designs were selling well and what preferences the customers showed. Production schedules would be regulated accordingly. After some initial difficulties the two factories began to work smoothly and the modest experiment was hailed as a major economic success. In 1965 the profit system was applied to about one third of the clothing and shoe industries, some four hundred factories in all, as well as to some food processing plants, restaurants, and retail stores.

. . . [In October 1965] the Central Committee of the Communist party approved a far-reaching series of economic reforms. The new emphasis on profit incentives and the elimination of unnecessary industrial controls received formal endorsement. Regional economic councils, which control all industries in an area, are to be abolished and replaced by centralized ministries, each one of which will be responsible for a specific branch of industry. In addition, new economic incentives are to be offered to workers and managers.

Do these changes hint that the Soviet Union may be going capitalistic? Communist China's Mao Tse-tung, in a bitter blast at the Soviet Union, declared that Russia was "facing an unprecedented danger of capitalist restoration." In fact, however, the adoption of more flexible methods of management is being carried out within the system of state ownership, and there is no justification for the view that the Soviet Union is adopting capitalism. In Marxist terms recent events would be put this way: increased prosperity has exposed contradictions between the system of state planning and the need for further development of the country's productive forces. Old methods, therefore, must be discarded if they no longer prove efficient.

Plant managers will not become capitalists; they will simply have greater operational freedom. The state will still own the producing units, and much of the capital for investment will be supplied directly from the state's budget. What has happened is that some of the flexible characteristics of capitalist management are being combined with the principle of state ownership and central control. Learn from the capitalists, Lenin advised. That is what Soviet leaders are apparently trying to do.

But these developments pose a set of interesting questions. How far is Libermanism to go? If certain industries can be put under the profit system to the advantage of the economy, then why not others? Why not even put the collective farms under some form of the profit system? And if a market economy gradually assumes a greater role in the Soviet Union, then what will happen to Communist control? Will ideology give way to a pragmatic approach to economic development?

The Soviet economy is no longer clamped in so tight a vise. It now appears to have been given room for maneuver. How might the evolution in the economy affect coexistence? If technocrats and administrators, rather than politicians and ideologists, assume more of the commanding positions, will they tend to favor, as a matter of practical economics, friendly coexistence so as to enable them to concentrate their energies and the country's resources on internal development? Could or should the United States do anything to encourage this situation?

2. The View from Peking

CHINA GOES IT ALONE [3]

After seven years of natural calamities, economic dislocation, and slow, painful recovery, China is moving again. Premier Chou En-lai has announced that a third Five-Year Plan will start in 1966. Three years late though it is, the new plan is a sign that the long period of "readjustment and consolidation" of the economy is almost over. The Chinese leaders are now ready to resume their "long march" toward a great industrial society, the equal of America and Russia.

Important deficiencies and stumbling blocks litter China's future course. China may not, for example, be able to produce or find enough oil to lubricate its policy of self-reliance. So far, ingenuity in factory and laboratory has been of little help in solving the perennial problem of the countryside, where 80 per cent of China's 700 millions produce the country's food and raw materials under the most primitive conditions. Even with grain imports and subsidiary foodstuffs, a generous calculation would not give the Chinese a daily average per capita consumption higher than 2,000 calories—a level that is some 200 calories lower than that of pre-war China. . . .

The last seven years have been a severe test of the resilience of the Communist regime and the cohesion of its leadership. The Party and governmental apparatus have all sustained shocks, but only temporarily and locally have their positions been threatened. Indeed, the major upheavals of the period, the Tibetan revolt of 1958-1959 and the apparently Soviet-inspired uprising among

[3] From article by Roderick MacFarquhar, editor of China Quarterly. Atlantic. 215: 69-75. Ap. '65. Copyright © 1965, by The Atlantic Monthly Company, Boston, Mass. Reprinted with permission.

minority races in the border province of Sinkiang in 1962, had little to do with the economic crisis. At no time was there any real question of the survival of the regime itself.

The manner in which Mao Tse-tung and his colleagues have weathered these storms is a striking proof of the continuing dynamism and revolutionary élan of this aging group of men fifteen years after seizing power. Not that their cohesion has been perfect. Defense Minister Marshal P'eng Teh-huai, commander of the Chinese People's Volunteers during the Korean War, has been dismissed, and onetime Senior Deputy Premier Ch'en Yun, fifth in the party hierarchy, has been demoted. Lesser men have also disappeared. Yet when one remembers the near chaos of the early months of the Great Leap, what is impressive is how well the ruling Party Politburo stuck together. China's leaders seem to have little need to look over their shoulders at one another. . . . They are far more concerned about their successors, wondering if the next generation will have the revolutionary zeal to carry on the Maoist line at home and abroad.

During the past year or two, as economic difficulties have eased, the problem of heirs and successors seems to have become Mao's primary concern. He had been disturbed for a long time by the fact that young people in general were without experience of the long revolutionary struggle. Unsteeled by the hardships of those days, they did not fully appreciate such benefits as the revolution had brought. But more recently, as the Sino-Soviet dispute has become acrimonious, Mao has grown alarmed that the next generation of Chinese Communist party leaders may fall into the quagmire of "Khrushchevite revisionism."

Russia's Creeping Capitalism

In analyzing Soviet society, Mao has formed a somber vision of the future of communism, a vision that was reflected . . . in the most startling anti-Soviet polemic yet to have emerged from Peiping [a variant form of Peking]. Implicit in the . . . denunciation of the "Soviet privileged stratum and the revisionist Khrushchev clique" was a deep-seated pessimism about the future of the entire European Communist bloc. While Western analysts examine the possibility of fundamental change in the Soviet system only with the utmost caution, the Chinese came right out and said that "the first socialist country in the world, built by the great Soviet people with their blood and sweat, is now facing an unprecedented danger of capitalist restoration." Much as some Americans talk of Afro-Asian countries going Communist, Mao was saying that Russia might go capitalist.

The evidence cited by the Chinese—reports culled from the Soviet press on embezzlement, black marketeering, speculative activities by chairmen of collectives, the organization of private workshops—was hardly likely to convince an outsider that a degenerate Soviet leadership was trying to overthrow communism. Indeed, the Soviet government has prescribed the death penalty for some "economic crimes." Mao may genuinely believe that such crimes are the harbingers of creeping capitalism, but his deepest worries are about phenomena more widespread in Soviet society.

The Chinese have noted that Russia's gradually rising living standards, the increasing availability of durable consumer goods and better housing, appear to be dampening revolutionary ardor. They have seen that the post-Stalin relaxation has permitted Russian intellectuals to survey the Western horizon with growing interest, though they are periodically checked by the Communist party. Finally, they know that such developments encourage and are encouraged by the easing of tension between Moscow and Washington. They may envisage a time when the Soviet Union, more prosperous at home and more respected abroad, settles down as a satisfied member of the world community, forgetting communism's revolutionary aims and expanding a dialogue with the West at the expense of consolidating communism at home.

If this is Mao's fear, he has good cause for it. Marxists who digested one reversal of the master's teaching when Communist revolutions occurred first in underdeveloped rather than in industrialized countries would be faced with an even greater and far more unpleasant shock if industrialization, far from strengthening the "revolutionary" proletariat, merely changed it into a satisfied bourgeoisie. For Mao, certainly, *embourgeoisement* would spell the doom of communism as he understands it. But since he too is committed to industrialization, instead of examining in Marxist fashion whether a nonrevolutionary Soviet leadership is the inevitable product of the kind of economic base Russia now possesses, he has to turn Marx on his head (not the first time the master has been so treated) and argue that the leaders are shaping economic developments rather than being shaped by them. . . .

Mao Calls for Militancy

The Chinese reaction to the fall of Khrushchev was consistent with Mao's stress on the importance of leadership. While Chinese propaganda had been emphasizing Khrushchev's personal role in masterminding the Soviet regression toward capitalism, there were no demonstrations of joy in Peiping such as one might have expected from his archenemies. Mao did not want to risk antagonizing further the new top men in the Kremlin, whom he had hitherto described as the Khrushchev clique, because now they could conceivably direct the Soviet Union back to the true revolutionary path. Instead, Peiping maintained a diplomatic silence while Premier Chou En-lai, who had led the two previous conciliation missions, hurried off to Moscow to sound out Brezhnev and Kosygin. It was only when Chou returned bearing nothing more than a possible offer of a standstill on polemics that Peiping began to rumble again, warning Moscow to expect no compromise on the crucial issues of the Sino-Soviet dispute, "imperialism" and revolution.

For five years now, Mao has been telling the Russians that the struggle between communism and "imperialism" (that is, the West) is irreconcilable. The West will not give in without a struggle. It will fight to recover what it has lost, as at Suez. War is inevitable; not necessarily a nuclear world war, but certainly local wars and wars of national liberation, as in South Vietnam. The Communist bloc must be vigilant, uncompromising, forceful. Much of what Mao says is the common coin of classical Leninism. But a century of Chinese humiliation at the hands of the imperialists infuses his arguments with an emotional certainty which the Russians—always the colonizers, never the colonized—can understand but can never really feel. . . .

No Third Road

The Russians accuse the Chinese of bellicosity, asserting that the local wars which Peiping supports could spark a nuclear war which would mean global suicide. Certainly the men in Peiping, first-generation leaders of a young revolution, are far more militant and more willing to risk war, if not provoke it, than the managerial bureaucrats and technocrats who are running the Soviet Union today. But Mao does not advocate false heroics in the face of stronger opponents. His guerrilla warfare maxim still applies: When the enemy advances (that is, because he is stronger), we retreat. When the Chinese Communists started their bombardment of the offshore islands in 1958, they gave every appearance of intending to invade Quemoy. But when it became clear that the United States would help the Nationalists defend the base, the Chinese preferred to lose face rather than to start something they could not finish. And it is noteworthy that while Peiping attacked Khrushchev as a capitulationist for withdrawing Soviet missiles from Cuba, it also denounced him as an adventurist for putting them there in the first place and taking up a position he was not strong enough to maintain.

There is a school of thought in the West that believes that Mao has never really appreciated the power of nuclear weapons, and that now that China is getting the bomb, the Chinese will sober up. In fact, the evidence suggests that from Hiroshima onward the Chinese Communists have been well aware of the importance of nuclear weapons. The appropriate Maoist maxim is: Despise the enemy strategically, but respect him tactically. It is foolish not to realize that *if used*, enemy nuclear weapons could do you great damage; but it is defeatist to believe that *even if used*, nuclear weapons could decide the fate of the world revolution. It is men, not weapons, however terrible, who are the decisive factor in history. More important, Mao, thinking in terms of the Korean War, probably assumes that the United States would never use nuclear weapons unless attacked with them. So he calls the atom bomb a paper tiger because it has not forestalled "liberation struggles" in such places as South Vietnam, the Congo, or Cuba. If the Americans were to dare to start a nuclear war, only they would be wiped out, while "on the debris of a dead imperialism the victorious people would create very swiftly a civilization thousands of times higher than the capitalist system and a truly beautiful future. . . ."

Furthermore, even if Mao had personally witnessed the destructive power of the Chinese nuclear explosion in the Takla Makan desert, it would not necessarily have changed his attitude on nuclear war. There is a significant difference between China and the four other nuclear powers, in that China is underdeveloped—"poor and blank" in Mao's phrase—and has far less to lose in terms of accumulated industrial and social capital. Mao may well think, as is often alleged, that China with its vast population would emerge better from a nuclear holocaust than the United States or the Soviet Union. However, none of this means that Mao will or would like to precipitate a nuclear war. It does suggest why China is prepared to take greater risks than the Soviet Union in backing revolutionary movements throughout the world. This is in fact the second major issue in the dispute between Moscow and Peiping.

Here again the history of the revolution does much to explain Mao's ideas and policies. The vicissitudes of his struggle with the "bourgeois" Chiang Kai-shek made it natural for Mao to accept the rigid Stalinist division of the world into two camps and to echo the Comintern denunciations of Nehru, U Nu of Burma, and, in those days, Sukarno of Indonesia as "running dogs of imperialism." There was a period in the mid-fifties when this attitude was put aside, but with the increased militancy of the Chinese general line after 1957, this attitude was modified, and a number of events reconfirmed Mao in his old prejudices against "bourgeois nationalists." China quarreled with Indonesia over its treatment of the overseas Chinese. Peiping was angered by Nehru's granting asylum to the Dalai Lama and India's hostile reaction to the Tibetan revolt in 1959. This deterioration of relations was undoubtedly one reason why the smoldering border dispute burst into flame later in the year for the first time.

This renewed Chinese antagonism toward the neutralist world ran up against Khrushchev's policy of wooing the uncommitted nations by aid and diplomacy. Peiping must have resented greatly the fact that Soviet credits to such countries deprived China of possible assistance, especially since these funds would help bolster bourgeois nationalist governments and put back the day when they might be overthrown by the indigenous Communist parties. Above all, the Soviet Union's ostentatious neutrality in the border dispute with India was regarded in Peiping as rank betrayal.

This combination of disagreements over policy toward the "imperialists" and toward the "bourgeois nationalists" in the third world of Asia, Africa, and Latin America is the bedrock of the Sino-Soviet dispute today, as it was five years ago when Peiping first brought it into the open. The Chinese motives are an inextricable mixture of Chinese national and Communist revolutionary aims. As a resurgent nationalistic state, China resents Soviet failure to support the Chinese in the Formosa Strait and on the Indian border. As a militant Communist state, it deplores Soviet willingness to relax Soviet-American tensions. If Mao were asked to specify the relative importance of nationalist and revolutionary components in Chinese foreign policy, he would probably simply say, What's good for China is good for communism.

At any rate, Mao is not jeopardizing the unity of the Communist movement just for points of doctrine. In their ideological barrage on Moscow, the Chinese have displayed great industry in researching into the Marxist-Leninist canon. But doctrine is a weapon for them, not an end in itself. Apart from the fact that ideology is the conventional language for Communist polemics, it happens that Mao's views do by and large coincide with Lenin's. And while the Russians can justifiably assert that Lenin would have despised anyone who used his analyses in a completely different world situation, there is no doubt that to be able to invoke Lenin's name is a powerful card in the world Communist movement. . . .

Mobilizing the Uncommitted Nations

But China's tug-of-war with the Soviet Union is not restricted to the ranks of the faithful. It encompasses the whole of that vast and amorphous area loosely known as the "third world," where China also sees itself as the only true leader in the struggle against American "imperialism." Mao pictures the world as a vast battlefield suitable for his kind of political guerrilla warfare. During the Chinese civil war, Communist troops would mobilize the peasants to gain control of the countryside and then to surround and capture the cities. . . .

Today Mao sees Africa as the most promising area for exploitation. An estimated two thousand Chinese officials and newsmen there, backed by the incessant multilingual propaganda of Peiping Radio, strive to project an image of China as another colored ex-colony anxious to support its black brethren against the rich white man's club of which Russia as well as the United States is a member. To some extent Peiping has reshaped its traditional two-camp theory. As Moscow has pointed out, the Chinese seem to think now in terms of a rich white camp and a poor colored camp; certainly the Chinese struggle vigorously to exclude the Soviet Union from all Afro-Asian solidarity organizations. . . .

Chinese Action in Asia

Although Mao considers Africa to be the present storm center of the "countryside," the Chinese have not been neglecting Asia, where China's national interests are most directly involved. Whether Mao thinks that China should regain the suzerainty over Korea, Indochina, Burma, and the other territories which he . . . [considers to have] been stolen from China by the imperialists will never be known. But he must still consider Southeast Asia, which sent tribute missions to Peiping in imperial times, as a legitimate and primary sphere of influence for China. Peiping is now infinitely more experienced in this area, and its diplomacy is correspondingly more restrained and sophisticated than in Africa. Secure in the memory of its traditional pre-eminence, China plays the role of the great power rather than the agent of revolution. While the general Maoist tactics—determined struggle against American "imperialism" and support for national liberation movements—apply here as elsewhere, the pattern of Chinese action in Asia is far more variegated, far better tailored to individual countries.

What China considers essential in Southeast Asia is the elimination of the influence of the United States. To this end Peiping encourages Ho Chi Minh in his prosecution of the guerrilla war against South Vietnam, but the American air strikes on North Vietnam present the Chinese with critical decisions. China's response will depend on the form, extent, and effects of any future attacks. The Korean experience suggests that China would back an invasion of South Vietnam with "people's volunteers" only if the very existence of the northern regime were threatened. But the fact of the air strikes might well indicate to the Chinese that the Americans were no longer operating under the Korean ground rules and that they might no longer stop short of bombing across the Chinese border. At this point, Soviet reactions would be crucial. In any event, Mao, as always, will move cautiously when faced with a superior foe. . . .

India is China's model of everything that a country of the third world should not be—neutral but sympathetic to Western democracy and heavily dependent on American aid, pro-Russian and anti-Chinese, a moderating influence in the Afro-Asian world, and intolerant of the pro-Chinese faction of the Indian Communist party, many of whose members were recently jailed. However, China's object in invading India's North East Frontier Agency in the fall of 1962 was not to topple the Indian government or to gain new territory, but only to teach India a decisive lesson in the border dispute.

China's current aim is to isolate India. It has concluded border agreements with their mutual neighbors, Burma, Nepal, and Pakistan, in an effort to show that Delhi is being unreasonable in not coming to terms. China's relations with Pakistan, which hitherto was strongly pro-Western, are based on a mutual dislike of India and are becoming increasingly friendly. If China were able to guarantee military support in the event of an Indo-

Pakistani clash, Pakistan might even leave SEATO. Friendship with Katmandu [Nepal] has been expressed through several aid projects, including a road linking Nepal and Tibet, but revelations by defectors from the Chinese road-building team about Peiping's ultimate hopes for revolution in the Himalayan kingdom have damaged relations.

Japan, as the only industrialized state in Asia, does not properly belong in the third world and occupies a special position vis-à-vis Peiping. Attracted to China by a mixture of emotions, including war guilt, traditional respect for the elder-brother civilization, and a desire to exploit the Chinese market, the Japanese could replace the Soviet Union as China's main supplier of capital goods. Last year, Sino-Japanese trade almost doubled, to $300 million. . . .

While the third world will remain China's main arena, Mao hopes to make inroads even in the heart of America's Western alliance. He has been encouraged by President de Gaulle's transfer of recognition from Taipei to Peiping, by his refusal to sign the test ban treaty, and by his anti-American policies in Europe and Vietnam. Since China will increasingly need Western European capital goods as well as Japanese as it seeks to end its dependence on the Soviet Union, there are good economic reasons for exploring such possibilities.

Throughout the whole tangled skein of China's foreign relations, there is one constant factor: hostility to the United States. Yet there are only two points at which the two countries meet—across the Formosa Strait and at the Warsaw conference table. China's main demand of the United States is the removal of the Seventh Fleet so that the Communists can finish off the Nationalists and finally end the civil war. To the Communists the presence of the American fleet is a humiliating reminder of China's former helplessness before the imperialist powers. Recognition, and even admission to the UN, are secondary issues. Indeed, even if Washington were to take the initiative, it is difficult to imagine that Peiping would agree to diplomatic relations with the United States prior to settlement of the Formosa issue. And

China would be highly unlikely to join the UN if Nationalist China were allowed to remain on some different basis.

Today China stands virtually alone against the United States and the Soviet Union. This has made Mao more militant, not less. He seems prepared to take on both countries in the interests of China and world revolution. But to do so he wants to be able to talk to them on equal terms. This is the true significance of the explosion of China's first nuclear device. Peiping pushed on with an immensely costly nuclear weapons program at a time when the national economy was already operating under great strain. The only safe assumption is that China will not stop until it has an armory of H-bombs and missiles which the United States and the Soviet Union will respect. However much Mao discounts the ultimate importance of nuclear weapons, he knows that without them he will always be at a disadvantage in negotiations with his major rivals.

Mao is . . . [more than seventy] and cannot expect to see his revolution completed. But the second generation of Chinese leaders, even if less militant, will surely continue to press toward Mao's goal of restoring China to its traditional position in the center of the world.

CHINA'S STRATEGY—A CRITIQUE [4]

Of the seventy-two years that Mao Tse-tung has lived on this earth, twenty-two of them, almost half his adult life, were spent in leading a protracted—and at times seemingly hopeless—armed struggle against a much superior foe. In 1927, after a brief period of collaboration with the Communists, Chiang Kai-shek turned on and decimated their cadres in the major urban centers. Mao picked up the pieces and from 1927 to 1933 waged guerrilla warfare against the Kuomintang from a number of rural bases in the mountains of south China. The Chinese Red Army, a relatively small and poorly-trained band, held out against five successive efforts by Chiang Kai-shek (with an army that by 1933 totaled one

[4] From article by D. S. Zagoria, of the Research Institute on Communist Affairs at Columbia University and author of *The Sino-Soviet Conflict*. *Commentary*. 40:61-8. N. '65. Reprinted by permission.

million men) to encircle it. By 1934, Mao's position was so precarious that he was forced to break out of it; it was then that he began the legendary Long March to the North. During the twelve months from October 1934 to October 1935, Mao's army covered a distance of about 7500 miles over rugged, often mountainous terrain, while simultaneously defending itself against the Nationalists. By the time it arrived in Yenan, it had been reduced to a fraction of its former strength, but that it had survived at all must, by any standards, be considered one of the most impressive feats of military history.

Within two years after arriving in Yenan, Mao took his army into battle against the most modernized, powerful military machine in Asia—that of the invading Japanese. By skillfully manipulating nationalist sentiment, mobilizing the peasants, and promoting guerrilla warfare throughout China, Mao played a major role in defeating Japan. At the same time he exploited the war to strengthen his position vis-à-vis Chiang. While nominally allied with Chiang's Kuomintang against the Japanese, Mao never let up in his political struggle against them; and he even fought three major military engagements with them (in 1939, 1941, and 1943). This was a classical example of the "unity with and struggle against the Nationalists" line which Mao has persistently recommended to other Communist parties ever since.

As a result of such tactics, Mao had by the end of World War II greatly altered the balance of power within China and had built his ragged army into a fighting force of a million men augmented by a militia of more than two million. It was this army that by a combination of guerrilla and conventional tactics went on to defeat the Nationalists in the civil war which followed. No other group of revolutionaries has ever overcome greater handicaps, survived greater defeats, waged a longer struggle, or showed such resourcefulness and fanatical determination in the course of winning power.

It would be difficult to exaggerate the impact of this achievement on the outlook of Mao and his comrades who survived the Long March—the few hundred men who now rule Communist China. First, it convinced them that all "reactionary" adversaries, no matter how powerful they may seem, have feet of clay: any revolutionary group, provided it is armed with the correct Marxist-Leninist-Maoist principles and strategy, can eventually beat a stronger enemy. This is the meaning of Mao's famous and often misunderstood concept of the "paper tiger." In applying this phrase to the Americans, as he once applied it to the Kuomintang and the Japanese, Mao means not that the enemy is weak but that, in the long run, it can be worn down and overcome.

Second, his own revolutionary experience conditioned Mao's view of the world revolution, which he and his comrades believe will succeed only if it imitates on a global scale their domestic strategy of surrounding the cities from the countryside. In this view, the underdeveloped countries of the world correspond to the villages of China and the more advanced countries to the cities. Just as Mao found the weak spot in Chiang Kai-shek's armor in the Chinese villages, where Nationalist control was ineffective, so he now sees the weak spot of American "imperialism" in Asia, Africa, and Latin America.

Third, the Chinese Communists' protracted armed struggle has left their revolutionary strategy, party organization, and style of thinking with a decidedly military bias. Mao and many of his colleagues are not only revolutionaries; they are also military leaders. They tend to look upon war as the highest form of revolution and to attach lesser importance to nonviolent forms of revolution. It was Mao who long ago urged every Communist to understand that "political power grows out of the barrel of a gun."

Finally, their own revolutionary success has convinced the Chinese Communist leaders that the strategy which brought them to power is applicable to other underdeveloped countries where the peasantry forms the great bulk of the population. Indeed, even before they finally defeated the Kuomintang in 1949, the Chinese Communists were highly self-conscious about their revolutionary strategy. And within months after they assumed power, they began, much to Stalin's dismay, to assert explicitly the validity of their own model for all "colonial" countries and to codify their experience so as to make it more readily available to other Communist parties struggling for power.

During the mid-fifties, when the Chinese were trying to seduce the Afro-Asian world by the "spirit of Bandung," and were hesitant about provoking the Russians, they de-emphasized their own revolutionary model. But since 1958, when the Chinese began to perceive a new revolutionary upsurge in Asia, Africa, and Latin America and became increasingly willing to challenge Soviet leadership of the Communist world, they have been systematically proposing to other Communist parties a revolutionary strategy based on their own experience.

. . . [An] article by Mao's defense minister, Marshal Lin Piao —written to commemorate the twentieth anniversary of the Chinese triumph over Japan and entitled "Long Live the Victory of the People's War"—can be viewed as a high point in this campaign. This 25,000-word statement represents the fullest, most authoritative, and most systematic effort yet made by the Long Marchers to sum up Chinese Communist revolutionary experience; and it is clearly intended as a guide for Communist parties throughout the third world. What does it say? Why was it issued at this particular time? What are its implications for American foreign policy?

Lin begins by declaring that the Chinese victory over Japan occupies an important place in military history because it was a case of a weak semi-colonial country winning against a strong imperialist power; moreover a "seemingly weak army"—that of the Communists—became the main force in the resistance movement. These two developments were made possible, says Lin, only by the Chinese Communist party's fidelity to the "people's-war" strategy formulated by Mao. Since the American imperialists are repeating on a worldwide scale the past actions of the Japanese imperialists in Asia, it has become an "urgent necessity" for the "people" (i.e., the Communists) in many countries to master this strategy.

Each of the first six sections of Lin's article is devoted to a different aspect of the strategy as illustrated by Chinese Communist experience in the fight against Japan and in the struggle with the

Kuomintang. Part I makes three essential points. First, Japanese aggression gave the Chinese Communists the chance to form a national united front (in the interests of which they soft-pedaled demands for radical social reform and class warfare). Second, protracted war was beneficial to China and harmful to Japan because Japanese imperialism could not sustain such a war. Third, protracted war afforded the Communists the opportunity to mobilize, organize, and arm the peasants.

Part II is a short course on united-front tactics. It is necessary, Lin states, to build the broadest possible united front. But such a front cannot be led by the nationalists; the Communists must lead it right from the outset. To ensure Communist leadership, the party must insist on maintaining its ideological, organizational, and political independence within the front, and must also insist on retaining control of its armed forces and of its bases in the rural hinterland. In short, no fusions or mergers with non-Communist parties—as are currently being recommended by Moscow—are permissible.

Lin goes on in Part III to elaborate on the importance of establishing bases in rural areas during a protracted war ("To rely on the peasants, build rural base areas and use the countryside to encircle and finally capture the cities—such was the way to victory in the Chinese revolution"). In Parts IV and V, he dwells on the importance of building a "people's army" under the absolute leadership of the party, and reiterates some of the well-known principles of Mao's theory of guerrilla warfare. And in Part VI, finally, he counsels self-reliance to all would-be revolutionaries. Revolution in any country should be carried out primarily by the masses in that country: "there is no other way." The local guerrillas must not depend on foreign assistance; they must be self-sufficient in food, clothing, and arms.

The remainder of Lin's article, Parts VII, VIII, and IX, carries the analysis directly into the present. North America and Western Europe, says Lin, may be called the "cities of the world," while Asia, Africa, and Latin America constitute the "rural areas of the world." In a sense, then, "the contemporary world revolution also presents a picture of the encirclement of cities by the rural areas." What is needed, therefore, is a worldwide united front against American imperialism. The main battlefield of this struggle is Asia, Africa, and Latin America, where the United States is most vulnerable.

It is in those areas, moreover, that a number of people's wars have already taken place (here Lin specifically mentions Korea, Vietnam, Laos, Cuba, Indonesia, and Algeria). The classes leading these people's wars may vary, he continues, "and so may the breadth and depth of mass mobilization and the extent of victory." But the important point is that these wars have "very much weakened and pinned down the forces of imperialism," and the more successful the development of a particular people's war in a given region, the larger the number of American forces that can be "pinned down and depleted there." When the Americans are hard pressed in one place, they have no alternative but to loosen their grip elsewhere. In short, American imperialism can be defeated "piece by piece" with some "striking at its head and others at its feet." However superior American weapons and technical equipment may be, "in the final analysis, the outcome of a war will be decided by the sustained fighting of the ground forces, by the fighting at close quarters on battlefields, by the political consciousness of the men, by their courage and spirit of sacrifice." It is at this point that Lin introduces Vietnam as the "most convincing current example" of how to defeat American imperialism in a people's war.

Lin concludes his article with an attack on the "Khrushchev revisionists" and their successors who have all "set themselves against people's war" and are "scheming to undermine it." The Khrushchev revisionists, says Lin, exaggerate the danger of a nuclear conflict growing out of people's wars. There have been many such people's wars throughout the twenty years since World War II, he declares, but "has any single one of them developed into a world war?" In any case, although war brings destruction and suffering, "the sacrifice of a small number of people in revolutionary wars" will bring security to entire nations and even the whole of mankind.

The revolutionary recipe offered up by Lin is not new in the sense of reflecting any major departures in Chinese thinking. The idea of "surrounding" North America and Western Europe—the "cities" of the world—by fomenting Communist and nationalist revolution in the former colonial areas—the "countryside"—has been implicit in Chinese strategic writing since 1958 and was explicitly stated on behalf of Peking by the Indonesian Communists more than a year ago. Nor, as we have already seen, is there anything very new in the revolutionary strategy itself. The only significant difference between past Chinese statements and Lin's is the unusual stress Lin places on armed conflict. In the past it was usually made clear that while armed struggle is the main and highest form of revolution, peaceful political struggle could become the main form in a certain period and under certain circumstances. The absence of any such qualification in Lin's article, and his heavy emphasis on the virtues of armed conflicts—no matter how successful or who leads them—seem to reflect Peking's growing interest not merely in promoting revolution but in tying the United States down in a series of debilitating protracted wars against local guerrillas throughout Asia, Africa, and Latin America.

This is not to suggest that Peking has in the past or will in the future indiscriminately foster armed revolution and civil war. Their main objective is to weaken their principal national enemy, the United States, and they will foment armed struggles wherever by so doing they can achieve that objective as a contribution to the ultimate aim of forcing a total withdrawal of the Americans from Asia and the rest of the underdeveloped world. Thus they will continue to concentrate, as they have in the past, on fostering armed struggles primarily in countries tied to the American alliance system—that is, on getting several "South Vietnams" going at once. In addition, they will try to fan the flames of any local war that might prove embarrassing to the Americans or implicate them (this was clearly their intention during the abortive Indo-Pakistani war). There is a double advantage here. First, if successful armed struggles can be launched in these countries, there is a good chance that the Americans will come in and get bogged down in an unpopular war against a colored people. Second, an incentive is provided for pro-American governments to accommodate themselves to Peking. For Peking is in effect blackmailing these governments by telling them to get rid of the Americans or else prepare for a protracted war led by local Communists.

This strategy, Peking believes, is already bearing fruit. The Americans are deeply bogged down in South Vietnam and therefore cannot afford to become involved so deeply elsewhere. To keep the Americans in this dilemma, the Chinese are, with some success, using all their influence in North Vietnam to prevent a negotiated settlement, while selectively fanning the flames of war elsewhere, most recently in the Indo-Pakistani conflict. Moreover, a strategy of overextending and exhausting a great power is ideally suited to the limited material resources of an inferior one like China: it requires no large investment either of Chinese manpower or material. And indeed, Lin Piao pointedly asserts that local revolutionaries cannot and should not expect much outside help, that they must win largely on their own resources.

Why was Lin's article released at this particular time? It is now clear that a decision was taken about a year ago by Hanoi and the Liberation Front to step up the battle in the South from a guerrilla to a conventional war. This effort has failed, and the question for Hanoi now is whether to go back to guerrilla tactics and fight a protracted struggle or to negotiate and try to take over South Vietnam by political means. Lin's argument is designed to support the former alternative. He is in effect telling Hanoi and the Front that, no matter how great the difficulties may seem now that massive American air and fire power have been introduced, they will triumph in the end. "Difficulties are not invincible monsters," says Lin: our liberated areas faced great difficulties from "savage attacks" by the Japanese and Kuomintang; we survived encirclement and the economic blockade; and we did this all by relying on our own resources.

The extraordinary importance Lin attaches to the virtues of self-reliance suggests an effort both to rationalize the lack of any substantial Chinese support to the Vietnamese Communists and to bolster those in Hanoi who argue that the Americans can be defeated even without much outside aid. In a particularly pointed passage, Lin says that reliance even on Socialist countries still committed to revolution—that is, China as opposed to Russia—is no substitute for self-reliance.

More generally, the Chinese are also seeking to reassure Communist revolutionaries not only in Vietnam but throughout the emerging areas that they can defeat the United States and its allies by protracted violence even though the price will be high and the path tortuous. Peking has persistently claimed, and Lin reiterates, that Vietnam is a crucial testing ground for the strategy of people's war.

Lastly, the fact that China's top military leader rather than a political figure was chosen to deliver a statement of such importance indicates that the statement has implications for the dialogue which has been going on for some time within the Chinese military between the "modernizers" and the "guerrillas." There have been a number of recent attacks on "modernizers" who want more professional, up-to-date armed forces equipped with the latest weapons as a deterrent against American attack. Lin's article could in part be the party's response to these critics, for it in effect says that China itself must in any case be prepared to fight a protracted guerrilla war in the event of an American attack on the mainland.

But if the Chinese strategy seems to be bearing fruit at the moment, in tying the United States down in Vietnam, is it in the long run realistic? My own belief is that it is not. Without denying the considerable Chinese capacity for mischief-making in the underdeveloped countries, I would say that their global strategic thinking is crude and growing more and more dogmatic.

The truth is that Mao's strategy has serious weaknesses on both of the two levels at which it operates. On the first level—where it is designed to turn Afro-Asian nationalism against the United States and optimally to foment war between the new nations and the United States—the strategy assumes that the American role in the underdeveloped areas can plausibly be equated with Japanese expansionism in Asia before and during World

War II. Now it is obvious that both the interests and policies of the developing countries are sometimes in conflict with those of the United States. Moreover, in a world where tensions between rich and poor nations are likely to grow, nationalist leaders will always be tempted to use the richest country on earth as a scapegoat. But American policy in the emerging areas is not static and is not dictated by the rapacious needs of an "imperialist" system, as the Chinese believe. Nor, by and large, do the nationalists in the third world view the United States as their main enemy, and neither are they anxious to see a complete American military, economic, and political withdrawal. The best recent indication of this is that the Chinese have not been successful in getting the majority of the Afro-Asian powers to condemn American "imperialism," as distinguished from ritualistic condemnations of "imperialism" and colonialism in general, as the main enemy. . . .

On its second level—where it is a design for local Communists to capture the nationalist movement during an armed struggle against the Americans or an American-supported government —the Maoist strategy has up to now worked only in China itself and in Vietnam. Two crucial factors were common to both these cases. First, there was an armed struggle with an outside enemy— the Japanese in China and the Japanese and then the French in Vietnam—which gave the Communists an opportunity to make a nationalist appeal against an imperialist or colonial power. Second, the nationalist opposition to the Communists both in China and Vietnam was divided, unimaginative, and without effective organization at the rice-roots level. Current Vietcong successes in South Vietnam are inextricably related to the fact that Ho Chi Minh, like Mao, was able to capture a weak nationalist movement during World War II.

Communist successes in China and Vietnam should not, however, obscure the more fundamental point that the Communists have been unable to seize control of a nationalist movement anywhere else in Africa or Latin America since the start of World War II. (Castro was not a Communist when he took power; he converted to communism afterward in order to obtain Soviet protection against American attack.) This is not a mere historical accident. It suggests that the Chinese and Vietnamese successes are not easy to duplicate even in the favorable circumstances of an anti-colonial armed struggle. Witness the fact that in none of the recent or current instances of such a struggle—Algeria and Angola, for example—have local Communists played an important role. All this means that Communist prospects of creating another "South Vietnam" are not as good as either Mao or the American adherents of the "domino theory" believe them to be.

In those Afro-Asian countries which have already achieved independence—and these, of course, constitute the vast majority—Maoist strategy runs into a number of even greater difficulties. First, the Chinese cannot woo nationalist leaders in order to turn them against the United States while simultaneously trying to subvert them. . . . Second, many of the Afro-Asian states have established one-party regimes which make it all but impossible for the local Communists to build up independent power bases. Third, even the local Communists in these areas are becoming increasingly aware that the Maoist revolutionary model cannot be mechanically adapted to their own situations.

In India, for example, the Communists are irrevocably split into pro-Soviet and pro-Chinese parties and the latter has been critically, if not mortally, wounded by the Chinese-Indian border conflict, which has robbed it of the chance to pick up the banner of Indian nationalism. In Indonesia, the local Communists have as of this writing been dealt a severe blow [the Communist party was nearly wiped out by anti-Communist forces—Ed.] after participating in a premature coup directed against the army. In Thailand and Cambodia, the local Communists are extremely weak. In Burma, although the local Communists have been waging an armed struggle against the Government for more than a decade, they are not now a serious threat to Ne Win's military government, and without substantial help from China (which they have not been getting), they are unlikely to become such a threat. In what remains of Malaysia, Communist influence is confined largely to the overseas Chinese, who are very unpopular with the Malays. A Communist-led insurrection there would thus most likely lead to a communal war between the Malays and that portion of the Chinese under Communist influence. This strategy failed in 1948 and there is no reason why it should meet with success now. What is more, in none of these Asian countries, with the exception of Indonesia, do the local Communists have a strong base among the peasantry, an indispensable prerequisite for launching a Maoist-style guerrilla war. [This base was considerably, if not completely, shattered in the aftermath of the attempted coup.—Ed.]

As for Africa and Latin America, one decisive fact stands out—great physical limitations on the Chinese ability to intervene directly or by proxy on behalf of local guerrillas. For all the Chinese talk about self-reliance, the truth is that their own aid to the North Vietnamese was decisive in Ho Chi Minh's victory over the French in 1954 and that external Communist aid is a necessity for any guerrilla force which wants to move from guerrilla to conventional war.

But not only do most of the Communist parties in the former colonial areas lack the capability to launch protracted wars against the Americans or American allies; many of them may not have the will. Indeed, they must now be wondering about the desirability of a Chinese strategy for fighting the United States with Vietnamese and other Asian and African lives.

In addition to all this, Peking's attempts to export protracted war are inhibited by the fact that Moscow is putting its still considerable influence in the world Communist movement largely on the side of evolutionary rather than violent change. The vehemence with which Lin denounces Soviet "arguments against people's war" and efforts to "undermine it," suggests that the Soviet influence is having a considerable impact on local Communist parties. It is noteworthy in this connection that in the past year, the North Koreans, North Vietnamese, and Cubans have all veered away from Peking toward a neutral position in the Sino-Soviet conflict.

All of which points up a general weakness in the Chinese approach—its almost obsessive preoccupation with violence and war as the key to social change. This may reflect the mood of desperation of an aging leadership in Peking, but it is doubtful that it accurately reflects the mood in most African and Asian countries, even among the radicals. There are large sections of the Asian Communist movement, for example, that are simply not psychologically prepared to fight in the swamps for twenty or thirty years. Moreover, some of these parties, notably the PKI in Indonesia, have made impressive gains by following a peaceful path. The results from South Vietnam are not yet in, but whatever the outcome, Peking will never be able to argue that Communist successes were purchased cheaply.

So far as the Soviet Union is concerned, its . . . efforts to bring a quick halt to the Indo-Pakistani war were in sharp contrast to Chinese attempts to throw gasoline on the fire. Clearly, Moscow is increasingly committing itself to stability in the underdeveloped areas. Not that it has given up hope of tilting the unaligned countries toward the East or eventually even of installing pro-Soviet Communists in power. But the Russians are more and more counseling non-violent revolutionary paths to Afro-Asian nationalists and Communists alike. In Vietnam, the Russians, unlike the Chinese, have been eager for a negotiated settlement from the beginning. They have given enough aid to Hanoi to maintain their credentials as Communists but have done little more. Indeed, Soviet restraint in Vietnam has been remarkable and has not been exercised without considerable cost to Moscow's worldwide prestige. Even its moderate Communist allies in Eastern Europe, who are not at all in sympathy with Chinese tactics, have been shocked by Soviet impotence in the face of an American attack against a "socialist" country. This Soviet humiliation in Vietnam could eventually produce strong pressures in Moscow, particularly among the military, to "stand up" to the Americans.

On the other side, the Soviets have their hands full at home in modernizing the economy and increasing what for the past few years has been an extremely slow rate of growth. To do this, and to raise their standard of living, is not compatible with an arms race or support of Communist-led protracted wars against the Americans. Nor is there any reason for Moscow to mortgage its foreign policy to Communist guerrillas in Africa and Asia.

What then are the implications of Mao's theory of people's war for American foreign policy? The Chinese are undoubtedly right in believing that armed violence in the form of civil, revolutionary, or local wars will occur in the future as it has in the past twenty years. But the experience of the past twenty years also suggests that such conflicts are not necessarily incompatible with American interests even when the Chinese themselves label them "people's wars." The Algerian war is a case in point. More important, recent experience also indicates that it will be very difficult for local Communists to take over the leadership of such armed struggles, which means that there is no reason for Washington to rush in with American military power out of fear of a possible Communist takeover whenever violence erupts in the underdeveloped countries (the Dominican Republic is a good example).

On the other hand, in countering the Chinese strategy, the United States would do well to help educate nationalist leaders and nationalist armies in the underdeveloped countries to subvert people's-war tactics by taking the appropriate military and sociopolitical pre-emptive measures early enough. To accomplish this, and in the long run to promote the stability and independence of these newly emergent countries, the United States cannot withdraw from these areas. Its continued presence is vital. At the same time, however, while reiterating its intention to remain in Asia, to protect allies and friends from attack, and to take serious steps to bridge the widening gap between rich and poor nations, the United States ought to begin laying the basis for a realistic relationship with Communist China (recognition, a seat in the UN, limitation of the trade embargo to strategic materials only) once the present leaders pass from the scene. Such a policy would in all likelihood be denounced by Mao and his comrades as an imperialist trick. But it would at least have the virtue of putting the onus for the impasse in American-Chinese relations on Peking's present leadership. More important, it would make available an alternative to Mao's anti-American policy for those who will come to power in China after his death.

3. Communists in Conflict

DIVISION OVER VIETNAM [5]

There is little evidence that the sudden removal of Nikita S. Khrushchev from power on October 14, 1964 has contributed to a settlement of the long-standing Sino-Soviet conflict. The new Soviet leaders have reaffirmed the basic Khrushchev policies which Communist China has long denounced. The Chinese Communists have retaliated by attacking the new Kremlin leaders as proponents of "Khrushchevism without Khrushchev." Mao Tse-tung's price for a Sino-Soviet rapprochement appears to be nothing less than Moscow's wholesale rejection of the Khrushchev line, particularly "peaceful coexistence" with the United States. But Khrushchev's successors have shown no intention of submitting to Peking's demands. Consequently, an early healing of the Sino-Soviet rift is a most unlikely event.

The embittered struggle between Moscow and Peking has become, in the eyes of many Western observers, an important factor in the Communist-initiated conflict in Vietnam. Some suggest that recent United States military moves in the Vietnam crisis, particularly the sustained and intensified bombing of North Vietnam, have been calculated to take advantage of the Sino-Soviet split. Others fear that the continuing United States air raids on the North, ever closer to the Chinese Communist frontier, may eventually bring the two Communist giants closer together. The evidence suggests that, to date, the Sino-Soviet rift has been aggravated rather than reduced as a result of Washington's direct, though measured, retaliation against North Vietnam.

Peaceful Coexistence Versus Wars of National Liberation

The Sino-Soviet dispute over the Vietnam situation stems from (1) disagreements regarding the strategies and tactics which the Communists can employ safely against the United States; and (2) the traditional contest for spheres of influence—in which, according to the Communists, only the "imperialists" engage. The

[5] From "The Sino-Soviet Dispute and Vietnam," by Tai Sung An, assistant professor of political science, Washington College, Chestertown, Md. *Orbis.* 9:426-36. Summer '65. Reprinted by permission.

central issue is "peaceful coexistence" versus "wars of national liberation." Moscow favors peaceful coexistence, a more cautious and devious drive toward world communism, as the proper strategy for the world Communist movement in the present era of thermonuclear terror. All other forms of Communist expansionism, including wars of national liberation, must be subordinated to the Soviet line of peaceful coexistence—although Moscow does not deny the importance of the former. Peking firmly insists that active support for wars of national liberation (the modern cover for guerrilla warfare) in the non-Communist underdeveloped areas is the surest road to world communism, even in the face of the West's nuclear superiority. For Peking, and presumably for Moscow as well, Vietnam has now become a major testing ground for these two seemingly divergent strategies.

Khrushchev, for all his noisy brandishing of rockets and nuclear weapons in the past, realized that the Soviet Union stood to lose all its painfully won political and material gains, as well as tens of millions of lives, should the struggle against capitalism touch off a nuclear conflagration. He and his successors believe that the advance of world communism must now depend less on overt armed aggression and more on skillful political, economic, and psychological warfare under cover of the Soviet nuclear deterrent. Accordingly, the Soviets tend to sanction Communist military adventures only when they can effectively control the risks.

The Chinese Communists maintain that the Khrushchev line of peaceful coexistence represents accommodation to "U.S. imperialism" and a shameful betrayal of revolutionary Marxist-Leninist principles. In its role as principal mentor of the Vietnamese Communists, Peking has been making every effort to discredit the Soviet policy of peaceful coexistence as applied to Vietnam. If South Vietnam should fall to the Communists, Mao Tse-tung will be able to use the victory as evidence that wars of national liberation can safely be supported and even multiplied in other parts of the non-Communist underdeveloped world without danger of courting a nuclear war. More important still, the Chinese Communist case against the Soviets would be strengthened in the eyes of many Communist party leaders throughout the world. Peking would score heavily in the Sino-Soviet conflict. . . .

Contrary to some views widely held in the West, the Chinese Communists in their dispute with the Soviet Union have never advocated policies which would deliberately provoke a nuclear war with the United States. Instead, they have insisted on controlled Communist "brinkmanship" in order to create favorable conditions for expansion. . . .

Peking has often accused Moscow of failing to run sufficient risks to help China and other Communist allies in Asia against the United States. The Chinese Communists have argued that, although "U.S. imperialists" might intervene on a limited military basis in Southeast Asia in order to suppress wars of national liberation, they would not run the risk of escalating these conflicts—*provided* the Soviets had clearly committed themselves to retaliate with whatever weapons were required. In Peking's view, Soviet nuclear strength is sufficient to deter the United States from raising the stakes in any local war and, therefore, "U.S. imperialism" would have to accept local defeats. Hence, Communist brinkmanship in "brush-fire" conflicts or local wars would involve a minimal risk of global nuclear war and would permit the Communists to press on to new victories in those areas "ripe for revolution."

Moscow is worried about Chinese Communist brinkmanship. The Soviets view local conventional wars as part of a continuous spectrum of conflicts leading to general war. They have repeatedly warned against the grave danger of local wars escalating into global nuclear conflict because of mistakes, accidents, and miscalculation, and assert that Communist expansion must and can be achieved without pushing the United States to the brink of initiating a nuclear war. Moscow, like Washington, contends that the dangers of nuclear escalation in the Cold War remain great, while Peking declares that the dangers are virtually nonexistent— or could be minimized if the Soviets knew how to use to advantage their nuclear deterrent. The Chinese seem bent on dragging the Soviet Union into a direct military confrontation with the United States in Vietnam and thus destroying, once and for all, the Soviet policy of peaceful coexistence with the United States. Such an eventuality would be further proof of the correctness of the Chinese Communist line of revolutionary belligerence. The avoidance of such a military showdown has been a cardinal aim of Soviet foreign policy.

The View from Hanoi

The over-all strategy of the Viet Cong insurrectionary movement in South Vietnam is directed by the Lao Dong Party (the North Vietnam Communist Party) under the overlordship of the Chinese Communists. While Peking has committed itself heavily to the Vietnamese Communists, Moscow's influence over Vietnam in recent years has been in sharp decline. The North Vietnamese Communist leadership has since early 1963 taken public stands favoring the Chinese Communists in the Sino-Soviet dispute. Hanoi has allied itself with Peking because the Chinese Communists were willing to support Hanoi's effort to unify all of Vietnam under its hegemony. At the present time, Hanoi and Peking have overlapping interests, the most important of which is to evict United States power from Southeast Asia.

The Communist insurrection in South Vietnam has not yet entered the third and final phase of guerrilla warfare, i.e., full-scale conventional military operations. Fully aware that they would be no match for regular units of the South Vietnamese and United States armed forces in conventional warfare, the Viet Cong have decided to stick to mobile guerrilla operations, hit-and-run raids, terror, and disruption—the second stage of the Maoist theory of protracted guerrilla warfare—at which they excel. Their only hope for victory is to produce complete political, social, and economic chaos in South Vietnam so that the United States is finally left with nothing to defend, or to rely on worldwide "peace movements" and other pressures to deter the United States from intensifying its military efforts against the Viet Cong. They recognize that total *military* victory is beyond their grasp as long as United States air and naval supremacy is maintained in Asia and United States ground forces are committed to defend South Vietnam. Victory on the battlefield has become even more

elusive since the United States began its air attacks on the "privileged sanctuary" of Viet Cong aggression, the sanctuary which
has always proved so vital to Communist aggression. A Viet
Cong military victory, therefore, would require heavy military assistance and support from both Communist China and the Soviet
Union, including the protection of Moscow's nuclear umbrella.
The present Sino-Soviet split and Moscow's nuclear "timidness"
render unlikely such a combined military effort.

North Vietnam's leaders may not welcome massive Chinese
Communist troop movements into their territory lest this should
lead to Chinese domination. The Vietnamese, both North and
South, have for centuries feared and disliked the Chinese. Ho
Chi Minh is reportedly opposed to calling for Chinese Communist troops and "volunteers" to help the Vietnamese Communists
—except in the utmost extremity. Many industrial plants and
streets of cities in North Vietnam are still named after Vietnamese heroes who won victories in the past over Chinese invaders. A
number of powerful Vietnamese Communist leaders retain this
strong traditional distrust and dislike of the Chinese. One such
person is General Vo Nguyen Giap, the hero of Dienbienphu,
who now directs the Viet Cong insurgents in South Vietnam.
Surely the worst nightmare Ho Chi Minh could have would be of
a massive United States retaliatory air bombardment followed by
a Chinese Communist military occupation.

It is probably this ingrained fear of China that prompts Ho
Chi Minh to resist Peking's heavy pressure for a complete break
with Moscow. He is well aware that the Soviet Union can supply
far more military and economic aid than can Communist China.
Moreover, he is anxious to keep the door open to Moscow in the
event that some day he might have to seek a counterweight to
Peking.

Ho Chi Minh has another important reason for wanting to
avoid direct Chinese Communist military intervention in North
Vietnam: He has political ambitions of his own in Indochina.
The ultimate aim of the Vietnamese Communist leadership is to
bring the whole of Vietnam, Laos, Thailand, and Cambodia under Hanoi's hegemony. The Chinese Communists certainly do

not look with favor upon the emergence of an independent-minded Communist power center in Southeast Asia. Peking may even want to see North Vietnam considerably weakened and thus inhibited in its political aspirations. This may be one of the reasons the Chinese Communists are advising Hanoi to endure United States bombing raids while pressing on with the Viet Cong insurrection until the anti-Communist regime in South Vietnam collapses and the United States is forced to withdraw. The protraction of the Vietnam conflict would leave two exhausted Vietnams much more susceptible to Chinese Communist influence, discredit the Soviet policy of peaceful coexistence, trim the influence of the pro-Soviet faction in Hanoi, and strengthen Peking's belligerent revolutionary line.

Peking's Strategy

Despite their continuing vituperative outcries against "U.S. imperialism," the Chinese Communists apparently do not want to become involved in a direct military confrontation with the United States in Southeast Asia. In response to the United States bombing of North Vietnam, Peking recently raised the specter of a Korean-type intervention by Chinese Communist "volunteers" in Vietnam, but Mao Tse-tung seems unprepared to carry out his threat. Communist China is unlikely to risk another Korean-type military adventure in Vietnam, unless South Vietnamese or United States troops cross the seventeenth parallel.

This conclusion is based upon several important factors. First, the United States has in the Western Pacific an immense concentration of air and naval power which could wreak great punishment on mainland China; and the Chinese Communists, given their view of "U.S. imperialism," no doubt fear that United States military commanders are just itching for an excuse to employ these weapons and thus to wipe out the memories of frustration remaining from the Korean War. Communist China herself possesses no retaliatory nuclear capability to reach the heart of United States power. Chinese leaders must realize that alone they could not win an all-out war with the United States.

Second, Peking probably has no assurance of automatic Soviet military and nuclear support in a confrontation with the United States—although Washington at the same time cannot safely assume that the Sino-Soviet rift has gone so far that Moscow would stand aside in the face of a massive United States retaliation against mainland China. But so long as Chinese leaders suspect that the Soviet Union hopes to profit from a Sino-American showdown and thus may not come to their aid, they will be cautious before committing their forces to battle. By and large, the Sino-Soviet conflict is a restraining influence on Communist China.

Third, Communist China can utilize its formidable ground power effectively in contiguous border areas, as it demonstrated in the Korean War as well as in the Sino-Indian border dispute of 1962; but it is seriously handicapped in carrying out sustained military operations at long distances. It has limited air and naval strength and severe transport and supply problems. For example, there are only two single-track railway lines from Kunming and Nanning in South China to North Vietnam.

Fourth, the Chinese Communists realize that if the Vietnam war is expanded by virtue of Communist China's active military intervention, they will not be permitted to operate from a privileged sanctuary as they did during the Korean War. The escalation of the Vietnam war would invite destruction upon Peking's major industrial installations, including, perhaps, the elementary nuclear complex in Sinkiang Province.

Fifth, Chinese Communist leaders are certain that Southeast Asia will eventually fall into their hands, one way or another, without a major war with the United States. They are prepared to wait with great patience for that moment.

Sixth, the Chinese are aware that Ho Chi Minh and the Vietnamese do not relish the idea of direct and massive military intervention by Chinese soldiers, and they probably prefer to extend their hegemony by more subtle means.

In the face of increased United States military pressures in Vietnam, the Chinese Communists have stepped up their threats of military intervention, but they have been careful in describing the conditions under which they would intervene. Their design is to deter the United States from expanding its increasingly destructive bombing and other military pressures against North Vietnam while giving themselves adequate room for maneuver.

South Vietnam is the logical target for Peking's expansionist drive, constituting as it does the weakest link of the non-Communist defense perimeter in Asia. Peking feels that the United States does not have vital national interests in Vietnam and thus would not risk national survival in a struggle over this area. The Chinese leaders believe, therefore, that they can safely continue to intensify their expansionist drive in the area at low levels of violence without having to worry about (1) the need for Soviet military and nuclear support; (2) the risk of inviting full-scale United States intervention and retaliation; and (3) the necessity of committing their own forces to battle. If they can keep the conflict in Vietnam at a low level of violence, the Chinese might convince the world's Communist parties that the Chinese model of "national liberation war" is not as risky as the Soviet Union has contended.

Moscow's Dilemma

Moscow's Vietnam policy has been ambiguous and ambivalent. By withholding effective support from Peking as well as Hanoi, the Soviets have forced North Vietnam to move closer to the Chinese Communists in the Sino-Soviet conflict. Officially, the Soviet Union has given political, diplomatic, and propaganda support to the Vietnamese Communists by condemning the United States role in Vietnam. At the same time, it has rebuked Communist China for pursuing its reckless policies in Vietnam and elsewhere in Southeast Asia. Moscow has accused the Chinese of damaging the Communist cause in Vietnam by increasing the pace of the war and thus giving the United States a pretext for retaliating in a much more telling manner, and it has warned Ho Chi Minh against actions which might tend to escalate the crisis.

In many ways Moscow, as head of the Communist bloc, is in a very uncomfortable position with regard to Vietnam. If the Soviets continue to provide only limited aid to Hanoi, they can be condemned for betraying a member of the Communist bloc in order to save their own skin and to pursue policies of "accommodation" with the West. Their passivity has already been exploited by Peking as a means of destroying Moscow's leadership in the world Communist movement. If, on the other hand, the Soviets intervene on an increasing scale, they might exacerbate the situation in Vietnam with the risk that it will get out of control. In doing so, they would have accepted implicitly the Chinese line of militant communism and, more important still, endangered the motherland. To extricate themselves from such a painful dilemma, there seems to be only one solution: to advocate a negotiated settlement of the Vietnam war.

Moscow probably favors a negotiated settlement which would remove the United States military presence from South Vietnam without a military triumph for either side, but it is reluctant to put direct pressure on Hanoi to enter into negotiations for fear of triggering fresh Chinese charges of treason. Through a reconvening of the Geneva Conference [which provided for the division of Vietnam], Soviet leaders would try to obtain the "neutralization" of South Vietnam (and even of North Vietnam, if necessary). Such a negotiated solution—opposed strongly by Peking—might protect North Vietnam against "satellitization" by the Chinese. It would also greatly enhance Moscow's image as a "peace-loving" nuclear power capable of acting with great restraint in the midst of an international crisis.

To the Soviets, nothing would be more disagreeable than the prospect of becoming entangled in a direct military confrontation with the United States in Vietnam, from which the chief beneficiary would most likely be the Chinese Communists. Moscow must view involvement in Vietnam as "the wrong war, in the wrong place, at the wrong time." There is no vital Soviet interest in Vietnam which must be secured by a belligerent policy that would cut across Moscow's larger design in world affairs and jeopardize its present détente strategy. Major entanglement in Vietnam would be a steep price for the Soviet Union to pay in order to salvage the interests of Communist China, its inconvenient ally and rancorous rival.

There is considerable evidence to support the conclusion that Soviet leaders want a negotiated disengagement in Vietnam. (1) Although the Soviet Union is building surface-to-air missile sites near Hanoi and providing limited amounts of other types of military and economic aid, its commitment does not appear to be any deeper than this. Most observers believe the Soviets are providing this much assistance in order to gain more control over North Vietnamese actions. (2) The Soviet reaction to increased United States military pressures, particularly the bombing of North Vietnam, has been relatively mild, confined so far to the usual broad threats. Moscow has spoken of bolstering North Vietnam's defenses and has pledged to send "volunteers" if Hanoi wants them. It is difficult to measure this latter threat. (3) Moscow, by and large, has refrained from its missile rattling or nuclear blackmail techniques which have become standard Soviet behavior in tense international situations, such as the Suez and Berlin crises. (4) The Soviets have not given any assurance of military and nuclear backing to Peking and Hanoi. (5) Moscow's belated harsh warnings to the United States so far appear to have been made for the public record, to protect it against the Chinese charge that the Soviets are willing to sacrifice the interests of other Communist countries to their policy of peaceful coexistence with "U.S. imperialism."

This is not to say that the Soviets are not pleased at the prospect of the United States committing several divisions of its finest troops to Vietnam, suffering a serious blow (deserved or not) to its image as a restrained, "peace-loving" nation, and perhaps absorbing a number of military setbacks in Vietnam. Moscow may even wish to see the war prolonged, provided it can be controlled. In addition, Moscow is fully aware of the danger of allowing Peking to appear as the only staunch champion of Communist revolution. The new Kremlin leaders in recent months have stepped up their efforts to regain influence in North Vietnam by adopting a more belligerent line in support of the Vietnamese Communists, by claiming that the Soviet Union is the real champion of the national liberation movements of Asia and Africa, and also by outdoing the Chinese Communists with promises of support for

North Vietnam. Illustrative of these efforts are Moscow's statements about "volunteers," promises to take the "necessary measures" to improve North Vietnam's defense capacity, and the recent decision to extend a sort of limited diplomatic recognition to the Viet Cong insurgents.

There is good evidence, on the other hand, that Moscow continues to recommend quietly that Hanoi take a more flexible attitude toward negotiations, so the Vietnamese Communists may be able to gain at the conference table what they cannot win on the battlefield. For example, the Soviet Union recently agreed to attend an international conference on Cambodian neutrality with the apparent expectation of using it as an informal forum for discussion of the Vietnam crisis. The Chinese Communists torpedoed the Cambodian conference and thus succeeded in blocking any Vietnam peace talks that might have developed there. The Soviet Union also seems to be nudging North Vietnam into a neutral stance in the Sino-Soviet conflict, trying to wean it away from Peking although not insisting on Soviet control. While the Soviets seem to have failed so far in both of these efforts, they have not given up hope of eventual success.

Conclusion

The Vietnam crisis is not likely to be the occasion for a restoration of unity between the Soviet Union and Communist China. The Sino-Soviet split appears irreparable, though neither side seeks a complete and final break. Unity could be restored only in the extremely unlikely event that the United States became involved in a general war with the Chinese Communists. The Sino-Soviet rift has made it impossible for the two giants of the Communist bloc to coordinate their policies and power in a joint offensive against the West. By skillfully using its military superiority in and around Vietnam, the United States can contain Communist aggression and force the Chinese and North Vietnamese Communists to abandon their designs on Southeast Asia. Such a victory might go far to blunt the Chinese Communist strategy of wars of national liberation and protracted guerrilla conflict and strengthen other Free World nations in Southeast Asia.

TO INTERVENE OR NOT TO INTERVENE? [6]

Paradoxically at first sight, Moscow is eager for intervention in Vietnam, while Peking objects to it. A first indication of this was given . . . when the Chinese were reported to have stopped at their frontier Soviet arms transports for North Vietnam. The Russians protested then and the Chinese, it was said, yielded and allowed the transports to pass. It now appears that they opened the road to only some of the Soviet transports, and that others had to return to the U.S.S.R. The affair is enigmatic, for both sides are extremely reticent about it, but it is virtually certain that the trains the Chinese allowed to pass carried only supplies of munitions. The mysterious cargo that returned to Russia is said to have consisted of military specialists and advisers detailed to Hanoi. According to information coming indirectly from a Chinese source (but not confirmed from other sources), Peking denied transit to no fewer than twenty thousand Soviet specialists and advisers. If this report is correct, then the Chinese Government has vetoed and, for the time being, frustrated a Soviet attempt to build up in Vietnam a military establishment that might match the American establishment.

Such an action may appear inconsistent on the part of Peking. The Chinese have repeatedly denounced Russian reluctance to aid North Vietnam and the Vietcong; why then do they themselves sabotage Soviet aid? On the other hand, how is one to square Russian "moderation" with Moscow's willingness to commit itself so heavily to direct intervention in Vietnam? These contradictions may not seem so strange if the following points of the Russo-Chinese controversy are considered:

1. The Chinese believe that the Vietcong can win the war in South Vietnam by its own forces. For this it needs generous aid in munitions, but no Soviet military establishment with thousands of specialists and advisers. Peking argues that with the support of an overwhelming majority of the local population, the Vietcong will be able to drive into an impasse any American expeditionary forces, even ones far larger than are at present en-

[6] From "Russia vs. China: Clash over Vietnam," by Isaac Deutscher, author of many books on the U.S.S.R. *Nation.* 201:3-4. Jl. 5, '65. Reprinted by permission.

gaged in Vietnam. They draw a parallel with the Algerian War, in which a French army, half a million strong and superbly equipped, could not defeat the partisans. The Vietcong is in this respect even better placed than was the Algerian FLN, which had to contend with the hostility of a huge mass of French settlers and *colons*.

The Russians are less confident of the Vietcong's chances. Nor do they believe that President Johnson will ever be able to afford admitting defeat and withdrawing in the way General de Gaulle admitted defeat and withdrew from Algeria. Moscow fears that the United States will go on pouring men and munitions into Vietnam and raising the stakes as long as its military power is confronted solely by the Vietcong. Only the presence of a Soviet military establishment in Vietnam, so the argument runs, can deter American escalation and eventually allow the Vietcong to obtain advantageous terms through negotiation.

2. The Chinese suspect that through their specialists and advisers the Russians may obtain control of all the key positions in North Vietnam, turn the country into its satellite, and eventually strike a bargain with the Americans at the expense of Hanoi's and Southeast Asia's revolutionary interests. The Russians do in fact favor some new version of the 1954 Geneva settlement. The Chinese, who at the time endorsed that settlement, now think that it gave undue advantages to the anti-Communists; and they refuse to repeat the experiment. They do not wish to be involved in any international bargaining, for they are convinced that in any such meeting the Vietcong will be "betrayed." They have vetoed Russian plans to appeal to the United Nations and the Security Council, and all attempts by neutral governments, especially by India, to act as umpires or mediators. The real belligerents in Vietnam, so the Chinese argue, are the Americans and the Vietcong; and the Americans and the Vietcong should be the only partners in any negotiations for armistice or peace. The Russians reply that as the Americans will never consent to such a loss of face, a negotiated settlement can be achieved only at an international conference, to which the Vietcong is brought by the major Communist powers.

3. Moscow and Peking disagree also over the prospects of American escalation. Here the Chinese are in a sense more moderate than the Russians. They fear that Russian intervention may precipitate escalation just as did Khrushchev's intervention in Cuba, and the installation of a Soviet missile base there. During the Cuban crisis they criticized Khrushchev for his "adventurism" (in needlessly provoking the United States), as well as for his "opportunism" (in meekly climbing down). "We want neither your adventurism nor your opportunism in Vietnam," the Chinese now say to Kosygin and Brezhnev.

4. Peking maintains that the Russians are secretly negotiating a Vietnamese settlement with the Americans. Hints to the same effect come occasionally also from authoritative American sources. It is difficult to say just how much truth there is in them; but even if Russo-American soundings are taking place, their effect has so far been negligible, because Moscow has had little or no influence on what is going on in South Vietnam.

It is therefore logical for Moscow to try to increase its influence by establishing a closer contact with the North Vietnamese Government. . . . The North Vietnamese are in a quandary: they must show Moscow their gratitude for the aid received; but they are wary of antagonizing Peking, and they hardly wish to see legions of Soviet "advisers" and "specialists" in Vietnam.

RIVALRY IN UNDERDEVELOPED AREAS [7]

In the rapid liquidation of colonial empires since the end of World War II, the Communists have discerned a great setback for world capitalism and have therefore applauded—and, on occasion, aided—what they call the national liberation movement. They have been reluctant to believe that the West would accept the loss of imperial domination without a struggle, and they accuse the Western powers of attempting to reinstate imperialist domination in new forms denounced by the Communists as "neo-colonialism."

[7] From article by Herbert Dinerstein, an expert on Soviet affairs. *Problems of Communism* (a publication of the United States Information Agency). 13:64-72. Mr.-Ap. '64.

Some events seemed to furnish evidence for such an interpretation: (1) the colonial wars in Indo-China and Algeria; (2) the brief Anglo-French-Israeli campaign against the Egyptian nationalization of Suez; (3) the United States' assumption of responsibility for keeping communism out of South Vietnam. However, the first two now appear to have been last stands, and it seems difficult to interpret the American presence in Vietnam as a resurgence of imperialism. But whether or not the Soviet leaders believe that their support of national liberation movements was important in discouraging a supposed Western attempt to turn back the clock of history, they are satisfied that every subtraction from the power of the enemy camp is a plus for them. Viewed in terms of these broad perspectives, the internal political order of the newly independent countries is of secondary importance. Consequently, whenever newly independent or developing countries became involved in quarrels with members of the NATO, CENTO, or SEATO pacts, they found the Soviet Union ready to sell them arms in large quantities on easy terms. Egypt, Indonesia, Afghanistan, and Cuba are only some of the examples.

The Soviet leaders also felt, especially after Castro turned his revolution into a Communist one, that successful national liberation movements could become Communist revolutions of a sort. This of course lent added attraction to the policy of supporting such movements, but the prospect of reducing the sphere of capitalism was sufficient by itself to justify the policy.

. . . The Chinese leadership sets more exacting standards for the success of the national liberation movement than does the Soviet. In Peking's view, it must also serve the goals of legitimizing the regime and safeguarding the gains of the revolution. The Soviet Union is the foremost military power in Europe, and the Communist gains made there in the 1940's are protected by that power. In the western Pacific, however, the United States is the strongest military power; consequently, in that area, China requires more from the underdeveloped countries than a generalized anti-Western or neutralist stance. It requires a positive neutrality that involves active support of Chinese policies.

For the Chinese, in areas far from the mainland of China, the encouragement of revolutionary activity in underdeveloped countries is the only way they have of coping with the totality of American power, whereas the Soviet Union has a varied range of instruments at its disposal—e.g., technological advances, especially in missiles and space; military preponderance in Europe; weapons test moratoria, a partial test ban treaty. In the Chinese view, a series of Communist uprisings all over the world is necessary to force the United States to disperse its strength. This is, in essence, an international variant of the strategy of the Chinese revolution: the weaker force wears down the stronger by guerrilla tactics until the latter's strength is reduced and it can be directly engaged.

Sino-Soviet competition for influence. Old-fashioned rivalry for spheres of influence also plays an important role in the Sino-Soviet conflict. The Bandung Conference of 1955, to which the Soviet Union was not invited marked a critical point in the development of this rivalry. The conference could have been interpreted at the time as signifying a division of labor: the Chinese Communists would play the major role in promoting anti-American neutralist policies in Asia, while the Soviet Union would bear the responsibility for the rest of the world. If this was indeed the understanding, it quickly deteriorated.

Whatever may have been the purposes of Peking and Moscow, the neutralist organizers of the Bandung meeting, especially the Indians, hoped to separate Communist China from the Soviet Union and its policies. . . . The Chinese representative certainly seemed to fall in with this plan. He . . . spoke of a peculiar Asian identity, and was quite willing to retire the slogan of coexistence in favor of others. . . . It is hard to fix the precise moment when uneasy Sino-Soviet cooperation and division into spheres of influence passed over into outright competition, but relentless conflict is now unmistakable. Not only in Asia, Africa, and Latin America, but even in Western Europe, the Chinese Communists are supporting pro-Chinese wings and factions within the local Communist parties.

Creating favorable conditions for the transition to communism. From the Soviet point of view, reduction of the Western sphere of control and rivalry with the Chinese are sufficient reasons for Soviet support of the national liberation movement. The creation of favorable conditions for the transition to communism is a welcome bonus when it happens, but it is not necessary to justify the policy. This lower priority accorded by the Soviet leaders to the promotion of communism is the issue on which the Chinese have criticized the Russians most. That Peking's own policy towards Cambodia, Nepal, Sikkim, and Indonesia follows the same order of priorities does not embarrass them. The Chinese complain that the Soviet Union expects the bourgeoisie to prepare the way for the revolution in the underdeveloped countries, and that instead the bourgeoisie consolidates its position and stifles genuine revolutionary movements. The Chinese criticism probably represents more than an attempt to score points in the ideological debate. It probably reflects a radically different experience in revolution.

The Soviet historiography of the Russian revolution, which has already been invested with the aura of revealed truth, depicts the revolutionary process in a special way. The old regime crumbles, rotted through by internal contradictions and shaken by war. The short-lived successor, failing to cope with the situation, permits the establishment of a dual power in which the Communist share grows. Then, at the correct moment, the Communist party seizes power. (In Soviet hagiography, Lenin is revealed as a saint of the dialectic because he struck neither one day too late nor one day too soon.) Once the Bolsheviks have taken power, the struggle begins in earnest, and it is in the Civil War that the Communist party is forged into an instrument able to defend the revolution and build communism.

The Chinese memory of their own revolutionary victory is totally different. . . . The critical phase of the revolution was the struggle with the bourgeoisie *before* it collapsed. In that struggle the Communist party of China was hammered into the weapon which made the revolution.

From this fundamental difference in outlook many corollaries flow. The Soviet Union claims that the parliamentary path to communism represents a realistic possibility; the Chinese, while accepting it theoretically, minimize its chances of success. The Soviet Union points to the danger of poorly prepared revolts that fail and slow up the revolutionary process; the Chinese Communists emphasize the demoralization of inactivity and collaboration with the bourgeoisie. The Soviet Union fears that Communist revolutions, if ill-timed, may provoke Western intervention and cause local wars; the Chinese view revolutionary struggles as creating the most favorable ground for the growth of Communist parties.

But one need not accept the claim of the Chinese that they always support revolutionary struggle while the Soviet Union always procrastinates in hope of a more opportune moment. We have already referred to the Chinese Communist policy of collaboration with bourgeois regimes in neighboring countries when Peking judges that China's immediate foreign policy interests should take precedence over the prospects for revolution. And it was Soviet economic and military assistance that played a major, if not the determining, role in the establishment of the Communist regime in Cuba, the first such victory since the Communist triumph in China in 1949. Soviet support of Castro, though hesitant, was tangible; the Chinese merely shouted encouragement from the sidelines. Moreover, as the CPSU [Communist party of the Soviet Union] program makes perfectly clear, the Soviet Union is not wedded to an exclusive policy of nonviolent revolution.

Sino-Soviet doctrinal disagreements over the proper tactics to adopt toward the bourgeoisie, supporting wars of national liberation, and accepting the risks of local wars have already been thoroughly described. It may be useful, therefore, to examine a specific case in which the Soviet and Chinese prescriptions on these issues came into conflict.

The Conflict over India

Future historians will probably view the Sino-Indian border conflict as an important turning point in Far Eastern international life. Although much has already been written about it, much is still obscure. . . . Nevertheless, enough is now known to permit an analysis of the conflict as a concrete example of Sino-Soviet disagreement. Perhaps there have been equally significant differences over policy toward Laos, Vietnam, and Indonesia, but not enough evidence has been revealed.

The Sino-Soviet conflict regarding India has centered largely on the Tibetan problem. The interests of China and India in Tibet are fundamentally different, and in the end they could not be accommodated to each other. For China the Tibetan question is essentially one of the legitimacy of Chinese rule and the attainment of China's "natural" borders; and the frustration of Communist China's aspirations in Taiwan has made victory in Tibet all the more important to her. Soviet opposition to Peking's policy in Tibet must have confirmed the Chinese Communists in their suspicion that Soviet support of their claim to Taiwan was only *pro forma,* while Soviet (and Indian) suggestions that the Chinese should direct their energies toward Taiwan and Hong Kong instead of Tibet have probably been regarded in Peking as the mockery and contempt that are the lot of the weak.

The requirements of India's Tibetan policy have been quite different. While the British determined that policy, it was to make Tibet a buffer state separating India from China and Russia. China accepted British recognition of her suzerainty (rather than full sovereignty) over Tibet since she was then too weak to contest the case and the concept of suzerainty left the door open for further Chinese claims in the future. . . .

Independent India also wanted to maintain Tibet as a buffer state, but the means at her disposal were more modest for three reasons: First, she renounced the British positions in Tibet as a survival of imperialism and confined herself to the borders she claimed. Second, Chinese power after 1949 was on the ascendant. Third, whatever resources India was willing to divert to the military establishment were primarily earmarked for the conflict over Kashmir which erupted with Britain's grant of Indian independence.

When the Chinese Communists occupied Tibet militarily in 1950-1951, India accepted Peking's assurances that Tibet would remain autonomous and that no territorial dispute or controversy existed between India and China. India seemed loath to consider the alternatives of improving her bargaining position vis-à-vis China by improving her military position. Instead India avoided raising the Tibetan issue with China, assuming that the latter would preserve the buffer status of Tibet.

In an effort to convince China that she had nothing to fear from India—and probably out of genuine conviction, too—India consistently supported Communist China's admission to the United Nations and her claim to Taiwan. The Chinese meanwhile did nothing to discourage the Indian expectation that Tibet would enjoy special status within Communist China. Assurances that the social revolution in Tibet would move slowly were repeated. For example, on one occasion in 1956, the Dalai Lama, who was in India at the same time as Chinese Foreign Minister Chou En-lai, was reluctant to return to Tibet because he feared that Chinese policy in that country was moving toward full-fledged communization. However, Nehru obtained reassurances from Chou, and when these were passed on to the Dalai Lama, he returned to Tibet. Although the Chinese Communists gave no formal undertakings to preserve Tibet's autonomy and not occupy it in force, they encouraged the Indians to believe that this would be the case.

This uneasy but nevertheless mutually acceptable arrangement became untenable, however, when Communist China's hold on Tibet was threatened by a spreading rebellion which started in Kham in 1955. . . .

The direct routes from western China to the areas in which the Khampa tribesmen live are poor and in wintertime impassable. The route from Sinkiang province southeastward to Kham is better and—most important of all—open in the early winter. It has the disadvantage, however, of first passing through the Aksai Chin, long recognized as Indian territory and then very close to the Indian border. If the Chinese Communists were to make this their main avenue for the military pacification and control of Tibet, not only would the Indians lose some territory, but all hope of keeping Tibet as a buffer region with small Chinese occupation forces would vanish.

By 1959, when the Indians learned that the Chinese had already occupied the remote Aksai Chin area, the earlier basis for agreement had disappeared. Peking charged that the rebellion in Tibet was inspired and supported by Indian, American, and Kuomintang agents, especially in Katmandu—a version which the Chinese Communists found it more congenial to accept than to acknowledge that the Tibetans had risen against Communist rule on their own. Thus, India, in Chinese eyes, had shifted from a position of positive neutrality to that of agent of the imperialists who wanted to prevent China from exercising legitimate control over her own territory.

Indian opinion became highly exercised over the Chinese occupation of the Aksai Chin, and Prime Minister Nehru had to defend publicly his Chinese and Tibetan policies. What worried the Indians was not only the realization that Tibet's buffer status was completely lost, but also the studied and deliberate vagueness of the Chinese claims with respect to India's northeastern frontiers. Did the Chinese encroachment in the border region represent the final Chinese claim, or the first in a series?

Communist China's communications to India in 1959 drew a distinction between Nehru and his "evil advisers," suggesting Chinese hope that Nehru could and would prevail upon Indian public opinion to swallow the bitter pill of the Chinese military presence on the frontier. However, Soviet intervention on the Indian side reduced the chances that such hopes would be realized. From the Chinese statements published in the summer of 1963 we learn that the Soviet Union notified the Chinese of Moscow's intention to publish a note charging that the Sino-Indian conflict had been instigated by those who wanted the then imminent Khrushchev-Eisenhower meeting at Camp David to fail. The Soviet purpose, obviously, was to get the Chinese to relax their pressure on India. The Chinese asked the Russians not to publish the note, calculating that public evidence of Soviet support for India would encourage Nehru to resist. Notwithstanding this appeal, the Soviet news agency Tass published the note on September 10, 1959.

Here, the essential nature of the Sino-Soviet conflict is revealed. The Soviet Union—in an adversary relationship with the United States—hoped, through negotiation with Washington, to gain a change in the status of West Berlin and to prevail on the United States to do less than its utmost in the arms race. The Chinese Communists, on the other hand, had nothing to gain from negotiations with the United States and confined themselves to the issue of the security of their Tibetan province. Although the Chinese remained in the Aksai Chin, the Indians, far from accepting the situation, took measures to improve their strategic position. By 1962 the Indians, with Soviet help, including even Soviet helicopters manned by Soviet personnel, had improved their communications to the area, suggesting the likelihood that in time it would become easier for them to support military operations in the area than for the Chinese.

Meanwhile, Soviet-Chinese relations were deteriorating steadily. The Chinese felt and said that the Soviet policy of negotiating with the United States had failed. Soviet economic and military aid to China dwindled. But if this Soviet action was designed to force the Chinese to submit to Moscow's direction, it had the contrary effect of making the Chinese feel there was nothing left for them to lose. When the Indians sought in 1962 to regain control over territory they had lost in 1959, they did so from a position strengthened by Soviet material assistance; but this aid was no more effective in changing Chinese policy than Soviet verbal support of the Indians had been in 1959. One Communist ally made war on India; the other furnished her military equipment and promised more.

Such completely opposed policies can be found at times in all alliance systems, including NATO. The Suez crisis and French refusal to accept the test ban treaty are two cases in point. But such conflicts are very much less disruptive in the Western alliance system because divergences of interest among its members are accepted as inevitable, even if awkward. In the Communist system, with its assumption that only one correct foreign policy line exists, divergence is much harder to manage.

It is not altogether impossible that with the disappearance of the chief Chinese or the chief Russian figure in the quarrel, the diverse interests of the two major Communist powers can once more be brought into some measure of harmony. More probably, however, matters have gone too far for genuine and lasting repair. Barring the development of some common threat to both regimes, each side can be expected to act upon its own divergent convictions.

But one should not simply expect the Chinese Communists to create revolutionary movements, and the Soviet Union to stifle them. It is more likely that the Chinese will be able to influence Soviet policy more effectively in open opposition than when forced to pretend to a common policy. Especially in areas remote from China's borders, such as Angola or Zanzibar, the Chinese may well force the tempo of Soviet involvement by threatening to pre-empt revolutionary leadership. The Soviet Union cannot fail to act without forfeiting its claim to that leadership. Thus the Chinese Communists though weak in resources and cast in the role of international pariah, might conceivably influence Soviet policy in the underdeveloped world more than ever before.

SINO-SOVIET COMPETITION IN AFRICA [8]

The Russians know that they are in serious trouble in the non-Western world today, and that many of their problems are caused not by the West but by their former comrades in Peking. The People's Republic of China, despite its substantial military and economic weaknesses, is now locked in a bitter struggle with the Soviet Union. It has already won some signal victories in Asia, particularly within the Communist movement, and it is now determined to make Africa the next major target. By the time the march toward independence has been completed on this continent, it is likely that some forty sovereign states will have emerged. This will represent approximately one third of the entire community of nations.

[8] From article by R. A. Scalapino, professor of political science, University of California. *Foreign Affairs.* 42:640-54. Jl. '64. Copyright by the Council on Foreign Relations, Inc., New York. Reprinted by permission.

Soviet leaders are thus well aware of the fact that the outcome of this struggle could be crucial to the ultimate balance of power both in the world and in the Communist camp. They also know that this struggle cannot be won by military means. They have begun to fight hard, using a variety of psychological, political, and economic weapons. But the battle is only in its opening stages, and it will surely grow more fierce. African leaders, meanwhile, watch developments with mixed emotions. There are certain advantages in being wooed vigorously by a number of suitors, but there are real dangers involved when complex international rivalries are transplanted onto the African continent.

Both the benefits and the dangers were illustrated by the . . . African trip of Chou En-lai. For nearly two months, beginning in mid-December 1963, the Chinese Premier and a sixty-man entourage visited ten states of North, West, and East Africa. An assessment of current Sino-Soviet rivalry in Africa might well begin with an evaluation of Chou's journey, which had three basic objectives.

The first was to involve China as fully as possible in the process of African emergence and to thwart all attempts at the isolation of China from whatever source. . . . Chou's basic argument was a simple one: whatever our ideological and cultural differences, we have two vital goals in common. We are all committed to the establishment of our full independence and to the fight against imperialism, colonialism, and neocolonialism. Furthermore, we are all involved in the common struggle against backwardness and for economic development. Afro-Asian solidarity can be successfully achieved by keeping in mind these two primary objectives.

Having set forth the common goals of China and Africa, Chou next addressed himself to the question of how China could assist the Africans in their attainment. . . . [He included] a firm guarantee of support in the fight against imperialism and "for the winning and safeguarding of national independence." Support was also pledged to the African policies of peace, neutrality, and nonalignment; to any form of regionalism or Pan-Africanism satisfactory to the Africans; to the settlement of differences by

l means; and to the struggle against interference "from
er quarter" in the internal affairs of African states.

In Mali, Chou advanced the . . . principles which, he asserted,
governed Chinese economic and technical assistance. These included the themes that aid must be extended upon the basis of
equality and mutual benefit, with no strings or special privileges
requested by the donor; that the most favorable terms should be
extended, with emphasis upon projects requiring minimal investment, yielding quick results, and aimed at launching nations on
the road to self-reliance and independent economic development,
not making them dependencies of China; that only equipment of
the best quality should be sent and indigenous personnel should
be fully trained by the Chinese; and that all Chinese experts
would live at the same level as the experts of recipient countries,
requesting no special favors.

China's . . . policy was intended to constitute a challenge to
the Soviet Union quite as much as to the West. At its heart,
Sino-Soviet competition in Africa will center on who is contribut-
ing most and demanding least. Who is prepared to make the
greatest sacrifices on behalf of the national liberation movement? Who will abstain to the greatest extent from interference
in the internal affairs of the African states and acknowledge most
fully their desire for equality? Who will offer the most generous
aid with the fewest strings?

China now uses in Africa the same arguments which she has
advanced repeatedly against the Soviet Union within the international Communist movement. She charges that the Soviet government . . . has at best given second priority to the liberation of
colonial peoples, preferring an accommodation with the imperialist West. She asserts that the Russians employ typically imperialist methods in dealing with small states, interfering in their internal affairs and seeking to dictate to them. Soviet economic aid,
according to the Chinese, is aimed at producing dependency upon
the Soviet Union and providing a basis for obtaining special concessions. The . . . principles advanced by Chou in Mali are in
reality a product of Chinese grievances against the Russians based
upon their experience with Soviet aid.

Before examining the Soviet answer, let us set forth briefly the other objectives of Chou's trip. A second major aim was to create in the African mind an image of China that would contradict the picture being painted by Peking's enemies. In this respect, Chou had a complicated task. In essence, he wanted to establish a series of dual images: a China dedicated to revolution and the over-throw of imperialism everywhere, but also a China committed to peaceful coexistence and noninterference in the internal affairs of states having a different social system; a China sharing a com-mon timing of revolution and common problems of backwardness with Africa and hence able to understand Africa's problems and to exchange experiences, but also a China which by virtue of its size and accomplishments had to be regarded as a major world power, a state that could not be ignored or shunted to the politi-cal sidelines.

Two . . . events had to be handled carefully by Chou—the Sino-Indian border conflict [see the preceding article "Rivalry in Underdeveloped Areas"] and the [nuclear] test ban treaty. Many African leaders, including some on the left, have taken a dim view of the Chinese attack upon India. Almost all African states, moreover, signed the test ban treaty despite Peking's violent at-tack upon it. Everywhere, Chou gave a spirited private defense of Chinese actions in the border controversy. In most states, he also made a public promise that China would strive for a peaceful and negotiated settlement of the dispute. . . .

Nor did Chou give ground on the test ban treaty. He ad-vanced the customary Chinese position on disarmament with vigor: the world should accept complete disarmament and the total destruction of nuclear weapons, with nuclear-free zones be-ing established as a preliminary step. Did not these positions, and the excellent relations which China enjoyed with such small neighbors as Nepal, Burma, and Cambodia prove that the Peo-ple's Republic was a peace-loving nation? The test ban treaty, however, was totally improper in two basic senses, according to Chou. First, it was a fraud that did not guarantee peace but rather gave American imperialism certain significant military ad-vantages. Second, it was a treaty negotiated essentially by the superpowers and then presented to the rest of the world to sign. Its primary purposes were to keep the nuclear club small and to perpetuate big-power control over the world.

Throughout his African journey, Chou played in contrapuntal fashion upon the themes of struggle and peace, backwardness and progress, weakness and power. Since imperialism and colonialism were the true threats to peace, he argued, the struggle against these forces was inseparable from the struggle for peace, and China stood in the forefront of both battles. A backward society itself, China could appreciate the revolutionary aspirations of the African people and their basic rejection of the status quo. If the have-not nations of the world hoped to have an influence in international affairs, they must overlook differences and achieve unity. Only then could separate weaknesses be turned into collective strength. And to impress Africans with the physical dimensions of the world's largest emerging society, Chou constantly told his audiences, "The 650 million people of China stand with you!"

Chou's African trip had one final objective, that of allowing a top Chinese leader to assess the situation first hand, preparatory to reviewing Chinese policy toward this important continent. Today, Communist China stands at a crossroads in Africa, and certain basic decisions must be made concerning the future. Peking's African policies up to date, while reasonably successful, have been very modest. Should commitments be expanded and, if so, in what direction? The pace of political change in this area renders answers to these questions all the more imperative.

The Chinese Communist Record

To appreciate this fact, let us briefly review the Chinese Communist record in Africa up to the present. The first substantial Chinese Communist contacts were in North Africa shortly after the establishment of the People's Republic in 1949. This was logical because "the liberation struggle" developed at an early point in this area; a sophisticated, articulate left existed in such countries as Egypt and Algeria; and Cairo in particular was a natural base for organizations such as the Afro-Asian Solidarity

Council. Making use of the fierce struggle being waged by North African leaders against the British, French, and Israelis, Peking proclaimed its full devotion to the Arab cause, hastened to establish relations with the Nasser government, gave support to the Algerian revolution, and made Cairo its headquarters for contacts with all African revolutionaries. This policy paid dividends. By the end of 1963 the People's Republic had achieved recognition from four states in this area—the U.A.R., Algeria, Morocco, and Tunisia. In the aftermath of Chou's visit, however, it was clear that Peking faced problems in North Africa. Only in Algeria did Chou come close to getting a response matching Chinese hopes, and even here there was an absence of full support for Chinese positions.

What were the difficulties? Three factors stand out. First, material needs and cultural ties both draw the nations of North Africa closer to the West or to the Soviet bloc than to the People's Republic of China. For this region, the revolutionary era is over and the era of construction has begun. Many unsettled problems remain, including some having dangerous international implications—like Arab-Israeli hostility. In general, however, North African leaders are now anxious to consolidate their power at home, create a unified nation, and push forward with modernization. Is the Chinese position conducive to these goals, and can China provide hardware for these tasks? Moreover, can she truly communicate with a political élite that has its cultural roots in the Western and Islamic worlds?

Related to this point is a second one: North African leaders . . . see their interests best served by maintaining a judicious balance between the West and the Soviet bloc. Such a balance is not aided by any marked degree of alignment with a China angry at almost everyone. . . . North African leaders, moreover, have their own ideas about the tactics and leadership of the African liberation movement. Nasser believes that Egypt has an important role to play both in the Arab world and in black Africa. Algeria shares its experiences and provides assistance to a variety of African revolutionaries. These states do not intend to allow Communist China to assume the leadership of the African revolutionary movement.

Indeed, even the "left" states of North Africa have had sufficient trouble with their own Communists to be on guard when embraced too warmly by foreign Communist leaders. In Morocco, ironically, accused Communists were coming to trial on charges of subversion even as Chou hailed the "growing friendship" of the Chinese and Moroccan peoples. Nasser's Communists are in jail, in exile or in retirement. . . .

China also faces certain problems in East and Central Africa today. Here, too, contact was relatively early in terms of the political evolution of these regions. The Chinese made their initial contacts, generally through Cairo, while colonialism still prevailed over much of the area. Their basic tactic—like those employed by the Bolsheviks three decades earlier in Asia—has been to invest seed money in promising individuals. Generally, Peking has concentrated upon journalists, politicians, and student-intellectual types. To those receptive, Peking has offered red-carpet trips to China, special training programs, and funds for a variety of purposes.

The mass media have received particular attention. A number of journalists and presses have been subsidized with the result that a pro-Peking flavor can often be detected in the radical African press. The Chinese have also established one of the world's most powerful transmitters so as to beam Swahili, Arabic, and English language programs into eastern Africa. Peking, however, does not confine its activities merely to propaganda. Increasingly, the Chinese have indicated a willingness to give substantial aid to revolutions against colonial or "reactionary" regimes.

The Chinese Communists appear to be involved, directly or indirectly, in every active revolution on the African continent at present. Perhaps the most striking example is the uprising led by Pierre Mulele in the Kwilu region of the Congo. Mulele, who only returned to the Congo in the fall of 1963 after two years in Peking, has sought to follow Maoist principles completely. He is seeking to develop a guerrilla movement based upon the support of the peasants. Instructions have been issued to the troops to cultivate the people, winning their confidence and support, so that the "Liberation Army" can swim in their midst as fish in the water—Mao's famous dictum.

Peking gives trips, funds, and training to other revolutionary movements. Rwanda exiles plotting a return to power receive Chinese Communist assistance. Certain leaders of the Zimbabwe African People's Union, which aims at African control of . . . Rhodesia, have been ardently wooed by the Chinese. Full support has been promised the African nationalists of Angola and Mozambique, and leading representatives of both these movements have been to Peking where they presumably have obtained aid. South Africa represents a natural target. On April 13, 1964, a typical Peking "rally" on behalf of South African "freedom fighters" was held, with various African speakers being featured. The radical portion of the South African National Congress is reportedly under strong Peking influence. Thus, as the revolutionary tide sweeps through central and southern Africa, the Chinese Communists are determined to be in the vanguard.

Peking, however, is anxious to play both sides of the street. It has balanced its revolutionary program with one of seeking formal relations with self-governing African states of widely varying political coloration. Apparently there is only one qualification: recognition of Nationalist China is unacceptable. To some of the East African states, moreover, Peking has offered economic and technical assistance. The campaign to win friends thus progresses simultaneously at different levels and via different tactics.

As in North Africa, Peking's East African policy has produced mixed results. Most states in this area have granted recognition to the People's Republic and established formal relations with it. Some of Peking's seed money, moreover, appears to have paid off. At least a few individuals aided by the Chinese have been in a position to repay their benefactors. Perhaps more importantly, African nationalists still struggling against white rule are undeniably gravitating to the left at present, and Peking has good reason to hope that it can achieve major gains here, both against the West and against the Soviet Union.

There is a debit side to Peking's ledger, however. A program of "buying" individuals is not very costly, but its long-run effectiveness may be questioned. Most individuals do not stay hitched. Either they are independent-minded men who will take funds but not orders, or they are opportunists whose "convictions" last only as long as the subsidies. A more serious question for Peking is whether the Chinese can simultaneously ride the two tides now running strongly in this region: revolution and stabilization. If Peking continues to invest in revolution, it will inevitably gain the hostility of the African moderates. Because they are already suspicious of Peking and anxious to keep foreign interference in Africa to a minimum, many East African leaders would prefer that the Africans themselves underwrite the remaining liberation movements. If Peking decides to invest more heavily in stabilization, a much greater outlay of funds will be required.

In West Africa, the Chinese Communists were relatively late in their arrival. Thus they were confronted with independent states many of which were using the designation "socialist." It was in this part of Africa, therefore, that Peking first experimented with official aid programs. Beginning in 1960, the Chinese advanced credits and shortly thereafter started to operate tea and rice plantations, promised to build cigarette and match factories, and undertook technical training programs. These activities were in addition to Peking's usual programs of cultural relations. In this area, there is little evidence of the seed-money approach; extensive unofficial ties would be dangerous—as Russian experience has shown—and they are also basically unnecessary.

Up to date, the Chinese Communists have scored their most significant gains in selected parts of West Africa. In considerable measure, this is a product of the political climate of the region. But it is also a product of the Chinese capacity to learn from the mistakes of others, and their ability in this region to keep their policies clear and unambiguous. Their aid programs have been successful partly because they have been small-scale and hence have not involved the Chinese in the total planning process, with all of the complications which this involves. The Chinese have been in pursuit of immediate political gains. From all indications, their technicians have made no demands, there has been no interference in domestic politics, and no obvious *quid pro quo* has been sought. Peking has shown a capacity to tolerate waste and inefficiency without complaint. Even in this region, however, the issues for the future are troublesome. Should and can present activities be expanded? More importantly, in the long run, can Peking rely upon the parties and leaders of the African left? It is significant that Chou En-lai refused to apply the term "socialist" to the governments of Ghana, Mali, or Guinea.

The Soviet Record

There can be little doubt that Communist China, despite the problems it faces, has scored significant gains in Africa during the past five years, some of them at the expense of the Soviet Union. How shall we assess the Russian position at present? Like Peking, Moscow has engaged in a wide range of activities: subsidization of journalists; training of revolutionaries; scholarship programs; and large-scale economic aid. In retrospect, it can perhaps be said that Russia was at the zenith of her *revolutionary* influence upon Africa in 1960. Prior to that time, she and her close allies stood as the sole alternatives to continued dependence upon the West. The Soviet Union, moreover, was able to outbid all external competitors in supporting national liberation movements, until the Chinese entered the field.

Even after 1960, the Soviet Union has continued to have certain significant advantages over the Chinese. As a major world power, it can confer a degree of prestige on a movement or government which Peking can scarcely offer. Moreover, unlike the Chinese, the Russians derive strength in the contest from industrialized allies. Finally, Soviet resources are infinitely greater than those of Peking. It is not surprising that Soviet operations have been on a much larger scale in almost all of the areas where these two nations are in serious conflict. According to figures believed reliable, Soviet credits extended to Algeria total $100 million whereas Chinese credits equal $50 million; Soviet aid to Somalia is $44 million in comparison with Chinese credits totaling $20 million; the figures for Ghana are $81 million and $20 million respectively; for Mali, $55 million and $19.6 million; and for Guinea, $80 milion and $24 million. Only in Zanzibar did the Chinese recently commit themselves to a more extensive aid program than the Russians, . . . [although] that commitment may be reexamined. If East European assistance were added to the Russian figures, the gap would be significantly wider.

In the competition for students, also, the Soviets are far ahead of the Chinese Communists. It is difficult to get reliable figures because many African students go to bloc countries "unofficially," but the evidence suggests that there are presently about 1,000 Ghanaian students in the Soviet bloc countries and no more than a handful (possibly 5–10) in China; there are some 600 Sudanese in the bloc and few if any in China; Guinea has about 600 students in the bloc, not more than 20 in China—and many of these may have returned home.

Both the Soviet Union and China have had difficulty in attracting good students and in satisfying those that they get. Indeed, in the light of Soviet experience, it may be doubted that having a large number of students is an asset. Relatively few Africans have thus far returned from the Communist world as enthusiastic supporters of the system. A significant number have been disillusioned. Linguistic and cultural barriers are formidable, but social and political problems have also been serious. While the situation is not as critical as some Western reports have indicated, African students are a somewhat dubious factor in the struggle for influence. There is no reason to believe, however, that the Chinese problem in this respect is less difficult than the Russian.

Weighing these various factors, we can state that the Chinese Communists are engaged in an uphill struggle to match the Soviet Union in volume of aid, influence, and general prestige on the African continent. Nevertheless, the Chinese have made recent gains, and the Soviets find themselves in trouble at many points. Perhaps the roots of the Soviet problem lie in three factors: racial-cultural differences; the developmental gap between the Soviet Union and Africa; and Soviet weaknesses or errors in diplomatic-political policies. Naturally, the Chinese have been quick to exploit these factors when they could do so. Thus, in some cases, they have thrown the Russians onto the defensive in spite of the much larger Soviet presence in the African scene.

Moscow has repeatedly charged Peking with using racism to advance it cause in Africa. There is some exaggeration in this charge, but it also contains an element of truth. The Chinese have rarely if ever resorted to straight racial appeals. To do so would be un-Marxian and probably unpolitic. As is the case with most people, Africans are primarily for the Africans. At the grass-roots level at least, there is no reason to believe that the Asian is regarded with any more enthusiasm than the European. A strong element of racialism does exist in contemporary Africa, but any direct appeal based upon this theme by the Chinese would probably backfire.

Nevertheless, the general thrust of the Chinese line in Africa has racial implications. The strong emphasis upon the unity of the Afro-Asian world, the heavy assault upon Western imperialism, even the slogan about the East wind prevailing over the West wind, suggest the unity of the black and yellow peoples against the whites. The unremitting attacks upon the Russians as non-Asians in the attempt to force them out of Afro-Asian organizations is clearly an effort by the Chinese to identify the Russian people with the advanced, Western world. Clearly, the many stories of discrimination in the Soviet Union against African students have done the Soviet image some harm. And it is possible that if anti-white sentiment in Africa were to be extended or increased by a series of bloody liberation wars in the south, Chinese advantages over the Russians might also increase.

However, the most telling blows struck against the Russians by the Chinese relate to the issue of Soviet methods and motives. The Chinese have not hesitated to charge Russia with being guilty of big-power chauvinism in Africa—ignoring the rights of small nations, interfering in their internal affairs, making economic aid a weapon of Russian power. These charges strike home, of course, because there is some substance in them. In the postwar era, the Russians came forward rapidly as a global power from a background of relative inexperience in formal diplomacy and a record of great highhandedness in dealing with the international Communist movement. As a result, the Russians have made numerous mistakes in Africa. They have interfered in internal affairs, as in Guinea; they have often appeared to favor major-power diplomacy at the expense of small states; and they have granted economic aid on less generous terms than might have been possible.

Like certain Western powers, moreover, the Russians have often found the experience of aiding underdeveloped societies terribly frustrating. The usual complaints have been voiced: the unwillingness of aid recipients to take advice; massive inefficiency, waste, and corruption; and lack of gratitude. The very scope of Soviet operations in some societies has presented a problem that the Chinese have not faced. The Russians have been intimately involved in the total economy, and hence forced to share the blame when general crises developed. In the final analysis, it might not be unfair to say that the Russians have faced the disadvantages of being *both* developed and developing in African eyes. On the one hand, Africans tend increasingly to group the Soviet Union with the advanced West, hence to doubt the applicability of the Soviet model and to view with suspicion Soviet economic and political objectives. But on the other hand, the Soviet Union frequently does not fare well when compared with the West in cultural or technological terms. This is important in a period when the African elite is still strongly influenced by Western civilization. . . .

Conclusions

What are the main conclusions to be drawn at this stage? Four basic points would appear to merit emphasis:

1. A bitter struggle for influence has now erupted on the African continent, a struggle between the Soviet Union and China in which all available political and economic weapons are being used. Fundamentally, the basic issues involved are the same as those that provoked the global Sino-Soviet split: a conflict over

organization, decision-making, and leadership in the revolutionary movement; sharply differing positions on the most appropriate tactics and strategy for Communist victory in the late twentieth century; and quarrels over the proper treatment to be given comrades and allies. Each of these basic issues reflects in some measure the different traditions, timing of revolution, stage of development, and degree of power that mark the two Communist giants.

Increasingly, the central tactic of the Chinese in Africa and elsewhere appears to be that of trying to couple the Soviet Union and the United States together, as the two imperialist superpowers which threaten the rest of the world. The Chinese seek to isolate their two primary opponents and to establish a series of "United Fronts"—one tying them with the Afro-Asian-Latin American world, another connecting them with selected "advanced" or "transitional" societies of Europe and Asia. Thus Peking will strive with all its capacity to read the Russians out of the Afro-Asian group, and present itself as the leading revolutionary model.

The Russians, on the other hand, are increasingly drawn to the strategy of banking upon *development* rather than revolution, in the belief that the leaders of post-independence Africa are primarily interested in political unification and economic modernization, and that socialism can be achieved only in the context of indigenous development. Thus their tactic is to underwrite certain lines of economic and political "growth" in Africa while charging that the Chinese are attempting to force the pace of African revolution on behalf of their own selfish bid for world power.

2. In assessing the tide of battle, one cannot ignore recent Chinese gains. In the past few years, Peking has made its presence felt throughout the African continent. Prior to 1956, no African state recognized Communist China. Today, that government is recognized by [at least] fourteen African states. . . . Now, however, the Chinese may well have reached a more difficult part of the road. Initial gains were easy; Peking could take advantage of Moscow's errors and mount modest programs having an impact far greater than their cost. (It should be noted, however, that Taipei [Nationalist China] also did well with limited

aid programs in selected African states.) But the Russians have advantages that cannot easily be overcome: Soviet power and resources are vastly more extensive; despite its troubles with Eastern Europe, the Soviet Government in its quest for African "votes" has allies upon whose ideological commitment and technical skills it can generally count; and whatever the record of Russian interference in African internal affairs, Moscow's current ideological-political line would seem to be more compatible with that of most established African leaders than the Chinese line.

The Chinese Communists have an interest in keeping the revolutionary fires stoked. Their greatest opportunity for influence is in areas of Africa which are not yet self-governing or where independence seems most incomplete. In the aftermath of successful revolution—in the cold, gray dawn of consolidating power and nation-building—Chinese competitive advantages sharply decline. Not only are Chinese resources very limited. The Chinese revolutionary model has limited applicability for Africa, despite the relatively common timing of the Chinese experience and certain common socioeconomic problems.

3. One basic political problem looms ahead for both the Soviet Union and the People's Republic of China. At what point will it be necessary or natural to encourage the establishment of more Communist parties? Today, there are only a few bona fide Communist parties in Africa and, without exception, the majority of their leaders appear to be inclined toward Moscow. As the importance of being able to count upon votes—to have disciplined supporters—in all parts of the world increases, both Moscow and Peking will be under greater pressure to create their own orthodox parties. It is entirely possible that rival factions will emerge almost simultaneously in a number of African states. Up to date, Soviet and Chinese Communists have managed to maintain cordial relations with governments which have taken a tough line toward their domestic Communists. If Russia and China get into a deadly struggle for the establishment and control of Communist parties throughout the African continent, it could have serious repercussions in their relations even with the leftist African states.

4. The overwhelming majority of African nations want to remain strictly neutral in the quarrel between the two Communist leaders. Their foreign policy is one of "positive neutrality," friendly relations with all—or almost all—nations. . . . As noted earlier, the Africans want maximum aid and minimum interference. The leftist states in particular are thus deeply troubled by the Sino-Soviet rift; it threatens to add new complications to an already complex foreign-domestic situation. It is not easy to maintain positive neutrality when the neat international divisions of yesteryear have been fragmented. Moreover, many African states can now feel the heat of the Sino-Soviet dispute since it has been carried onto their own soil, and they can feel the increasing pressures to take sides, at least on some issues. This they will resist as long and as fully as possible. The most basic theme underlying African politics will continue to be "Africa for the Africans." Ironically, however, one by-product of the Sino-Soviet competition in Africa may be greater opportunities for the West to play a significant role in future African development. After the Russians and Chinese have slashed at each other for a while, the French, the British—and even the Belgians—may not look so bad to those newly emerging African states in quest of help.

YUGOSLAVIA—IS IT GOING BOURGEOIS? [9]

One of the principal issues between the Chinese and the Russian Communists has been that of Yugoslavia, more precisely whether Yugoslavia continues to be a socialist state or whether in fact it has not abandoned socialism and become an *agentura* of the imperialists. To put it bluntly, the Chinese Communists denounce the Yugoslav comrades for having abandoned the world revolution. This is a very serious charge, even if untrue, and deserving, one might think, of more Western attention than it has received. . . .

[9] From "Yugoslavia: Has Tito Gone Bourgeois?", by R. V. Burks, professor of history, Wayne State University, Detroit. *East Europe.* 14:2-14. Ag. '65. Reprinted by permission.

The Chinese Indictment

Is Yugoslavia a socialist country? Essentially what the Chinese say is that there has taken place in Yugoslavia a degeneration of state and party power which has resulted in a loss of control by the proletariat and the emergence of a . . . *bourgeoisie* made up of managers and experts. The Chinese indictment concentrates on the reforms which the Yugoslavs have introduced in the economic field.

The basic change here, according to the Chinese, was the introduction of what the Yugoslav revisionists please to call "workers' self-management." The essence of workers' self-management consists in handing over the factories to "working collectives," with each enterprise operating independently, purchasing its own raw materials, deciding on the variety of its output and the prices of its product, determining its own wage-scales and distributing a part of its income. Actually, say the Chinese, workers' self-management is a device by which real authority over the productive process is placed in the hands of bureaucrats and managers, who control both the property of the enterprise and its personnel. . . . [China] argues in effect that the Yugoslav party is no longer in command of the economy.

As proof of this basic contention, the Chinese itemize the following charges:

First, the abandonment of unified economic planning by the state.

Second, the use of profits as the primary incentive in the operation of the enterprises. . . . The aim of production is not to meet the needs of society but to seek profits, just as in any capitalist enterprise.

Third, following the policy of encouraging capitalist free competition. . . .

Fourth, the use of credit and the banks as important levers to promote capitalist free competition. . . .

Fifth, relations among the enterprises are not socialist relations of mutual support and coordination under a unified government plan but capitalist relations of competition and rivalry in a free market.

All this has undermined the very foundation of socialist planned economy.

The Chinese point out in addition that the state no longer has a monopoly of foreign trade, that there are some 115,000 privately-owned craft establishments in Yugoslavia, and that in 1951 the Tito clique openly abandoned the collectivization of agriculture.

One result of these grave sins, the Chinese continue, has been the increasing dependence of Yugoslavia on the great capitalist states, and particularly on the United States. From 1945 to 1963 the imperialist powers gave Yugoslavia $5.5 billion in aid. About half of Yugoslavia's exports of magnesium, lead, zinc, and antimony have gone to the United States since 1957. Yugoslavia has factories which do nothing but assemble products the parts for which have been manufactured by Western monopolies. . . .

Put in Western terms, what the Chinese say is this: by abandoning the central administration of the economy and permitting limited play of market forces, and by returning to private property in land and in the service industries, the Yugoslav Communists have abandoned the world revolution. In so doing they have, objectively speaking, gone over to the side of the imperialists, since they have provided the world with an example of how, under the cover of revisionist preaching, a Communist regime may gradually and peacefully evolve into a non-Communist regime. By providing the first example of the abandonment of power by a revolutionary party, the Yugoslavs endanger the forward march of the world revolution. A serious indictment indeed!

What worries the Chinese most of all is the tendency of Khrushchev and his successors to borrow from and imitate the Tito clique. Tito denounces Stalin in order to oppose Marxism-Leninism in its very fundamentals. So do the Russian leaders. Tito plays up the horrors of nuclear war in order to intimidate the people of the world into abandoning the revolutionary struggle. So do Khrushchev and his heirs. Both Tito and . . . [the Russians] preach that a world without weapons and without wars can be brought into existence while imperialism still exists, and both proclaim that the possibility of peaceful transition from capitalism to socialism has increased. The Tito clique sabotages wars of national liberation in every way. . . . [The Soviet Union] opposes such wars on the ground that any local war could escalate into a general conflagration. The Tito clique has renounced the dictatorship of the proletariat. Khrushchev . . . invented the doctrine of "the state of the whole people." The Tito clique denies that the Communist party should be the vanguard of the working class. Khrushchev announces that the CPSU has become "the party of the entire people." . . . In short, the Soviet Union itself is about to abandon the world revolution.

Most observers do not, however, take the Chinese indictment all that seriously. They view the charge that Yugoslavia has abandoned the revolution (and that the Soviet Union is hard on its heels) as a propaganda gambit, a maneuvering for position within the world movement. They do not believe that the Chinese believe what they say. In fact, most observers would doubt that any Communist party would abandon the revolution, especially after it had come to power. . . .

But one certainly cannot say that the Chinese fears are groundless. On the contrary, there is much to justify them. The Chinese fear that the Yugoslav League of Communists [LCY] is moving steadily along the line from Stalinism to revisionism to liquidation; in short, that the LCY is opting out of the revolutionary game. The Chinese also fear that the Soviet Communists are following (at a safe distance) the Yugoslav heretics on this road to perdition.

Let us attempt to measure the distance already covered by the Yugoslavs, counting up the firsts they have to their credit (or, if you like, their discredit):

1. The Yugoslav party was the first satellite party in history to escape from Soviet control.

2. The Yugoslav party was the first party in history to decollectivize a fully collectivized agriculture.

3. The Yugoslav regime was the first to dismantle the central planning apparatus and move toward the development of a socialist market economy.

4. The Yugoslav party was the first to abandon the use of administrative measures, a normal means of maintaining ideological conformity and enjoining physical obedience. In this connection, Yugoslavia was the first Communist state to open its frontiers, both to incoming tourists and to outgoing seasonal labor.

5. The Yugoslavs were the first to declare for a truce in the ideological cold war; this is the meaning of their doctrine of "active peaceful coexistence."

6. The Yugoslavs were the first to dilute the leading role of the party. Theirs was the first party in power to reform the party statutes along democratic lines, to upgrade parliament, to hold semi-free elections of any kind at any level, and to introduce a separation of powers. . . .

If the Chinese position on Yugoslavia is thus susceptible of more convincing demonstration than Chinese authorities have yet produced, this is not the same thing as saying that it is correct. In order to establish a proper balance, we may counter . . . with a brief rejoinder.

In the first place . . . the extent of revisionist ferment in Yugoslavia . . . [tends to be overstated]. Furthermore, the revisionists in general are primarily intellectuals. The party *apparatchiki*, on the other hand, are practical politicians who are not accustomed to discussing political philosophy in public places. . . .

In the second place, the stronger forces, numerically and politically speaking, are on the side of the party and its apparatus. The strength of the apparatus is to be found in Serbia, Bosnia, Montenegro, and Macedonia, i.e., in the Orthodox and economically more backward parts. The Serbs alone constitute 40 per cent of the population and have traditionally played a leading role in Yugoslav affairs.

In the third place, the relaxation of central control and the de facto abandonment of administrative measures has been accompanied by a revival of tension among national groupings. There has emerged a species of local national communism. The First Party Secretary in Croatia, for example, . . . openly proclaims himself the defender of Croatian national interests. A basic issue between the nationalities is that of investment policy, i.e., the extent to which the better-off republics and provinces are to subsidize the industrial development of the poorer and more backward. The quarrel is bitter and complicated. Can the nationalities problem be kept in hand if dictatorship is abandoned? . . .

Fourthly, it seems farfetched to suggest that democratic institutions are developing out of Communist dictatorship. No dictatorship in history has ever peacefully surrendered its authority. The party is still in control. It is the party which dismantled the central planning machinery, set up constitutional courts, encouraged and managed semi-free elections. The party pulled back hard on the reins in 1962, and can do so again. It is more than slightly preposterous to suggest that the first abandonment of revolutionary dictatorship will occur in a backward Balkan country, one on whose territory live a variety of nationalities inimical to each other, one whose economy requires continuing foreign subsidies, one in which the democratic tradition has little root. It would make more sense, but not too much, to argue that the Czechoslovaks might in the long run move slowly back to democratic institutions. At least Czechoslovakia is an advanced industrial country which, during the interwar period, was governed democratically.

Finally, it should be emphasized that the Soviet and other brotherly parties would use all their not inconsiderable influence to prevent abandonment of the dictatorship of the proletariat in Yugoslavia—or anywhere else for that matter. It is precisely the Communist merit of the Chinese that they have brought to the attention of the world movement the dangers inherent in the Yugoslav situation. The abandonment of socialism by any population or any party would be a severe blow to the cause of the revolution, perhaps as severe as the Great Schism itself!

CHINESE SETBACKS [10]

It's said that each night after dinner the half dozen old men who guide Red China's fortunes gather in Peking for lengthy discussions of plans and policies. Nowadays, at least when the talk turns to foreign affairs, their words must drip bitterness and frustration.

For the current anti-Communist campaign in Indonesia is only the latest in a yearlong series of foreign policy reverses for the militant Chinese regime. Other setbacks for Peking:

Its bid to dominate Afro-Asian affairs and create a united anti-American front has failed; some Africans now complain about Chinese diplomats meddling in their affairs. . . .

Its efforts to drive Americans out of Vietnam and all Southeast Asia—thereby buttressing Mao Tse-tung's "war of liberation" theories—are stalled.

Its recent blustering about alleged border violations by India, followed by what can only be interpreted as a backdown from an ultimatum presented to the Indian government, hurt Peking's international standing and achieved little for its new ally, Pakistan.

Sums up an Asian diplomat: "The Chinese have tried a diplomatic 'great leap forward'—and failed."

Happier Days

All this contrasts sharply with the prestige China enjoyed only one year ago [in 1964]. Then it had just exploded an atomic device, giving it the political benefits of nuclear-nation status. "Revisionist" Soviet Premier Nikita Khrushchev, whom China claimed had sold out Russian communism to the West, had been bounced abruptly from office. China had good reason to believe 1965 would see the Vietcong defeat Saigon and United States forces in South Vietnam. And a North Atlantic Treaty Organization nation, France, recently had recognized the Chinese Communist regime.

[10] From "Peking Loses Face: The U.S. Could Benefit as Red China Suffers Setbacks Around the Globe," by Robert Keatley, staff reporter. *Wall Street Journal.* p 1+. O. 29, '65. Reprinted by permission.

The dismal diplomatic harvest China has reaped of late is, in the view of most analysts, the inevitable result of its continued adherence to a dogmatic, somewhat xenophobic view of the international scene. Chinese theorists divide the world into "imperialists," led by the United States, and the "people," led by China. It is the job of the people to destroy the imperialists. It is also the duty of the people to oppose regimes that, while not formally in the United States camp, do not hew strictly to the Chinese line and thus are classed as American "agents"; in this category are the Russians. The militancy with which Peking diplomats preach this doctrine has irritated some governments that are basically sympathetic towards China's efforts to modernize its rural economy.

But experts on Chinese affairs don't believe Peking officials have learned much from their recent reverses. They say China is now stiffening its already tough foreign policy and will try even harder to persuade, or browbeat, others into joining its world-wide campaign against "American imperialists and their lackeys." Those who reject this call to action could find themselves threatened by new pro-Chinese revolutionary movements.

Missionary Zeal

"When the Communists marched into Peking in 1949, they were singing songs about world revolution," says a diplomat who was there at the time. "Now they will try to export revolution, with the same missionary zeal they had sixteen years ago."

Paradoxically, this could benefit the United States. Such aggressiveness may well antagonize already suspicious governments that now question Chinese motives and wonder if Peking doesn't have some imperialist aims of its own. It could force China into isolationism against its will, diminishing its world influence. And continued attacks on Russian communism, with its new emphasis on profits and productivity, would keep the Marxist movement divided and perhaps weaker than otherwise would be the case.

But China's present situation also may hold peril for the United States and its allies. Some authorities see Peking as so frustrated that it may order drastic steps to reverse its fortunes. There is a minority view in the State Department, for example, that China might enter the air war over North Vietnam, perhaps initially by offering refuge to North Vietnamese MIG's fleeing American jets and later by sending up its own air force, most of which is obsolescent. Such developments could lead to United States operations over the Chinese mainland, something Washington carefully has avoided so far. There are also hints in the Chinese press that Peking may try stirring up new trouble in Laos and Thailand to take some heat off the Vietcong.

"As Vietnam gets worse, the Chinese are under heavy pressure to do more for Hanoi," warns one specialist. "Attacking United States planes might not sound logical, but the Chinese are nothing if not unpredictable."

Though the future is uncertain, there is no doubt whatever that China's international stature has diminished in the past year. This has been especially obvious in Africa. Only a year ago there were dire predictions that pro-Peking governments would soon pop up across that continent; today China's African policy is in a state of disarray.

The cause of China's troubles in Africa is not hard to find. Though Peking's stress on nationalism and its "poor against the rich" theme have considerable appeal in Africa, several of the newly independent nations have become alarmed at Peking's attempts to subvert governments they consider unreliable allies in the global struggle against the United States. Leaders of Kenya, Niger, and Malawi have criticized Red Chinese efforts at subversion, and Burundi went so far as to sever diplomatic relations with China, charging that Peking had backed an anti-government coup.

When Malawi's blunt prime minister, Dr. Hastings Banda, was chided . . . for having closer relations with "imperialist" Britain than with "socialist" China, he replied: "I am less afraid of Queen Elizabeth II than I am of that Kubla Khan II in Peking."

China's only top leaders who travel abroad, Premier Chou En-lai and Foreign Minister Chen Yi, have toured Africa repeatedly . . . to sell their line, but with little success. They insist that the Vietnam war is of vital concern to Africa and that the United States plans to extend the war to China itself.

"In that event, what grounds are there for thinking the British and other imperialists will not return to their former colonies in Asia and Africa?" demands Foreign Minister Chen. But his tortuous reasoning apparently makes little impression in Africa today, and most leaders there—while not particularly happy about Vietnam—have refused to parrot the Chinese line. China's seeming eagerness to pick a fight with India over minor border problems and its recent bitter denunciations of the United Nations, which African leaders regard as a valuable forum for their countries, have contributed to African disenchantment with Peking. . . .

China also has problems closer to home. . . . The Chinese foreign ministry has felt it necessary to warn Indonesia of serious consequences if the current anti-Communist and anti-Chinese drive isn't halted. There seems little chance that army leaders will abandon policies that worry the United States, such as Indonesia's antagonistic stand toward Malaysia. But they apparently will be more hesitant about seconding Peking's propaganda line; they have good reason to believe Chinese Communists have been plotting against them.

Fears of the United States?

South Vietnam is another bitter disappointment to the Chinese, analysts say. Communist progress has been checked by massive American intervention, and Chinese statements now betray real fear that the United States will attack the mainland.

"They are scared to death about what America might do next," claims a Western diplomat. "China will swallow as much escalation as possible without fighting back—there's not much else it can do." Peking now realizes, it's said, that a few major bombing raids could wipe out most industrial progress made since the Reds took power in 1949.

China's Latin American ventures also have run into trouble lately. Harsh economic realities have made Cuba's Fidel Castro, at heart a militant revolutionist, swing away from Peking and closer to the more restrained Russians; China simply can't match Soviet aid, which Cuba needs to prop up its faltering economy. Elsewhere in Latin America, the Chinese have failed in efforts to control left-wing organizations.

According to some observers of Chinese affairs, a key reason for China's recent setbacks is its aging leadership. Most of the leaders are old men who have never seen the outside world they so blithely, and inaccurately, denounce. The average age of the Politburo's standing committee, the real seat of power, is over sixty-five.

In their approach to world affairs, these belligerent oldsters cling to the conspiratorial tactics and terminology of their guerrilla days of thirty years ago; they constantly call for the "countryside" (underdeveloped nations) to surround and destroy the "cities" (North America and Europe). But the leaders of many new nations are too sophisticated to buy Peking's outdated theories—and they also realize that the Chinese view them merely as temporary leaders who eventually must be overthrown to make way for a Communist regime.

III. DOCUMENTING THE RIFT

EDITOR'S INTRODUCTION

In sheer volume, the correspondence between Moscow and Peking relating to the rift is staggering. Both sides are in the habit of dropping 25,000-word bombshells on each other. Much of the exchange of accusations and charges is written in the high-pitched language of ideologues who have made a crusade out of the defense of obscure and esoteric points and who brandish clichés like spears to hurl at the enemy. The verbiage and posturing, however, should not obscure the deadly intensity and seriousness with which this battle is being waged.

In this section the protagonists speak for themselves. Some of what they say is crude propaganda and should be recognized as such. But beneath the propaganda lies the material from which the schism has sprung and on which it feeds. The section opens with a piece from the New York *Times* comparing the Soviet and Chinese positions on several key issues. This is followed by short selections taken from Chinese and Soviet sources. Two longer articles from Peking spell out the gist of the Chinese grievances against Khrushchev and his successors, who are bitterly accused of betraying the world Communist movement, of revising Marxist-Leninist theory to suit their own needs, and of a multitude of other sins.

The Soviet Union retorts with its own accusations in subsequent selections. It is the core of the Soviet argument that the Chinese have stuck to the letter of what was written by the Marxist philosophers in the last century and have chosen to ignore objective reality, to which presumably the Soviet Union is more capable of responding. The Chinese leadership, Moscow charges, prefers "to close its eyes to the problems posed by life." Peking has also, in the opinion of Soviet leaders, invoked the specter of racism by attempting to rally the nonwhite people to its side against the white world, which includes the Soviet Union.

The last article in this section, taken from *Problems of Communism,* evaluates the arguments and puts them into historical perspective.

AS THE COMMUNISTS SEE IT [1]

The most naked clash of national self-interest [between the Soviet Union and China] is visible in the Chinese charge that the Russians stole 1.5 million square kilometers (more than 500,000 square miles) of Chinese territory in the nineteenth century and the implied demand that this vast area be returned. Here is the way Mao Tse-tung put the matter . . . and here is the authoritative Soviet answer as printed in *Pravda:*

CHINESE VIEW: "The places occupied by the Soviet Union are too numerous. The Soviet Union, under the pretext of guaranteeing the independence of Mongolia, actually placed this country under its domination. . . . The Soviet Union occupies an area of 22 million square kilometers, while its population is only 2 million. . . . The region east of Lake Baikal [formerly Chinese territory] became Russian territory about one hundred years ago, and since then Vladivostok, Khabarovsk, Kamchatka, and other points have been the territory of the Soviet Union. We have not yet presented the bill for this account."

SOVIET VIEW: "Do those who question whether an area of more than one and a half million square kilometers belongs to the Soviet Union think of how these claims will be regarded by the Soviet people who have lived and worked on this land for several generations and consider it their homeland, the land of their ancestors? . . . It is hard to believe that [Mao] does not know the very dangerous consequences that could arise from any attempt to recarve the map of the world in present conditions. Mao Tse-tung pretends to be threatening the interests only of our country, but it is obvious to everybody that such a provocative appeal to revise borders (if taken seriously) would inevitably generate a whole series of mutual demands."

[1] From "Communist Split: as Both Sides See It," by Harry Schwartz, member of the New York *Times* editorial board and specialist in Soviet affairs. New York *Times.* p E5. Mr. 14, '65. © 1965 by The New York Times Company. Reprinted by permission.

Racism

The racism issue is in some ways the most sensitive one between the Soviet Union and China. The Russians see the explosive possibilities of Peking's attempt to win leadership of the nonwhite peoples of the world, realizing that this equates white Russians and white Americans. The Chinese, denying Soviet charges on this score, suspect the Russians of feeling closer to Americans than to Chinese because of the difference in color between the Russians and the Chinese. The Soviet indictment below is from a speech of Mikhail A. Suslov, member of the Soviet Communist party Presidium. . . . The Chinese reply is from another authoritative statement in *Peking Review*:

Soviet view: "For Lenin's idea of uniting the anti-imperialist forces of all countries . . . the Chinese theoreticians would like to substitute an appeal for setting the peoples of the East apart on a nationalistic and even racial basis. Their slogan . . . is clearly calculated to inflame nationalist and even racial moods among the peoples fighting against colonialism.

"The long years of enslavement and exploitation by the imperialists and their scoffing at the honor and national dignity of the oppressed peoples have engendered and are nurturing among part of the population of the former colonies and semicolonies a mistrust of people of the white race. The Chinese leaders are trying to fan these feelings."

Chinese view: "Having used up all their wonder-working weapons for opposing the national liberation movement, the leaders of the Soviet Communist party are now reduced to seeking help from racism. . . . They describe the correct stand of the Chinese Communist party in resolutely supporting the national liberation movement as . . . 'playing upon the national and even racial prejudices of the Asian and African peoples'. . . .

"When they peddle the 'theory of racism,' describing the national liberation movement in Asia, Africa, and Latin America as one of the colored against the white race, the leaders of the Soviet Communist party are clearly aiming at inciting racial hatred among the white people in Europe and North America."

Averting War

In the thermonuclear era both the Soviet Union and China face the question of what risks they dare take in the face of American power. The Soviet Union, which backed down in the Cuban crisis of 1962, seeks to justify its own caution by painting the critical Chinese as willing to set off a thermonuclear Armageddon. The Chinese, denying this, assail the Russians as overly cautious and insist greater risks than Moscow is willing to take are possible even in the age of hydrogen bombs. The Soviet view is from the Suslov speech mentioned earlier; the Chinese view is from the Chinese Communist party's official statement on the problem of war in the present era.

SOVIET VIEW: "It is possible to avert a world war even before the complete victory of Socialism on earth. . . . The Leninist principle of the peaceful coexistence of states with different social systems is the unshakeable foundation of the foreign policy of the Socialist countries. . . .

"In waging their struggle against the Leninist course of peaceful coexistence and opposing to it the path of "prodding revolution through war,' the Chinese Communist party leaders have gone so far as to assert that war is an acceptable and even, in essence, the only means for resolving the contradictions between capitalism and socialism. . . . Not one party that truly cherishes the interests of the people can fail to be aware of its responsibility in the struggle to avert a new war. Yet the Chinese leaders . . . are even bragging that they are ready, allegedly 'for the sake of the revolution,' to consent to the annihilation of one half of mankind."

CHINESE VIEW: "[The Soviet leaders] vigorously propagate the view that all wars can be prevented. . . . Their purpose . . . is to make people believe that permanent peace can be realized under imperialism and thereby to abolish revolution and . . . revolutionary wars. . . . The heart of the theory of the Soviet Communist party leaders on war and peace is their thesis that the emergence of nuclear weapons has changed everything. . . .

"In order to cover up their error, the Soviet Communist party leaders . . . assert that by advocating support for the peoples' wars of national liberation and revolutionary civil wars the Chinese Communist party wants to provoke a nuclear world war. This is a curious lie. . . ."

Issue of Vietnam

With the Vietnam crisis still in midpassage, neither the Soviet nor the Chinese side has yet produced a complete and candid statement of its position.

The Soviet Union has made it evident that, if at all possible, it wishes to avert a Soviet-American war over Vietnam. While promising, and . . . now delivering, military equipment to North Vietnam, the Russians have in effect pleaded with the United States not to spoil the détente by continuing strikes against North Vietnam.

For their part, the Chinese have also been much more militant in word than in action on the Vietnam issue. They have tried to imply in some statements that the Soviet Union, as the most powerful Socialist state, has an obligation to meet American military actions by military reprisals. But basically the Chinese seem confident that the United States will not dare inflict really serious harm on North Vietnam and that the American position in South Vietnam will continue to deteriorate.

LONG LIVE LENINISM [2]

The question is not whether the proletariat is willing to carry out a peaceful transformation; it is rather whether the bourgeoisie will accept such a peaceful transformation. This is the only possible way in which the followers of Lenin can approach this question.

So, contrary to the modern revisionists [a reference to the Soviet government—Ed.] who seek to paralyze the revolutionary will of the people by empty talk about peaceful transition, Marxists-Leninists hold that the question of possible peaceful transition to socialism can be raised only in the light of specific

[2]From article published in *Red Flag*, theoretical journal of the Chinese Communist party. Ap. 16, '60. Text from *Mao Against Khrushchev* by David Floyd. Praeger. '63. p 270.

conditions in each country at a particular time. The proletariat must never allow itself to one-sidedly and groundlessly base its thinking, policy and its whole work on the calculation that the bourgeoisie is willing to accept peaceful transformation. It must, at the same time, prepare for alternatives: one for the peaceful development of the revolution and the other for the nonpeaceful development of the revolution. Whether the transition will be carried out through armed uprising or by peaceful means is a question that is fundamentally separate from that of peaceful coexistence between the Socialist and capitalist countries; it is an internal affair of each country, one to be determined only by the relation of classes in that country in a given period.

ON NATIONAL LIBERATION: PEKING'S VIEW [3]

The oppressed nations and peoples of Asia, Africa, and Latin America are faced with the urgent task of fighting imperialism.

History has entrusted to the proletarian parties in these areas the glorious mission of holding high the banner of the struggle against imperialism, against old and new colonialism and for national independence and people's democracy, of standing in the forefront of the national democratic revolutionary movement and striving for a Socialist future.

In these areas, extremely broad sections of the population refuse to be slaves of imperialism. They include not only the workers, peasants, intellectuals, and petty bourgeoisie, but also the patriotic national bourgeoisie and even certain kings, princes, and aristocrats who are patriotic. . . .

On the basis of the worker-peasant alliance, the proletariat and its party must unite all strata that can be united and organize a broad united front against imperialism and its lackeys. In order to consolidate and expand this united front it is necessary that the proletarian party should maintain its ideological, political, and organizational independence and insist on the leadership of the revolution.

[3] From letter sent by the Communist party of China to the Communist party of the Soviet Union, June 14, 1963. Published in *Peking Review*. Je. 21, '63. Text from *Problems of Communism* (a publication of the United States Information Agency). 13:68. Mr.-Ap. '64.

ON NATIONAL LIBERATION: MOSCOW'S VIEW [4]

There is yet another important question— . . . the relation between the struggle of the international working class and the national liberation movement of the peoples of Asia, Africa, and Latin America. . . .

How do the Chinese comrades solve this question? This is apparent from a new "theory" of theirs according to which the basic contradiction of our time is . . . the contradiction not between socialism and imperialism, but between the national liberation movement and imperialism. In the opinion of the Chinese comrades, it is not the world system of socialism, not the struggle of the international working class, that acts as the decisive force in the struggle against imperialism, but once again the national liberation movement.

Thereby the Chinese comrades apparently hope to win popularity among the peoples of Asia, Africa, and Latin America. . . . But let no one be deceived by this "theory." Its actual sense, whether the Chinese theoreticians want it or not, consists of isolating the national liberation movement from the international working class and . . . the world system of socialism. But this could represent a huge danger to the national liberation movement itself.

STRUGGLE FOR SUPREMACY [5]

First, we would like to ask the leaders of the CPSU [Communist party of the Soviet Union]: You say we want to seize the leadership. From whom? Who now holds the leadership? In the international Communist movement is there such a thing as leadership which lords it over all the fraternal parties? And is this leadership in your hands?

Apparently the leaders of the CPSU consider themselves the natural leaders, who can lord it over all the fraternal parties.

[4] From open letter by the Communist party of the Soviet Union. Published in *Pravda*. Jl. 14, '63. Text from *Problems of Communism* (a publication of the United States Information Agency). 13:68. Mr.-Ap. '64.

[5] From article in Chinese publications, *Jen-min Jih-pao* and *Hung Ch'i*. F. 4, '64. Text from *Problems of Communism* (a publication of the United States Information Agency). 13:15. Mr.-Ap. '64.

According to their logic, their programs, resolutions, and statements are all infallible laws. Every remark and every word of Khrushchev's are imperial edicts, however wrong or absurd they may be. All the fraternal parties must submissively hear and obey and are absolutely forbidden to criticize or oppose them. This is outright tyranny. It is the ideology of feudal autocrats, pure and simple.

However, we must tell the CPSU leaders that the international Communist movement is not some feudal clique. . . . The history of the international proletarian revolutionary movement shows that, owing to the uneven development of the revolution, at a particular historical stage the proletariat and its party in one country or another marched in the van of the movement. . . . [But] even the vanguard position . . . does not remain unchanged for a long time, but shifts according to changing conditions. This shift is decided not by the subjective wishes of any individual or party, but by conditions shaped by history. If conditions change, other parties may come to the van of the movement. When a party which formerly held the position of vanguard takes the path of revisionism, it is bound to forfeit this position despite the fact that it has been the largest party and has exerted the greatest influence. . . .

By embarking on the path of revisionism and "splittism," the CPSU leaders automatically forfeited the position of "head" in the international Communist movement. If the word "head" is now to be applied to them, it can only mean that they are at the head of the revisionists and splitters.

KHRUSHCHEV THE "BETRAYER" [6]

In its proposal concerning the general line of the international Communist movement, the Central Committee of the Communist party of China has pointed out that, in accordance with Marxist-Leninist revolutionary theory, the basic experiences of the October Revolution and the revolutionary principles of the 1957 declaration and the 1960 statement [references to Communist party docu-

[6] From an article distributed by Hsinhua, the Chinese Communist press agency. N. 6, '64. Text from "Excerpts from Peking Denunciation." New York *Times.* p 9. N. 7, '64.

ments], the general line of the international Communist movement at the present stage is:

Workers of all countries, unite; workers of the world, unite with the oppressed peoples and oppressed nations; oppose imperialism and reaction in all countries; strive for world peace, national liberation, people's democracy and socialism; consolidate and expand the Socialist camp; bring the proletarian world revolution step by step to complete victory; and establish a new world without imperialism, without capitalism, and without the exploitation of man by man.

To realize this general line, it is necessary to strengthen, under the banner of the October Revolution, the unity of the Socialist camp and the unity of the international Communist movement.

In order to safeguard and strengthen the unity of the international Communist movement, an uncompromising struggle must be waged against all forms of opportunism which betrays Marxism-Leninism, especially modern revisionism, which is the main danger to the international Communist movement today.

Khrushchev is the chief representative of modern revisionism. He has betrayed Leninism, betrayed proletarian internationalism, betrayed the path of the October Revolution, and betrayed the interests of the Soviet people.

The Soviet people and the Communist party of the Soviet Union recently removed Khrushchev from the leading posts he held in the party and the state. This is a very good thing and it has the support of Marxist-Leninists and revolutionary people of all the world.

Facts have repeatedly borne out that the great wheel of history cannot be reversed by imperialism and the reactionaries nor by Khrushchev revisionism.

Anyone who runs counter to Leninism, to proletarian internationalism, to the path of the October Revolution, and to the interests of the people will inevitably, sooner or later, be spurned by the people. This was so in the past, is so at present, and will be so in the future.

The imperialists and reactionaries are extremely hostile to the friendship and unity of the Chinese and Soviet peoples. The nefarious United States imperialists and their lackeys regard the unity between China and the Soviet Union, the unity of the Socialist camp, and the unity of the revolutionary peoples the world over as the biggest obstacle to their conquest of the world.

Therefore, United States imperialism tries in a thousand and one ways to split the unity between China and the Soviet Union, unity of the Socialist camp, and unity of the revolutionary peoples of the world so as to break them one by one.

While stepping up its aggression against and control over the extensive intermediate zones between the United States and the Socialist camp, United States imperialism is, on the one hand pushing ahead with its so-called peaceful evolution policy in the vain hope of restoring capitalism in the Socialist countries and, on the other, is preparing to mount armed attacks on the Socialist camp.

In the face of the common enemy, the common interests of the Chinese and Soviet peoples demand that the Chinese and Soviet parties and the two countries unite on the basis of Marxism-Leninism and proletarian internationalism and wage common struggles.

The Communist party of China and the Chinese people have always worked untiringly for preserving and strengthening the unity between China and the Soviet Union.

Through no fault of ours, nor of the Soviet people's, the relations between the Chinese and Soviet parties and the two countries have met with difficulties and suffered impairment in the past period. This is contrary to the common aspirations of the Chinese and Soviet peoples, the peoples of the countries of the Socialist camp and of the whole world.

We are convinced that the difficulties that have temporarily appeared between China and the Soviet Union and between the two parties are, after all, only a historical episode and can be gradually resolved. The unity between the two countries can undoubtedly be restored and steadily strengthened.

The fraternal and militant friendship between the Chinese and Soviet peoples is eternal. No one and no force can destroy this friendship. The . . . Chinese people are the most reliable friends of the Soviet people by whose side they will stand firmly in all circumstances.

SOVIET REVISIONISM DENOUNCED [7]

The experience of the Chinese revolution shows that the tasks of the national-democratic revolution can be fulfilled only through long and tortuous struggles. In this stage of revolution, imperialism and its lackeys are the principal enemy.

In the struggle against imperialism and its lackeys, it is necessary to ally all anti-imperialist patriotic forces, including the national bourgeoisie and all patriotic personages.

All those patriotic personages from among the bourgeoisie and other exploiting classes who join the anti-imperialist struggle play a progressive historical role: they are not tolerated by imperialism but welcomed by the proletariat.

The Khrushchev revisionists are now actively preaching that socialism can be built without the proletariat and without a Communist party. And they have cast the fundamental tenets of Marxism-Leninism to the four winds. The revisionists' purpose is solely to divert the oppressed nations from their struggle against imperialism and to sabotage their national-democratic revolution, all in the service of imperialism.

The Chinese revolution provides a successful lesson for making a thoroughgoing national-democratic revolution under the leadership of the proletariat: it likewise provides a successful lesson for the timely transition from the national democratic revolution to the Socialist revolution under the leadership of the proletariat. . . .

The Khrushchev revisionists have come to the rescue of U.S. imperialism just when it is most panic-stricken and helpless in its efforts to cope with the people's war [a reference to national liberation movements]. Working hand in glove with the U.S. imperialists, they are doing their utmost to spread all kinds of arguments against the people's war, and wherever they can, they are scheming to undermine it by overt or covert means.

[7] From a statement by Marshal Lin Piao, Communist China's Minister of Defense. Distributed by Hsinhua, the Chinese Communist press agency. S. 3, '65. Text from "Excerpts from Peking Declaration Urging World 'People's War' to Destroy U.S." New York *Times*. p 2. S. 4, '65.

The fundamental reason why the Khushchev revisionists are opposed to the people's war is that they have no faith in the masses and are afraid of U.S. imperialism, of war, and of revolution.

Like all other opportunists, they are blind to the power of the masses and do not believe that the revolutionary people are capable of defeating imperialism.

They submit to the nuclear blackmail of the U.S. imperialists and are afraid that, if the oppressed peoples and nations rise up to fight the people's wars or the people of Socialist countries repulse U.S. imperialist aggression, U.S. imperialism will become incensed, they themselves will become involved, and their fond dream of Soviet-United States cooperation to dominate the world will be spoiled.

Ever since Lenin led the Great October Revolution [of 1917] to victory, the experience of innumerable revolutionary wars has borne out the truth that a revolutionary people who rise up with only their bare hands at the outset finally succeed in defeating the ruling classes who are armed to the teeth.

The poorly armed have defeated the better armed. People's armed forces, beginning with only primitive swords, spears, rifles, and hand grenades, have in the end defeated the imperialist forces armed with modern airplanes, tanks, heavy artillery, and atom bombs.

Guerrilla forces have ultimately defeated regular armies. "Amateurs" who were never trained in any military schools have eventually defeated "professionals" graduated from military academies, and so on and so forth.

Things stubbornly develop in a way that runs counter to the assertions of the revisionists, and facts are slapping them in the face.

The Khrushchev revisionists insist that a nation without nuclear weapons is incapable of defeating an enemy with nuclear weapons, whatever methods of fighting it may adopt.

This is tantamount to saying that anyone without nuclear weapons is destined to come to grief, destined to be bullied and annihilated, and must either capitulate to the enemy when confronted with his nuclear weapons or come under the "protection" of some other nuclear power and submit to its beck and call.

Isn't this the jungle law of survival par excellence? Isn't this helping the imperialists in their nuclear blackmail? Isn't this openly forbidding people to make revolution?

The Khrushchev revisionists assert that nuclear weapons and strategic rocket units are decisive while conventional forces are insignificant, and that a militia is just a heap of human flesh.

For ridiculous reasons such as these, they oppose the mobilization of and reliance on the masses in the socialist countries to get prepared to use the people's war against imperialist aggression.

They have staked the whole future of their country on nuclear weapons and are engaged in a nuclear gamble with United States imperialism, with which they are trying to strike a political deal. Their theory of military strategy is the theory that nuclear weapons decide everything.

Their line in army building is the bourgeois line which ignores the human factor and sees only the material factor and which regards technique as everything and politics as nothing.

The Khrushchev revisionists maintain that a single spark in any part of the globe may touch off a world nuclear conflagration and bring destruction to mankind. If this were true, our planet would have been destroyed time and time again. . . .

In diametrical opposition to the Khrushchev revisionists, the Marxist-Leninists and revolutionary people never take a gloomy view of war.

Our attitude toward imperialist wars of aggression has always been clear-cut. First, we are against them, and secondly, we are not afraid of them. We will destroy whoever attacks us.

As for revolutionary wars waged by the oppressed nations and peoples, so far from opposing them, we invariably give them firm support and active aid. It has been so in the past, it remains so in the present and, when we grow in strength as time goes on, we will give them still more support and aid in the future.

It is sheer day-dreaming for anyone to think that, since our revolution has been victorious, our national construction is forging ahead, our national wealth is increasing, and our living conditions are improving, we too will lose our revolutionary fighting will, abandon the cause of world revolution, and discard Marxism-Leninism and proletarian internationalism.

Of course, every revolution in a country stems from the demands of its own people. Only when the people in a country are awakened, mobilized, organized, and armed can they overthrow the reactionary rule of imperialism and its lackeys through struggle; their role cannot be replaced or taken over by any people from outside.

In this sense, revolution cannot be imported. But this does not exclude mutual sympathy and support on the part of revolutionary peoples in their struggles against the imperialists and their lackeys. Our support and aid to other revolutionary peoples serves precisely to help their self-reliant struggle.

The propaganda of the Khrushchev revisionists against people's war and the publicity they give to defeatism and capitulationism tend to demoralize and spiritually disarm revolutionary people everywhere.

THE "ATTACK" ON WORLD SOCIALISM [8]

The CPC [Communist party of China] leaders no longer limit their actions to the sphere of ideology. They have carried over ideological differences to interstate relations, to the realm of the practical policies of the Socialist countries and the Communist parties. Striving to weaken the unity and solidarity of the Socialist commonwealth, the CPC leadership is permitting itself every kind of maneuver and contrivance to undermine the economic and political relations between the Socialist countries, to introduce discord into their actions in the international arena. The undermining, schismatic activity of the Chinese leaders in the world Communist movement has recently been sharply stepped up. There is no longer any doubt that Peking has plotted a course toward a split in the Communist parties, toward the creation of factions and groups hostile to Marxism-Leninism. . . .

[8] From a report by M. A. Suslov, a leading Soviet theoretician on Communist philosophy, delivered before the Central Committee of the Communist party of the Soviet Union on February 14, 1964. Published in *Pravda*. Ap. 3, '64. Text from *World Communism Divided*, pamphlet by W. E. Griffith. (Headline Series. no 166) Foreign Policy Association. 345 E. 46th St. New York 10017. Ag. '64. p 44-6.

Attempting to conceal their departure from the positions of Marxism-Leninism, the Chinese leaders have recently been maneuvering intensively, masking their objectives and schemes and talking at length about their "revolutionism," "boldness," "resoluteness" and so on. But the further events develop and the more hysterical becomes the tone of Chinese propaganda, the more obvious it is that the true plans of the Chinese leadership have nothing in common with Marxism-Leninism, with the interests of world socialism. It is becoming increasingly clear that under the cloak of ultrarevolutionary phrases and slogans, the CPC leadership is now waging a furious attack upon the gains of world socialism, concentrating its main fire not against the imperialists but predominantly against the CPSU and other Marxist-Leninist parties.

True, the Chinese leaders still have a lot to say about their desire for the unity and solidarity of the Socialist commonwealth. But their deeds are completely divorced from these words.

They trumpet about unity, but all their actions pursue another purpose: to disorganize and split the Socialist camp, to undermine the ideological foundations and the organizational and political principles that rally and unite the peoples of the Socialist commonwealth. They are striving to impose on the Socialist countries a "Sinicized" socialism, an adventurist course in foreign and domestic policy, and the ideology and practice of the cult of the individual. . . .

The Chinese leaders run on and on about how it is they who are the most reliable and tested friends of the national liberation movement. However, anyone who believes this will be profoundly deceived. The scheme of the CPC leadership reduces to imposing its adventurist concepts and methods on the peoples of Asia, Africa, and Latin America, opposing the peoples to one another on racial principles and disrupting the alliance between the national liberation and the workers' movements, which can in fact only disorganize and weaken the national-liberation movement.

. . . The CPC leadership does not confine itself to slander. In the actions it has undertaken both on the state level and in various international democratic organizations, it is concentrating its efforts not on strengthening the unity of the anti-imperialist forces, but on a struggle against the CPSU and other countries of socialism. . . .

At . . . [an Afro-Asian Solidarity Conference] Liu Ning-yi, head of the Chinese delegation, said in a conversation with our representatives: "The countries of Eastern Europe should not interfere in the affairs of Asia and Africa. . . . We regret your having come here at all; why are you needed here? It is an insult to the movement for the solidarity of the African and Asian countries. . . . Do as you like, but we will oppose you." The Chinese delegates at this conference suggested to the representatives of the African and Asian countries that inasmuch as the Russians, Czechs, and Poles are white "you can't rely on them," that they will allegedly "always be in collusion with the Americans—with whites," that the peoples of Asia and Africa have their own special interests and must create their own separate associations.

The Chinese leaders have recently set about the creation of separate organizations for the countries of Asia, Africa, and Latin America (organizations of trade unions, journalists, writers, students, sportsmen and so on), which they intend to counterpose to the World Federation of Trade Unions and other international associations.

In the light of the Chinese leaders' practical activities in recent years, the true political meaning of the slogan they have advanced—"The wind from the East is prevailing over the wind from the West"—has become especially clear. As long ago as . . . [1960] this slogan was subjected to resolute criticism as being nationalistic, one that substitutes for the class approach a geographical and even a racist one. It plainly bespeaks a belittling on their part of the role of the world Socialist systems, the working class, and popular masses of Western Europe and America.

For Lenin's idea of uniting the anti-imperialist forces of all countries and continents—expressed in the slogan, "Proletarians of all countries and oppressed peoples, unite!"—the Chinese theoreticians would like to substitute an appeal for setting the peoples of the East apart on a nationalist and even racial basis. . . .

The long years of enslavement and exploitation by the imperialists and their scoffing at the honor and national dignity of the oppressed peoples have engendered and are nurturing among part of the population of the former colonies and semicolonies a mistrust of people of the white race. The Chinese leaders are trying to fan these feelings, in the hopes of setting the peoples of the former colonies and semicolonies against the Socialist countries, against the working people in the developed capitalist countries, and of presenting themselves as the sole defenders of the interests of these peoples. . . .

PEKING'S "DISTORTIONS" [9]

In their theoretical speculations, the Chinese leaders are revising Marxist-Leninist teaching, distorting the views of Marx, Engels, and Lenin, and repudiating one of the most important principles of Marxism-Leninism—the creative attitude to theory. . . .

Indeed, in what have the CPC leaders seen the "revisionist sin" of the Marxist-Leninist parties? As they themselves explain, in the fact that these parties have adopted the "course of so-called peaceful coexistence," "peaceful competition," "peaceful transition," "the state of the whole people" and "the Party of the whole people." There is hardly any need to say that the general line of the Communist movement is by no means reduced to the above-mentioned propositions. . . .

Different things are at stake—the principles of the foreign policy of the Socialist states; the character of the state in the period of the transition from socialism to communism; the roads of Socialist revolution; and the social character of the Party after the complete victory of socialism. There is, however, one common aspect to all these diverse questions—in every case, the points at issue are theoretical problems, in the elaboration of which the Communist parties, in accordance with the demands of the epoch, have introduced many new elements, particularly over the past few years.

[9] From "What Chinese Leaders Are Trying to Impose upon the Communist Movement under the Guise of Marxism-Leninism." *Pravda*. My. 11, '64. Text from *Soviet Documents* (Crosscurrents Press). 2:10-17. Je. 1, '64.

It is against this practice that the CPC leaders have directed their offensive first and foremost. They appraise all propositions of creative Marxism advanced by the present generation of Marxist-Leninists from the viewpoint of their conformity to what was written one hundred, fifty, or thirty years ago. This approach matches their method of criticism, which completely ignores objective reality and boils down to designating individual quotations from the works of Marx, Engels, and Lenin referring to another epoch and another historical situation. Chinese theoreticians, judging by their own pronouncements, think Marxism-Leninism is a set of hard-and-fast rules, principles, and slogans valid for all time, which Communists have to abide by as strictly as churchmen by the Old and the New Testaments.

Such an approach to theory was basically alien to Marx, Engels, and Lenin. The founders of Marxism-Leninism did not see their theoretical task as being that of remaining loyal to the letter of books written earlier, but that of being loyal to the spirit of the scientific world outlook of the working class, of carefully analyzing changing reality, of generalizing new experiences gained in the struggle, and of creatively solving the tasks that each new epoch puts on the agenda.

That is the same approach that modern Marxists also take toward the teaching of Marx, Engels, and Lenin. In their eyes, Marxism-Leninism is not only a collection of classical works, and not only truths expressed by authorities decades ago, but also achievements of modern Marxist thought that have stood the test of practice. That is the kind of Marxism we uphold.

Can one visualize the scientific theory of the working class today . . . without the conclusions drawn by the parties in their programmatic documents, without the truths that have emerged from the revolutionary battles of the past few years? The subtraction of all this from Marxism would infinitely impoverish it, deprive it of that very thing which bears the imprint of the epoch and which is particularly important to the struggle of the working people. Our generation of Marxist-Leninists would be unworthy of their brilliant teachers were they not to do their duty to the working class in the field of theory. . . .

One may well ask the Peking theoreticians: Where does the present enter the picture here? Although all the theses that they have advanced are important, they have to do with every epoch and call for concretization at each specific stage in history: namely, how to bring about a union of the proletarians of all countries at the present stage; how to wage the most effective struggle against the imperialists under given conditions; and how to struggle for the full victory of the world proletarian revolution today.

The Marxist-Leninist parties considered it their primary task to answer these concrete questions. Their answers constitute the political line of the Communist movement, its strategy and tactics. But under cover of general declarations that repeat universally known truths, the Chinese leaders reject everything new that has been added to revolutionary theory by the collective experience of the fraternal parties. Meanwhile the new evaluations and conclusions are more than just "pure" theory. They are a guide to action, a generalization of the working class movement's new forms of struggle, an exposition of new methods for waging an onslaught against the positions of imperialism. Rejection of the new conclusions not only reveals theoretical stagnation but also leads to idle talk and inactivity in policy, to rejection of the new powerful levers that exist for the revolutionary transformation of the world.

For the first time in the history of our movement, the Communist party of the Soviet Union has been faced with the task of all-out Communist construction. Naturally, the Party had to answer a number of new questions brought forward by this stage, especially those pertaining to the historical destiny of the state and the Party on the approach to communism. The Chinese leaders, who did not even bother to analyze the essence of the problems touched upon, hastened to anathematize the new theses advanced by our Party.

After the war the Communist parties of the developed capitalist countries found themselves confronted with new conditions for struggle, conditions that resulted from the aggravation of the general crisis of the capitalist system, from the defeats it had sustained in the peaceful competition with socialism, from the growth of state-monopoly trends, from the upsurge of working class and democratic movements. It was only natural that these parties paid particular attention to evolving new tactical lines in order to make more effective use of new possibilities to defend the interests of the working people, fight the monopolies, and bring the masses nearer to the Socialist revolution.

Again the Chinese leadership preferred to close its eyes to the problems posed by life. . . . They preferred to cling dogmatically to quotations, true of a different epoch and under different conditions, taken out of context and presented in a distorted light.

Nor did they want to see the new tasks that were facing the national liberation movement and the peoples who had won political independence—tasks of struggling for economic independence, of overcoming century-old backwardness, of embarking on noncapitalist development. The Chinese leaders keep reiterating that these peoples have, as before, only to follow the one road of further armed struggle, although the Chinese leaders fail to explain against whom this struggle should be waged today in such countries as Algeria, Mali, Ghana, and Burma, among others.

Many general problems, among them the problem of war and peace, have today appeared in a new light before the world Communist movement. Again the Chinese leadership, posing as the champion of Marxism-Leninism, preferred to resort to old quotations and launched an attack against the concerted stand of the fraternal parties.

The CPC leaders attempt to cover their break with Marxism-Leninism by referring to the history of the Communist movement; they draw parallels between the struggle Lenin and the Bolsheviks waged against the opportunists of the Second International and their own splitting activities in the world Communist movement. But again the Chinese leaders are treading on thin ice.

Indeed, what was it that Lenin so ruthlessly fought in the Second International's activities? Along what basic lines did the ideological and political struggle proceed between the Communists and the social-reformists?

Lenin formulated the law of the uneven economic and political development of imperialism and drew the major conclusion on the possibility of a break in the imperialist chain in one country. Adopting doctrinaire, dogmatic positions, the leaders of the Second International accused Lenin of departing from Marxism. They tried to use antiquated quotations against Lenin.

Lenin and the Bolshevik party led the people to socialism after the victory of the Great October Socialist Revolution. The thesis on the possibility of achieving the complete victory of socialism in one country has become the historic achievement of revolutionary thought. These conclusions of Lenin's were also dogmatically and persistently opposed by the leaders of the Second International.

Lenin's analysis of imperialism and its contradictions, his plan for building socialism, and his tremendous contribution to the treasury of Marxist thought were viewed by leaders of the Second International as encroachments on Marxism. Actually, it was precisely the struggle against the fossilization of theory and for a creative Marxism, constantly enriched by revolutionary practice, that lay at the heart of the bitterest ideological battles Lenin waged. . . .

Closer examination of the theoretical concepts advocated by the Chinese leaders, thoughtful analysis of their recent ideological evolution, will compel the conclusion that the path the Chinese leadership is following is one of flagrant distortion of Marxism-Leninism and revision of its basic principles.

The revisionist essence of the positions adopted by the Chinese leaders leaps into particularly bold relief in their reestimation of that vital point of Marxist-Leninist theory, the question of the historic mission of the proletariat and its place in the world-wide process of emancipation.

The CPC leaders are, in effect, discarding the Marxist-Leninist thesis regarding the world-historic role that the working class plays in the revolutionary transformation of the world, a thesis that has stood the acid test of decades of class struggle. Though the Chinese leaders are attacking this paramount conclusion of revolutionary theory from all sides, their one and only purpose in doing it is to prove that hegemony in the world revolutionary process is shifting, or has already shifted, from the working class to the social strata comprising the mass at the foundation of the national liberation movement, namely, the peasantry, the radical intelligentsia, and the national bourgeoisie. Now Marxist-Leninists greatly value the revolutionary potentiality of the peasantry. It was the peasantry that, after they started making history, became the staunchest ally of the international labor movement in its struggle against imperialism. However, the Chinese leaders are not talking about this obvious fact, but are preaching a regrouping of revolutionary forces which dispenses with the vanguard role of the international working class.

This is the specific purpose of Peking's "concept" alleging that the zone of the national liberation movement, upon which the destiny of the world Socialist revolution now wholly depends, presumably, has become the main center of all world contradictions. The Chinese would-be theoreticians are trying to borrow Lenin's authority to back up this point. But actually they are going against Lenin's ideas. Because when Lenin spoke of the great significance of the national liberation movement, far from opposing it to the revolutionary struggle of the proletariat, he, on the contrary, explained the unbreakable alliance between the two forces, placing particular emphasis on the role and importance of the labor movement in all revolutionary processes.

But what is Peking doing? It is peddling the claim that today the peasantry has, supposedly, become the most consistent revolutionary force. While, in the opinion of the theoreticians acting as apologists for the Chinese leadership, the world working class has been "infected" with social-reformism and has thereby relinquished its revolutionary birthright.

Although such talk may flatter the ego of certain immature, nationalistically-minded, petty-bourgeois politicians, what can it have in common with Marxism-Leninism?

The Peking leaders are not only shouting from the house-tops about the "special" role that national liberation plays in the world proletarian revolution, but at the same time they are also trying in every way to minimize the revolutionary role of the world working class and its offspring, the Socialist system.

Such is the big idea behind all the talk about it being impermissible to attach decisive significance to the competition between world socialism and world capitalism, because that attitude is allegedy nothing but "revisionism." Such also is the big idea behind the charges of "social reformism" being leveled against the Communist parties of the developed capitalist countries. The Chinese leaders actually discount the working class movement in these countries and refuse to recognize its revolutionary force, its revolutionary potentialities.

A rather odd picture that: to see the people who deny the revolutionary potentialities and world-historic mission of the working class donning togas as the sole defenders of the revolutionary theory of that class!

Just how far the new-fangled "orthodoxists" go in their revision of Marxism is shown by the fact that the Chinese leaders do not stop short of distorting the ultimate goal of the revolutionary struggle of the working class, its Socialist ideal.

The pronouncements and political activities of the CPC leaders give us a notion of the type of society they are striving for, a society that actually contradicts the basic principles of Marxist-Leninist theory and the proletarian character of socialism, although it is presented as a paragon of socialism.

The men in Peking do not consider a high level of industrial development to be an inalienable feature of socialism. Improvement of the living standards of the working people is declared unnecessary, even dangerous, as it allegedly entails "bourgeois degeneration." The principles of Socialist democracy are constantly neglected in both theory and practice. The very notion of Socialist democracy is, in effect, absent in the verbose material Peking publishes. But then the Chinese leaders make a fetish of violence in every way and cultivate the personality cult, which is alien to the very nature of the dictatorship of the proletariat and socialism. They are carrying out "militarization" in every aspect of life and look upon the masses as a "blank sheet of paper" (as Mao Tse-tung put it) on which the leader may "write" what he wills.

The Chinese leaders' idea of socialism is most unusual—they visualize it as a society devoid of developed industry, democracy, and respect for the rights of the individual, a society perpetuating the poverty and privations of the working masses. But is it really this type of "socialism" that Marxist-Leninist theory offers? Is it really this type of socialism that millions of working people all over the world are fighting for? Not for nothing do the CPC leaders throw mud at the banner of humanism the Marxist-Leninist parties are holding on high. They have no use for it because they no longer visualize socialism as a society created for the working man, in the name of his happiness.

The Socialist revolution, Lenin pointed out, replaces the private ownership of the means of production by public ownership and introduces planned organization of social production to ensure the well-being and the all-round development of all members of society. Socialism is built in the name of the people, for their good.

No matter what the Chinese leaders may say, no matter how they may extol themselves, the real facts refute their claims to the role of the law-givers of Marxism. The facts convincingly testify to the opposite: the Chinese-style version of Marxism-Leninism, which underlies the ideological and theoretical platforms of the Chinese leadership, is nothing but a betrayal of the basic principles of the international revolutionary theory espoused by Communists in all countries, betrayal of the great teaching of Marx, Engels, and Lenin.

A VIEW OF THE POLEMICS [10]

Somehow there is a general impression that the Chinese disputants are more "orthodox" and consistent, "purer," less "commonly human" . . . than their Soviet antagonists. This impression is somewhat doubtful.

[10] From "The Polemics Seen by a Non-Polemicist," by Benjamin Schwartz, professor of history and government, Center for East Asian Studies, Harvard University. *Problems of Communism* (a publication of the United States Information Agency). 13: 102-6. Mr.-Ap. '64.

There is, to be sure, one issue on which the Chinese seem to be clearly on the side of orthodoxy, namely the question of war and peace. Yet even here all is not so clear as it appears. It is true, of course, that the Soviet Union and Communist China have adopted different foreign policy postures vis-à-vis the United States, but when we consider the theoretical question of coexistence as understood by Lenin complications arise. There is one *locus classicus* for Lenin's views on coexistence and world war which runs:

The existence of the Soviet Republic side by side with imperialist states for a long time is unthinkable. . . . One must triumph in the end, and before that end supervenes, a series of frightful collisions between the Soviet Republic and the bourgeois states will be inevitable.

Here we have an unqualified prediction of world wars. Most other pronouncements on coexistence can be reinterpreted to fit Soviet needs, but a statement of this kind from the Soviet point of view requires the application of "Marxist-Leninist creativity."

How have the Chinese interpreted this statement? They have occasionally cited it, . . . usually to project an image of the "imperialists" much like the one in Lenin's statement. The "imperialists," it is implied, are like lemmings rushing toward the sea. They cannot help but make war. In actuality, however, the Chinese do not seem to have accepted the clear meaning of Lenin's assertion. Mao has, to be sure, deprecated the horrors of a nuclear war. . . . But the fact remains that the Chinese have retreated from adopting publicly the plain meaning of the Leninist formula for obvious reasons of public relations if not from a genuine desire to avoid the holocaust. Also, while their image of the "imperialists" seems to be that of the lemmings, it is in fact somewhat more complicated.

Why "war maniacs" with nuclear weapons in both hands should refrain from using them when threatened with extinction is somewhat of a puzzle. Yet the Chinese continue to insist that war is not inevitable, provided that the "correct" approach prevails. Even while minimizing the effects of a new world war, Mao is also quoted as saying in Moscow in 1957 that "the East wind prevails over the West wind and that war will not break out." The Chinese view, therefore, is that if the "imperialists" can be intimidated and thrown off guard by a steady stream of "national liberation wars" and "people's revolutionary struggles," they will ignominiously shrink to nothingness without ever flinging their bombs. The "imperialists" are, after all, capable of being paralyzed with fear and vacillation, and this may be sufficient to inhibit the remorseless workings of the "imperialist system." All that the Soviet position adds to this is the notion that in addition to their capacity for fear, the "imperialists" may also be capable of sober calculation. . . .

The Soviet side freely admits that Khrushchev has modified Lenin's position on this matter and simply claims that it has creatively applied Leninism to a new unanticipated situation. Such "creative applications" of Marxism-Leninism have been the prerogative of the CPSU ever since Lenin began indulging in *his* creative applications of Marxism. We are all familiar by now with Mao Tse-tung's numerous claims to creative applications of Marxist-Leninist-Stalinist truth in all of which the same procedure is invariably involved. What had previously been considered a universal truth—a proposition applying to all places and all time in modern history—is suddenly relativized and limited in applicability to certain places and certain limited segments of time. Lenin's doctrines concerning the inevitability of world wars, state the Soviet theoreticians, were true only for the period of time preceding the emergence of nuclear military technology. According to China's ideological spokesman, Chou Yang, however:

The leaders of the CPSU who boast of having developed Marxism-Leninism in a creative manner permit themselves and their followers to revise Marxism-Leninism while they try to prevent others from developing it in a truly creative fashion. . . . Even while adulterating Marxism-Leninism at their own discretion, they demand that the other Communist parties follow their steps and repeat their words as if their adulteration were an imperial edict.

The guileless Chou Yang is evidently unaware that during the long reign of Stalin Moscow's claims to creativity *were* "imperial edicts" based ultimately on an assumption of superior authority.

What, then, about Mao Tse-tung's claims to creativity? Can one really find in the copies of Lenin's and Stalin's writings proof texts for all of Mao's "innovations"? To take one of the most recent themes of Chinese propaganda, what would Lenin have made of a Socialist world made up of sovereign nation-states, each developing its own economy in complete "self-reliance" and autarchy? The reasons for Peking's adoption of this bit of "creativity" are obvious, but whether Lenin would have considered it more "creative" than Moscow's position on coexistence is open to question. Both the Chinese and Soviets, of course, appeal to "life" to verify their respective creative applications of Marxism-Leninism, and life obligingly tells both of them exactly what they want to hear.

Turning from the question of peace and war to the question of ideological policy vis-à-vis the nonaligned world, we find a very muddy-looking picture indeed. The notion of a consistent Chinese posture in this area will hardly bear close scrutiny. During the period of the Chinese rise to power—roughly from 1948 to 1954—both Moscow and Peking seemed to be equally hostile to the newly emerging "bourgeois nationalist" regimes in Asia and equally inclined to dismiss them as lackeys of imperialism. There was a similar tendency to favor only nationalist movements under Communist party control. . . .

In the period 1950-1955, however, we see on both sides a gradual drift from this approach. . . . With the death of Stalin, the end of the Korean war, the rapid unanticipated retreat of colonial power, and the rise of numerous non-Communist nation-states, both the new Soviet leadership and the Chinese found it in their interest to cultivate the new neutralist regimes and to acknowledge their independence in spite of the lack of "proletarian hegemony" anywhere in the ex-colonial world. To be sure, both Moscow and Peking continued to cherish the hope of proletarian hegemony in the future, but during the whole period from 1955 to 1959 Peking was quite willing to push its previous doctrine of the universal relevance of the Chinese model [of revolution] into the background and to indulge in ardent wooing of all the established regimes in Asia, Africa, and elsewhere. . . .

This article has focused on Chinese manipulation of ideology because of the widespread impression that the Chinese have been less cavalier and more rigidly doctrinaire than the Soviets in their ideological stance. On the whole, it is true that they have attempted to give an impression of greater toughness, but toughness has no necessary relationship to rigidity. In none of this do I mean to imply that the Soviet side of the controversy will bear close scrutiny.

Contrary to Soviet assertions, as already pointed out, the Chinese have not clearly committed themselves to world war, nor have they in any of their public statements emphasized color or race. The Chinese also seem quite correct, it seems to me, in their claim that the Soviets still clearly aspire to "wave the baton" in the Communist world in spite of their frequent protestations that there is no longer any "center" in that world. The Soviet claim to ascendancy now simply takes the form of alleging the "unanimity" of all Communist parties in accepting the decisions of all recent Soviet party congresses as binding upon all of them. It is precisely the Chinese refusal to accept the binding nature of these decisions that has shaken the whole structure of authority in the Communist world to its very foundations.

IV. DEALING WITH THE COMMUNIST WORLD

EDITOR'S INTRODUCTION

Few foreign affairs issues evoke quite as much passion in the United States as the question of what policies to follow toward the Communist world. One school of thought would have the United States pursue a friendly course toward the Soviet Union while trying to isolate China. Another school regards it as something akin to treason to talk of détente or to think of making any concessions to the Communists. Still another group would have the West do everything possible to heighten the bitter feelings between Moscow and Peking on the theory that the more hostile the two Communist countries are toward each other the greater are the dividends for the West. In between these theories are numerous variations.

This section presents a group of articles on how the West has reacted toward the Communist world and what the West might do in the days ahead. The first selection reviews our policy towards China and offers a sampling of the debate on where the West should go from here. Should Washington give diplomatic recognition to Communist China? What about a UN seat for Peking, assuming that the Chinese would even accept membership?

The next piece, by W. E. Griffith, discusses a number of recommendations regarding Western policy and the Sino-Soviet split. But our first and most important task, the author states, is to understand the schism itself. The concluding essays in this volume treat a broad array of policy issues. The *Atlantic* article deals with some of our major objectives towards the Soviet Union on the one hand and China on the other. The article also discusses Vietnam and suggests that our best course might be graduated conversations aimed at ending the war, combined with a careful escalation of the military methods we employ so as to convince the Chinese that their theory on wars of liberation will not necessarily prove valid. The New York *Times Magazine* piece asks whether the West can find enough common ground with the Soviet Union so as to provide for a further relaxation of tensions —and warns that though Moscow advocates peaceful coexistence, it still opposes the West in every part of the world.

Whatever else may be said of it, the Sino-Soviet rift has already had a momentous impact on the course of foreign affairs, an impact which may well grow to even larger proportions in the years ahead.

WHAT CHINA POLICIES? [1]

Despite the absence of formal diplomatic ties, the United States and Red China have conducted intermittent negotiations through their respective ambassadors to Poland for the past seven years. The talks have resolved few, if any, substantive issues, but they have provided Washington and Peking with a sort of diplomatic "hot line," useful in preventing miscalculations of one another's policy intent. Last April the retiring Chinese ambassador to Warsaw, Wang Ping-nan, met with his United States counterpart for the last time before returning to Peking. Emerging from the talks, he told newsmen: "We believe the differences now existing between China and the United States will eventually be settled."

Yes, but, How?

The questions worrying United States diplomats are: How will those differences be settled? And in whose favor?

The Peking regime has been rattling its sword at the United States almost continuously for fifteen years. It has talked a great deal about the need for force and violence. And it has backed these words with deeds—in Korea, Tibet, India, etc.

It wants the United States out of Asia and rolled back in the western Pacific to Hawaii. It wants the Far East recognized as a Chinese preserve. Nor do the differences end there. It wants the United States—and all other white powers, for that matter—out

[1] From *Great Decisions 1965*. (Fact Sheet no. 1. Red China—Menace or Paper Tiger?) Foreign Policy Association. 345 E. 46th St. New York 10017. '65. p 13-14. Reprinted by permission.

of the underdeveloped countries, and it wants the Chinese Communists in. And for a crowning difference, it wants a violent worldwide revolution toppling "reactionaries" and "imperialists" everywhere and substituting instead the Maoist way of life.

Just as it is hard to imagine a more ambitious program, so it is hard to imagine two nations separated by more fundamental differences than Red China and the United States. Secretary of State Dean Rusk expressed concern in this regard . . . when he said: "We think it would be a serious matter for the authorities in Peking to believe that a policy of militancy brings dividends, is profitable, makes gains, because on that issue may turn the peace of the world, and we are interested in somehow trying to build a peaceful world."

United States policy toward Communist China today can be broadly characterized by one word: *isolate*. In concert with Nationalist China, and with some unbargained-for assistance from the U.S.S.R., the United States has sought to counter Peking's drive for power by erecting a political, economic and military wall of isolation around the mainland.

Politically, the United States has led in the effort to block Peking's admission to world councils—particularly the United Nations—and has used its considerable influence to dissuade other nations from establishing diplomatic ties with the Communist regime. It has stood fast in its support of the Nationalist claim to represent the legitimate government of China. "We are loyal to our commitments to the government of the Republic of China," Secretary Rusk has said, "and we will never abandon the twelve million people of Taiwan to Communist tyranny."

Economically, the United States has imposed a strict embargo on all American trade with Communist China. It has also sought and obtained a ban on the shipment of strategic goods from its major allies (Japan, Britain, France, etc.) who carry on limited trade with the Peking regime. The list of strategic goods barred from Red China under this program is far longer than a similar list governing trade with the U.S.S.R. The United States strongly opposes Peking's bid to expand trade with Western Europe.

Armed Encirclement

Militarily, the United States has ringed the Chinese mainland with a system of bilateral and multilateral alliances, all aimed at the containment of Red Chinese aggression. It has established bilateral defense treaties with South Korea, Japan, and Nationalist China. Under the multilateral Southeast Asia Treaty Organization (SEATO), it has entered into additional mutual security arrangements with Pakistan, the Philippines, Thailand, Australia, New Zealand, Britain, and France. To shore up local defense efforts against the Chinese threat, the United States provides large-scale military aid to India, South Vietnam, South Korea, and Taiwan. American military bases and installations encircle the mainland from South Korea to Thailand. The nuclear-armed Seventh Fleet commands the sea off China's coast.

Despite these and other efforts, however, . . . Peking broke through the political and economic barriers raised against it to establish new diplomatic and trade ties with France and closer ties with Pakistan. Among "nonaligned" nations . . . Cambodia moved closer to the Chinese camp. In South Vietnam, America's economic and military aid seemed of little avail in stemming the tide of guerrilla activity. And, due in part to policy clashes between the United States and France, the SEATO alliance appeared headed toward a state of grave disrepair.

Though the United States has maintained a firm policy of strict opposition to Peking's aims, there have been recent indications that a new approach may be in the making. In a major foreign policy address on December 13, 1963, Roger Hilsman, Jr., then Assistant Secretary of State for Far Eastern Affairs, said that the United States was "determined to keep the door open to the possibility of change" in the Peking leadership. Mr. Hilsman indicated that American hopes for an accommodation with Red China rested on the belief that a new generation of Chinese leaders would prove less recalcitrant and dogmatic than Peking's current crop. He suggested that there was awareness among some second-echelon Communist officials and intellectuals that Peking's militant policies were unrealistic. These remarks came shortly after the late President Kennedy had announced, in mid-

November, that the United States "is not wedded to a policy of hostility to Red China"—a remark that provoked outcries of indignation on Taiwan.

Hard Line or Soft?

Such remarks—indeed, any suggestion that our China policy may be softening—also provoke outcries from Americans who believe that a hard line is essential in our approach to Peking. These Americans argue that any hope for accommodation with China's fanatical Communists is doomed to disappointment. Being "tough" themselves, the Communists in Peking best understand and respect toughness in return, they maintain.

These advocates of a tough approach would urge the following: (1) stepped-up assistance to all anti-Communist elements in Asia, particularly the Nationalist government on Taiwan and the government of South Vietnam; (2) renewed United States efforts to block Red China's admission to the UN (even to the point of withdrawing from that body ourselves if Peking is seated) and to prevent other governments from according diplomatic recognition to the Communist regime; (3) new efforts to extend the trade embargo and to pressure our allies into joining it (even to the point of retaliating economically against those who do not).

Some in this group still put forward the idea of "unleashing Chiang" for an attack upon the mainland with United States support. Now is the time, they say, before Chiang leaves the scene and before Moscow and Peking have a chance to patch their quarrel.

Advocates of a more flexible United States policy on China argue that such a hard line toward Peking would only stiffen the hostility of Mao and his group, increase tensions in Asia and lose the United States some key opportunities for exploiting fissures in the Communist movement. They say that a change from the rigid hostility that has characterized United States policy in the past is long overdue.

Few advocates of a more flexible China policy believe we should abandon Chiang Kai-shek, extend recognition to the

Peking regime on its own terms, or let down our guard against Chinese aggression. Rather, they believe that United States policy should seek in other ways to bring China into closer contact with the West—not only with an eye to exploiting the Sino-Soviet split but also for the purpose of "educating" the Chinese leaders on world realities, of shattering that Stalinesque habit so faithfully adopted by Peking and described by Khrushchev thus: "If Stalin said anything, it meant it was so."

What would this approach mean in terms of concrete measures? According to its proponents it would mean that the United States should put out feelers for trade and cultural contacts with Peking. It would mean that negotiations for exchanging news reporters be undertaken. And it could mean that Peking's admission to the UN and other world councils would prove more beneficial than disastrous for world peace and for the United States itself in the long run.

Some would argue, in addition, that a dialogue between Washington and Peking on the nuclear issue is now both essential and inevitable. But others are just as firmly convinced that Red China's nuclear capabilities constitute a new and urgent reason for Washington to redouble its efforts to isolate the mainland regime.

The Recognition Problem

Some Americans maintain that on a purely practical basis, United States refusal to recognize the Peking regime as the legitimate rulers—no matter how tyrannical—of the Chinese people is absurd. They argue we should "swallow our pride" and exchange ambassadors with Red China just as we have with the Soviet Union. Most authorities believe, however, that the problem of recognition is far more complicated than this. For one thing, Peking has several times indicated that it would *refuse* United States recognition unless and until the problem of Taiwan is settled—in Peking's favor.

As Secretary Rusk indicated, it would be morally reprehensible to abandon the people of Taiwan to Communist rule. But beyond that, such an act of betrayal by the United States of one of its closest allies would undoubtedly have disastrous political consequences all around the globe, wherever people depended on United States support to maintain their freedom. The initiative for recognition clearly lies in Peking's and not Washington's hands, therefore.

A similar problem arises with regard to a seat for Peking at the UN. Chinese Communists have never seemed overly eager to join the UN, although they may have enjoyed watching the United States struggle each year to keep them out. In October 1963, Foreign Minister Chen Yi announced that China had no intention of seeking a seat at the world body because "under present circumstances" China had "no role to play in the UN."

Here again the problem focuses on Taiwan. To bring Peking in, UN members may have to expel Taipei—not only from the Security Council but from the General Assembly as well. The Peking position is unequivocal: "China will not participate in any international conference, organization, or undertaking in which representatives of the Taiwan local authorities are participating, no matter by what name they call themselves."

Nonetheless, many Western observers remain convinced that a "two Chinas" formula, which would provide membership for both regimes, will ultimately resolve the UN seating problem. Much hard bargaining would be required, as well as a more conciliatory stance by both sides. What would be Taipei's status under such an arrangement? Should UN supervised elections determine the future of the island? And who would get China's permanent seat on the Security Council?

Exploiting the Rift

The policies we adopt toward Red China may also depend greatly on an accurate appraisal of the Sino-Soviet rift. . . . Generally, there are two schools of thought as to the course United States policy should take in the event of continued discord between Peking and Moscow. One holds we should support the weaker antagonist, the Chinese, against the stronger, the Soviets, in order to encourage a widening of differences between the two powers and, as a fringe benefit, perhaps draw China closer to the

West. The other view holds that China, though weaker, is actually the more menacing of the two powers, the greater threat to Western interests. It is China, after all, that militantly hawks national liberation struggles, while the Soviet Union has sought out points of accommodation with the West. In this view, then, the United States should follow a hostile policy toward Red China in order to pressure Peking into moderating its stand.

THE COMMUNIST CAMP AND WESTERN POLICY [2]

What can and should the West in general and the United States in particular do about the Sino-Soviet split? Our first task, and probably still our most important one, is to understand it. Many of us unconsciously still tend to think in terms of "the international Communist movement," "the international Communist conspiracy," the "Sino-Soviet bloc," etc. But, like so many other clichés, these now obscure rather than illuminate the actual state of affairs. There is no longer one united international Communist movement, nor is there likely ever to be just one again. . . .

Slow Awakening

Why were most Americans, and indeed most Westerners, so slow to realize the extent and seriousness of the Sino-Soviet rift?

In the first place the Communist take-over in China seemed to those who had always been strong ideological opponents of communism, and to those who became hostile to it as a result of Soviet action after 1945, . . . just another, if more important, extension of Soviet influence, like that which occurred in Eastern Europe in 1945-1948. Chinese Communist support of Soviet policy up to 1956 seemed to confirm this impression. Secondly, America's traditional ties with pre-Communist China were often colored more by sentiment than by realism: our government and our public opinion consistently underestimated the weakness of the Chiang Kai-shek regime and the strength, fanaticism, and

[2] From *World Communism Divided*, pamphlet by W. E. Griffith, director of the International Communism Project at the Massachusetts Institute of Technology and author of *The Sino-Soviet Rift*. (Headline Series. no 166) Foreign Policy Association. 345 E. 46th St. New York 10017. Ag. '64. p 35-41. Reprinted by permission.

independence of the Chinese Communists. The Korean war, and apparent Sino-Soviet cooperation in waging it, solidified still further the image of international communism as a unified Moscow-directed conspiracy. Many experts on China in the State Department or in the academic world had been subjected to public attack as "too soft on the Chinese Communists," and their predictions that Sino-Soviet amity would not survive in the long run had thus been disregarded. In addition, the frustrations of the Korean war and the McCarthy period of the early fifties led to a demonization of Stalin. Even many Soviet affairs experts tended to look at Stalinism in Russia and total Soviet domination of world communism as something permanent. Finally, American scholars' and journalists' lack of access to Communist China frequently added ignorance to emotion. Thus the American image of Mao's China was in some respects removed from reality, nowhere more so than in the field of Sino-Soviet relations.

One must beware, however, of believing that the rift between China and Russia means that they are no longer a danger to the free world. . . . In some areas of the world the initial result of the Sino-Soviet split may well be an intensification of the most radical kind of Communist activity in terms of arms aid to, and guerrilla training of, radical nationalists, particularly in Africa and Latin America. Sino-Soviet competition for the underdeveloped world could thus create dangerous conditions of instability which might involve the West. Furthermore, communism in any given country may now become more attractive to the discontented as the growth of polycentrism frees local parties from the disadvantage of operating under foreign control and permits them to tailor their programs to suit local conditions.

In general, there are two schools of thought, here and in Western Europe, about the course Western policy should take in respect to the Sino-Soviet split. One holds the view that we should support the weaker antagonist, the Chinese, against the stronger, the Soviet Union, in order to assure that the split will deepen still further and that in due time the Chinese will moderate their now all-pervasive hostility toward the West. The other view holds that China, although weaker, is presently more dangerous to us because of its advocacy and support of national liberation struggles; while the Soviet Union, although stronger, is deterred by our thermonuclear superiority and in any case is so preoccupied with the Chinese challenge that it cannot afford to complicate its problems by aggravating its differences with the United States. Therefore, this second school holds, we should remain hostile to China but become more conciliatory toward the Soviet Union, with the objective of easing dangerous tensions with the U.S.S.R.

Both of these positions are, in the writer's view, oversimplified. We should not assume that the relative moderation of the Soviet Union on such issues as peaceful coexistence means that it is necessarily less dangerous a foe than China or that, as some argue, Soviet economic and industrial growth will erode the ideological convictions of Khrushchev and his successors and in time make Russia a "contented" power with which we can live in peaceful tranquillity. There are some important areas of common interest between the United States and the Soviet Union (preventing the spread of nuclear weapons and avoiding nuclear war, for example), as has been shown by the signing of the partial test ban treaty, but these are likely to remain limited in the foreseeable future. As the Chinese have pointed out, it was Khrushchev, not Mao, who put the missiles in Cuba. Nor does industrial growth necessarily lead to moderation, as the examples of pre-World War II Japan and Nazi Germany should remind us.

The leadership of the Soviet Union remains ideologically hostile to the United States and to the West and, as the Cuban crisis showed, is capable of taking dangerous risks. Khrushchev is quite as committed as Mao to burying us. [Khrushchev's successors seem to be giving less emphasis to talk of burying the U.S.—Ed.] Nevertheless to say that the Sino-Soviet dispute is only about *how* to bury us is greatly to underestimate its significance and possible consequences. On the one hand, it is worth recalling that the dispute between Catholicism and Protestantism over how to achieve the salvation of the soul convulsed Europe for decades in the slaughter of religious war. On the other hand, since means and ends are related, increasing differences between

Moscow and Peking over the means or tactics to employ in dealing with the West may in time lead to significant divergence in final goals.

The Importance of Strength

Meanwhile, a fundamental requirement of American security remains the maintenance of decisive superiority in strategic military strength over the Soviet Union. Moreover, while we need no longer worry that some action on our part, except perhaps a United States invasion of mainland China, will reunite Moscow and Peking, it is in our interest to make the Sino-Soviet rift as wide as possible and so further the process of disintegration within the international Communist movement. Since, of the two major Communist powers, China is in a more aggressive phase, particularly with regard to its support and advocacy of national liberation movements in Asia and elsewhere, it is essential that the United States contain Chinese-backed aggression, particularly in South Vietnam. China's Communist leaders are not carrying out what they consider to be a policy of high risk in this area. A continuing firm United States stand in East Asia may not only save the area from Chinese-dominated Communist control but may force China's leaders to develop greater respect for the United States and may eventually convince them of the wisdom of moderation in their dealing with this country.

A somewhat similar logic applies to the Soviet Union as well. One of the main Chinese arguments against Soviet policy is that Moscow consistently overestimates the risk of forceful American action and that therefore Soviet leaders tend to exaggerate the risks of Communist guerrilla warfare and subversion in general. Were the United States to make unilateral concessions to Moscow in vital areas, such a policy would seem to justify the Chinese thesis that the United States is a paper tiger and perhaps convince Moscow that it had overestimated American willingness to use its power or defend its interests. Therefore, the United States must not only contain the Chinese to demonstrate to the international Communist movement that aggression does not pay but it must also contain the Russians for the same reason. At the same time, since Soviet and Chinese tactics are different, we should respond differentially. Certainly we should seek to encourage accords with the Russians in areas of mutual interest and in areas which promise to reduce tensions. Such agreements are not only mutually beneficial, but indicate a realistic willingness on our part to encourage the U.S.S.R. to give more than lip service to peaceful coexistence. However insignificant a given agreement may seem in the over-all context of present Soviet-United States hostility, the accumulation of agreements, one by one, may in the long run be important. For virtually no serious students of international affairs think that a genuine settlement of United States-Soviet differences will take place suddenly. If it ever does come, it is much more likely to be the cumulative result of a change of atmosphere brought about by "little" agreements over a period of many years.

Détente Diplomacy

Despite friction between Washington and Paris, we are in a far better position, if we act intelligently, to profit from a relaxation of tensions than are either the Russians or the Chinese. Détente leads to more, not less, liberalization in the Soviet Union and in the Soviet-influenced states in Eastern Europe, and this, particularly in Eastern Europe, is in our interest. The Sino-Soviet split allowed us, for example, to undertake trade negotiations with Rumania, a country which, though it was until recently still internally Stalinist, has asserted its near-complete independence from the Soviet Union. (We should remember that in 1948, when Tito broke with Moscow, his regime was still repressively Stalinist —indeed radically so; only in 1951 did he begin to liberalize at home.) We can encourage cultural exchange and expand nonstrategic trade with the Soviet Union and with Eastern Europe. The fear of revived West German irredentism leads Poland and Czechoslovakia to seek Soviet protection. We may reduce this fear, and thereby increase the possibilities of maneuver by the two Eastern European countries, by attempting to persuade the West Germans to move toward recognizing the Oder-Neisse line.

Caution, however, is here very much in order. Our security interests make our alliance with West Germany most desirable; West Germany's interests make alliance with us essential. Bonn understandably regards the reunification of Germany and the preservation of the present status of West Berlin as vital national interests. To insure the stability of the American-West German alliance, so should we. Since we cannot improve the status of West Berlin in the near future, we should maintain the status quo. As to German reunification, it will not come about as the result of liberalization within East Germany, although this may ease relations between West and East Germany. Only long-range, basic changes in Soviet policy can bring German reunification about; unless and until they occur, we should continue to refuse to recognize East Germany and do everything to encourage other nations to refuse to do so as well.

In the Far East, we should, as has been stated above, contain China, North Korea and, most urgently, North Vietnam until they learn that aggression does not pay. We should provide India with the arms required to defend itself against Peking, but also encourage it to negotiate with Pakistan over Kashmir.

In Latin America, we should fulfill the aims of the Alliance for Progress. But we should refuse to accept the status quo in Cuba. Castro's aim of fomenting revolution throughout the Western Hemisphere is one he may temporarily soft-pedal but will not abandon. We should therefore intensify pressure on Cuba by all means short of invasion.

In Africa and the Middle East we should do what we can to prevent major Soviet or Chinese Communist gains arising out of the Israeli-Arab feud and the potentially more dangerous struggle of black African nationalism for Southern Africa.

The strength of the West and particularly of the United States has contributed to deepening the Sino-Soviet rift. The maintenance of our strength and a sophisticated diplomacy will enable us to profit from the disunity of our enemies and to meet the challenge of the coming decades of instability in the Southern Hemisphere.

CONTAINING COMMUNISM EAST AND WEST [3]

The October 1962 Cuban missile crisis was the great watershed for American foreign policy. The United States demonstrated decisive strategic superiority in second-strike missile deterrents and also local conventional superiority. Above all, we conveyed the clear determination to use them if need be. Since then our military lead over Moscow has grown larger. Rather than trying to close this gap, the new Soviet leadership seems to have intensified Khrushchev's post-1962 shift from heavy industry to consumer goods. The whole post-Stalin Soviet shift at home from terror to incentives and the emphasis on preventing thermonuclear war require at least atmospheric détente with the West.

Moreover, American strategic superiority, the Sino-Soviet split, and the reassertion of Eastern European nationalism confront Brezhnev and Kosygin with far more serious problems of imperial readjustment than Stalin's successors faced. Our alliance problems fade into relative insignificance when compared with their dilemma: the longer Moscow tries unsuccessfully to excommunicate China in order to contain Mao's rising influence, the more Russia's allies, notably Rumania and Cuba, can assert against Soviet wishes their increased autonomy (given them by Moscow lest they support Peiping [a variant form of Peking]), and therefore the fewer reliable allies Moscow has to contain Peiping.

Moscow's strategic pause is also prolonged by the Chinese challenge to Russian territorial integrity and national interests and to Soviet hegemony in the international Communist movement. The Sino-Soviet split thus works in our favor, except in areas where neither Moscow nor Peiping can pre-empt major influence, such as Africa (most recently, in the Congo), where the Chinese drive makes Moscow more aggressive.

Our foreign policy toward the Soviet Union should have three major objectives: (1) preventing thermonuclear war by (2) containing Soviet power within its present limits . . . and thus (3)

[3] From article by W. E. Griffith, director of the International Communism Project at the Massachusetts Institute of Technology and author of *The Sino-Soviet Rift*. *Atlantic*. 215:71-5. My. '65. Copyright © 1965, by The Atlantic Monthly Company, Boston, Mass. Reprinted with permission.

gradually replacing the U.S.S.R.'s present nationalistic and ideological expansionism by moderation and protection of its true national interests.

Our major current policy problems with the Soviet Union are the control of nuclear weapons, Germany, and Cuba. The first is the most general, and potentially, although not immediately, the most important. General and complete disarmament is unlikely in the near future. As long as the Soviets remain expansionist, we must maintain decisive strategic superiority over them. Also, since agreements with Moscow are unreliable if there is no provision for inspection, we must not give up on-ground inspection as a prerequisite. Soviet authoritarianism and strategic inferiority compel them to secrecy. Even so, peripheral arms-control measures remain desirable, if only to make miscalculated or accidental thermonuclear war less likely and to consolidate détente—which, among other things, is a precondition for liberalization in the Communist world. The partial test ban treaty, signed in August, 1963, not only furthered these aims but also greatly intensified Sino-Soviet hostility, since it proved to Peiping that Moscow preferred détente with Washington to support of China against the United States. . . .

Underdeveloped Areas

After we foiled the Kremlin's 1960 attempt to gain predominant influence in the Congo, Moscow was until recently relatively quiet in the Afro-Asian area. But new Soviet opportunities in the Congo, plus Chinese competition there and elsewhere, have reawakened Soviet ambitions. We must not allow Moscow to enjoy détente with us and simultaneously support national liberation struggles. Were it not for Soviet and Chinese intervention, we might well leave Africa and Asia to their own devices. But we still must attempt to contain Soviet and Chinese expansionism; the strategic and economic prizes that could fall to the Communists in the underdeveloped world deny us the luxury of indifference. We must do what we sensibly can to prevent Soviet- or Chinese-armed rebellions from capturing major countries in "the third world."

Our problems in Africa are particularly serious for two reasons. First, the South African white redoubt is so strong and the black Africans so weak that only outside help can overcome South Africa, and only Moscow (or perhaps Peiping) can and may give this help. Second, the resultant conflict would be racial war at its worst, and this would inevitably nourish our racial problems at home. We cannot proclaim integration at home and support white supremacy in South Africa. We must therefore find ways to reestablish good relations with moderate African nationalists. We should try, for example, to disengage from our unholy alliance in the Congo with South African white mercenaries. We must also add deeds to our words against Portuguese, South African, and Southern Rhodesian white domination, which cannot last, in any case, for these whites are on the losing end of history. Specifically, we should begin to discourage American investments in the white supremacy countries of Africa.

Support of the United Nations remains in our interest, because the UN can limit some local wars, and thus aids containment of Moscow and Peiping; for the same reasons, Moscow obstructs the UN and Peiping tries to destroy it. No longer, though, can we rely on a safe majority in the General Assembly. It is in our interest, then, to abandon our recent insistence on compulsory assessments for UN peace-keeping expeditions. Those that are in our interest are worth our contributions. Those that are not in our interest—and we are approaching a time when an unfriendly majority can vote them into existence—we should not arbitrarily be required to pay for. We may not like the principle in the abstract, but in practical terms we can be no more willing in the future than are the Communists now to tie our interests to a hostile majority of the 115 United Nations countries.

China

How dangerous to us is China, and how may we best deal with it? We fought World War II in part to prevent a hostile major Asian power, Japan, from conquering East Asia and threatening us in the western Pacific. We fought a limited war in Korea to prevent a similar threat. We are now confronted with another such challenge, this time by a China with an immense land army and the beginnings of an atomic capability which may eventually threaten our physical security.

Unlike imperial Japan, Communist China is socially revolutionary as well as anticolonialist, and its ambitions, although also centered in East Asia, are worldwide in scope. China centers its worldwide revolutionary drive in the nonwhite underdeveloped regions, but its propagandists are even at work to exploit its racist appeal within our own country, among the American Negroes. (The underdeveloped world is not alone a threat to us, because it is too weak; but if China should capture it, and also bring Japan into its orbit, our peril would be great.)

Mao's determination to displace Moscow at the head of a purified international Communist movement has been most successful in East Asia. The 1962 Chinese victory over India scared much of the rest of Southeast Asia into neutrality or a pro-Chinese position. . . .

Long-range Chinese goals begin with expansion to the previous limits of imperial Chinese influence, including Southeast Asia, the Soviet maritime provinces, and Taiwan. These aims make China hostile to Russia and, unless we turn Taiwan and Southeast Asia over to them, to us. Chinese pressure now centers in South Vietnam and Laos, but China's revolutionary activity is not limited to East Asia. Peiping supports its Adriatic ally, Albania, the first East Asian foothold in Europe since the Mongols. It is splitting Communist parties throughout the world, including North and South America, where the Chinese support *Fidelista* activity against the pro-Soviet Latin-American Communist parties. In Africa the Chinese give radical anti-Western elements money, arms, and training. China everywhere preaches and acts on Mao's doctrine that the United States cannot win in guerrilla warfare and will eventually have to abandon it.

Our strategic choice, therefore, is between two alternatives. The first is to contain China within its present limits of geographic influence, in order, through prolonged frustration, so to moderate its geographic ambitions and its atomic threat that we may eventually achieve with China something like our partial precarious modus vivendi with the Soviet Union. The second is to abandon, as gradually and with as much face-saving as possible, Southeast Asia and Taiwan but continue to defend India and Japan by our sea and air power. Immediately, this means that we would leave Saigon.

South Vietnam is far away; the war there is dirty and bloody, and Americans have a deep revulsion, confirmed in the war with the Japanese in the Pacific and with the Chinese in Korea, against fighting fanatical troops in Asian jungle wars. Furthermore, the argument for abandonment goes, there is no viable anti-Communist, to say nothing of a democratic, government in South Vietnam; the Vietnamese are weary of the war, and its extension would only bring in millions of Chinese troops. Let us, therefore, leave Vietnam, and fight, if we must, where there are strong popular governments on our side—in Thailand, Malaysia, or even India or Japan.

Those who advocate the second alternative miss the main point: the nature and extent of Chinese ambitions. . . . China's rulers are totally hostile to the United States. Such men's appetites, history teaches, are whetted by victory, never satiated by their foes' concessions. Furthermore, the longer we wait effectively to contain them, the closer they come to effective atomic delivery capability. Today Mao and his associates are very confident. They beat us, they think, in the Korean war. They faced down the worst the Russians could do to them and still gained influence every year. They humiliatingly defeated India. They are the first Asian, colored, revolutionary power to explode an atom bomb. Their influence in Africa is rising rapidly. Finally, we have been steadily losing and they have been gaining in South Vietnam. If they will not stop now, why should they stop if and when we leave Saigon? And why should anyone believe we would keep pledges to other Asian countries after we break them with Saigon? Thus everywhere time works for China and against us: the sooner we decide on containment, therefore, the better.

In Vietnam, as toward China altogether, we can expect little help from our allies. Britain is fully occupied in Malaysia. . . . France, convinced we will leave Saigon, favors neutralization—

that is, saving as much face as possible while adjusting to Chinese victory. Germany and Japan are inactive. India, still suffering from the shock of the Chinese Himalayan victory, needs our aid. Whatever we decide needs to be done in East Asia, we must do ourselves.

As for the Soviets in East Asia, the Sino-Soviet split has greatly reduced Soviet power and influence there. In areas where it cannot bring military power directly to bear, Moscow will therefore probably offer little more than verbal protests to American containment of Chinese expansionism, so long as we do not attempt to invade and occupy either North Vietnam or China.

South Vietnam is far from the most favorable terrain on which to contain China, but the alternatives—the loss of Southeast Asia to China, the encirclement of India, the threat even to Japan: in short, Asia's adjustment to our withdrawal and Chinese advance—would all be worse. Therefore, to hold South Vietnam is our most important present priority in containing China. Can we? And how?

Our objective should clearly be limited to holding South Vietnam and ending the guerrilla warfare there—specifically, to return to the 1959 status quo, before Vietcong guerrilla action became extensive; it should not include the overthrow of the North Vietnamese regime. We need not, and should not attempt to, achieve that. In South Vietnam the cards are still stacked against us, and our position there may well continue to worsen. We must intensify our efforts all the more. Furthermore, instability in Saigon is best remedied by demonstrated firmness on our part.

Peace in Korea on the basis of the *status quo ante,* let us remember, came from the credible American threat to Peiping that we would otherwise begin air strikes on Manchuria. The war in South Vietnam is different, but the principle is the same: we must borrow strength from our opponents' weakness—North Vietnam's vulnerability to air and sea attack. Furthermore, Ho Chi Minh, although under predominant Chinese influence, hardly wants to fall under total Chinese domination, which would be inevitable if he had to call in major Chinese forces to defend him and if our bombing destroyed the industrial capacity he has with such difficulty built up. Our leverage on North Vietnam is considerable, but only if our intentions as well as our capabilities are made clear to Hanoi.

Opponents of escalation reply that even if Hanoi wanted to, it probably could not stop the Vietcong; most of the rebels' supplies come from South Vietnam itself. This is true, and Vietcong troops are mostly nationalist and social revolutionary rather than Communist; but it is far more important, as the overwhelming weight of expert opinion holds, that the Vietcong are directed from and controlled by Hanoi. Ho Chi Minh called off the guerrilla war once, after the French left in 1954; he began it again in 1959; if he wishes, he can call it off again.

And what, opponents of escalation ask, of Chinese intervention? In the first place, Chinese policy is not high risk but low risk. As analysis of captured Chinese military documents has shown, Peiping is quite aware of the threat of American conventional and thermonuclear capacity, the more so since it can no longer depend on Soviet aid against us, and it has no intention of engaging us in these fields. Moreover, its advocacy and support of guerrilla warfare, in South Vietnam and elsewhere, are based on its assessment that we cannot win such a war and will withdraw rather than escalate it.

Moscow seems to believe, on the other hand, in the reality of our determination to escalate, and therefore believes the guerrilla warfare is too risky. It is of the utmost importance for us not only to prove the Chinese wrong, and thus to contain them, but also to prove Moscow right, lest the Russians also renew their broad-scale support of guerrilla struggles.

Our best course in Vietnam is neither negotiation . . . nor all-out attack; it is, rather, careful, graduated conversations *and* escalation. This seems to be the choice President Johnson has made. At each stage, we should privately convey to Hanoi, Peiping, and Moscow our goals and our methods. We should make clear to Hanoi and Peiping that we can and will continue to escalate, unless and until they are prepared to go back to the 1959 status quo, to the gradual destruction of North Vietnamese ports and then of industrial installations. More may be necessary —Chinese intervention would force us to consider extending our air strikes first to south China and then to their atomic potential; this possibility should be made clear to Red Chinese leaders. We should emphasize to the Russians our self-imposed limitation on our objectives and also make clear that while we want détente with them, as we hope eventually to obtain it with China, any substantial military intervention by them will risk the use of our ability to blockade not only Cuba but the Dardanelles and the Baltic Sea as well.

China's drive for power centers in the colored underdeveloped world. Peiping has especially great hopes in Africa and is investing much effort there. We must therefore move rapidly and intelligently to prevent the racist Chinese, as well as the Russians, from fishing too successfully in these waters.

This may seem a tough and dangerous policy. It is. But Demosthenes vainly warned the Athenians about Philip of Macedon, "if any man supposes this to be peace, which will enable Philip to master all else and attack you last, he is a madman." Appeasement now will mean not lasting peace but major war later.

CAN WE MAKE COMMON CAUSE WITH RUSSIA [4]

The rift between Moscow and Peking has faced the United States with the chance and the need to make new choices in foreign policy. For roughly fifteen years, from 1947 to 1962, United States policy was dominated by the struggle against "world communism"—a hackneyed phrase but one that expressed the reality of a Communist bloc under Soviet leadership which acted as a single, powerful, and menacing enemy of the West. With the end of world communism and coordinated Soviet-Chinese foreign policies, we are now confronted with the radically different reality of two Communist great powers, distinct in their world outlook and power potential, their methods of action and their

[4] From article by Richard Lowenthal, professor of international relations at the Free University of Berlin. New York *Times Magazine.* p 34-5+. N. 21, '65. © 1965 by The New York Times Company. Reprinted by permission.

priority interests, and engaged in serious conflict with each other as well as with us.

Seen from Washington, the constellation of world affairs no longer appears bipolar but triangular, offering the West a chance to side with one Communist giant against the other in order to gain its most important objectives and avert the most urgent dangers.

But the use of that opportunity depends first of all on a clear definition of these objectives and dangers—on a careful choice of our own priorities. And it is by no means a foregone conclusion that those priorities will be seen in the same light by all the members of the Western alliance.

If we cannot reach agreement on this crucial choice, the Sino-Soviet split may result in losses rather than gains for the United States. The breakup of the Soviet bloc would then emerge as a decisive factor in the breakup of the Western alliance, long before the vital aims of that alliance are achieved.

The choice of enemies—or, more precisely, of the issues on which the United States could line up with one major Communist power against the other—is thus the most crucial decision on long-term policy this country has confronted since the beginning of the cold war. Like President Truman's decision to oppose further Soviet expansion, it will determine the course of world affairs for a long time to come.

Nothing could be more dangerous for Washington and the West than if this decision were made half-consciously, so to speak—hastily under the pressure of daily events or carelessly in a mood reflecting vague popular assumptions never fully examined in public debate.

Yet . . . [certain symptoms suggest] that just such a "decision by drift" may be under way at the present moment. The bitter, protracted war in Vietnam is focusing the attention of the Administration and the American people on Red China as the one irreconcilable enemy. On the other hand, the greater caution shown by the Soviets since their defeat in the Cuban missile crisis of 1962 and the real, if slow, long-term changes in the Soviet regime feed an impression that serious conflict between the

United States and Russia is virtually at an end. A growing number of Americans seem to take it for granted that the major task of United States diplomacy is now to persuade Moscow to cooperate with the United States in a new common cause—openly or tacitly—on the theory that the Soviets and the West are equally threatened by the Chinese.

Supporters of this view argue that the Soviets, in contrast to the Chinese, have abandoned the hope of dominating the world by promoting Communist revolutions everywhere; that they are tending to become a "satisfied" power whose main interest is the preservation of the status quo; that they are conscious of the risks of nuclear escalation of local conflicts and presumably would like to end the war in Vietnam while the Chinese favor its indefinite continuation; that they are concerned about preventing the proliferation of nuclear weapons and interested in reducing the burden of the arms race in order to afford a better standard of living for their own people.

If such analysts admit that a number of issues still remain in dispute between the Soviets and the West, and that negotiations with Moscow have not brought agreement on any specific issue since the partial atomic test ban was signed two years ago, the stalemate is explained by the persistence of hardened traditional attitudes which it is the task of diplomacy to overcome . . . by some concessions to Soviet demands, if necessary.

The trouble with this argument is not that it is all wrong. Much of it is quite true. But more significantly, it contains only part of the relevant truth. It is valid, broadly speaking, to say that Soviet objectives have become more limited and Soviet methods more cautious in recent years, and that both points distinguish Moscow's policy from Peking's.

But it is equally true that the remaining points of conflict between Russia and the United States involve areas more vital to American security than any conflicts that could arise in the near future between China and the United States. Moreover, the power Russia can wield in pursuit of her interests is incomparably greater than China's at least for a long time to come. Clearly, a realistic American foreign policy for dealing with the new triangular constellation in world affairs must take account of these basic differences.

To begin with the Soviets, it seems safe enough to assume that they no longer seriously hope to achieve world domination by world revolution. Experience has taught them that a Communist power can be a formidable rival and even a potential threat to their security, and that even a small Communist country like Castro's Cuba which depends on their subsidies and protection cannot be effectively controlled. Experience has also shown them that the risks of escalation involved in a policy of worldwide intervention may be prohibitive and the costs excessive—though we must not forget that this factor making for Soviet moderation depends on the West's maintaining the present relation between its power potential and that of the Soviet Union.

As a result, though the Soviets still oppose the West in every part of the world, they now seek to limit their risk in most regions by confining themselves to indirect intervention (of which the supply of arms remains the most dangerous form). It is only in Europe that their commitment to preserving the power sphere created by Stalin after World War II cannot be maintained without the permanent presence of Soviet troops, at least in the case of artificially divided Germany. This presence, while ostensibly serving the defense of the status quo, remains a major cause of international tension and conflict. For the status quo of European partition has the fatal flaw of being inherently unstable.

On one side, the presence of Soviet troops in the heart of Europe inevitably threatens the security of Western Europe, thus creating the need for an equally permanent presence of American troops. On the other, the present partition could not be accepted as final or legitimate by the West without leading to the demoralization of West Germany, the opening of Western Europe to Soviet influence and a consequent major shift in the balance of power in favor of the Communists.

The conflict between the Soviets and the United States is therefore now primarily a conflict about Europe, and it cannot be solved by stabilizing the status quo. The Soviet objective, in effect, is not simply United States acceptance of Moscow's predominance in Eastern Europe (including East Germany) but the disintegration of the Atlantic alliance and withdrawal of the American presence which protects Western Europe. The American objective, conversely, should not be the overthrow of Communist regimes as such, but withdrawal of those Soviet garrisons that make American protection necessary—a withdrawal that would, however, be bound to lead to the disappearance at least of the East German regime, however smooth the transition might be made by common consent.

Because the confrontation in Europe between the two leading nuclear powers is so direct, and because Western Europe is politically stable, the Soviets cannot pursue their aim by the same methods the Chinese use in Southeast Asia—by guerrilla-type military action. Instead, Moscow confines itself to threats and harassment, as during the Berlin crisis, and to diplomatic pressure against American "foreign bases," as in the disarmament negotiations.

But this does not alter the fact that the unsolved struggle for Europe remains a permanent cause of military tension, and a major cause of the arms race between Russia and America. Nor is this surprising—for the industrial, technological, and military resources of Western Europe are far greater than those of any other contested region in the world.

The conflict between the United States and Communist China is waged differently, for different prizes. The Chinese Communists evidently believe in world revolution, and they seek to promote it primarily by armed struggle. This does not mean that even Peking would welcome or actively seek a nuclear world war; it means that Peking is promoting "wars of liberation" in the underdeveloped regions of the world without restraint, regarding the risk of escalation as negligible.

The Chinese rightly consider that social and political instability in many underdeveloped countries offer a far better soil for armed revolution than conditions in advanced industrial countries. They hope the stability of developed nations—the United States in particular—will ultimately be undermined by the drain on their blood and treasure caused by endless guerrilla warfare in far-flung lands. In their own civil war, the Chinese Communists first gained control of the countryside before undertaking the final assault on the cities. Similarly, they now hope, by conquering first the underdeveloped "countryside of the world," to isolate and weaken the "world cities" of the West.

This obviously means that the Chinese attitude toward the United States is far less reconcilable than the Soviet attitude. Peking really wants war—war of its favorite type—not only the fruits of war. But it also means that for the time being, at least, Red China's limited technological resources limit its objectives. China's primary aim is to force the United States out of Southeast Asia and Taiwan; its secondary hopes depend on the repercussions of a United States retreat on Japan and India.

But for all their militant talk, the Chinese Communists have not so far tried to force their control on neighbors by open aggression across the frontier. (The Indian adventure served a more limited purpose.) But the success of guerrilla war depends primarily on the internal condition of the country under attack—as the contrast between developments in Vietnam and those in the Philippines and Malaya has shown. Hence, the conflict with China at the present stage seems to call for a major United States effort to strengthen the stability of the threatened countries, rather than for the multiplication of American military commitments—which the Chinese Communists themselves evidently count on.

What is at stake, at least in the present decade, is not American or Chinese control of a major part of the world's technological, industrial, and military potential. It is the future orientation of the peoples of Southeast Asia toward dependence on China and hostility to the West, or toward an independent development with Western help, with United States military protection in the background as the . . . [last resort].

Of course, the nature and gravity of the Chinese threat will change if and when Peking solves its problem of industrialization —if it acquires, not just a few atomic bombs, but the full military-industrial arsenal of a modern world power. If that happens (and the economic obstacles are still formidable), and if Peking's belligerent outlook has not changed in the meantime, Communist China will become a truly worldwide threat to the West instead of a regionally limited one. It will also become a physical threat to the Soviet Union, instead of a mere rival for regional and ideological influence. But that time is not yet.

If such are the nature and scope of our separate conflicts with the two Communist great powers, what is the scope for cooperation with one against the other?

In Europe, where the military proximity of the Russian colossus overshadows everyone's thinking, "development aid" for Chinese industrialization is sometimes recommended by certain Gaullist circles and by some right-wing politicians in West Germany. The stronger Peking becomes, they argue, the more Moscow will be forced to divert military strength toward its Eastern frontier and to relax its grip on Eastern and Central Europe.

This expectation may well prove true in the long run, but a strengthened China also would be in a better position to exert even more powerful pressure on her neighbors, thus increasing the immediate danger to important Western interests. For Western Europe to aid China while she is locked in an acute conflict with the United States would be the quickest way to destroy the Western alliance.

The idea that the United States and U.S.S.R. have a common interest in slowing down the growth of Chinese power seems to have more immediate applications. Moreover, the attractiveness of such cooperation to sections of American opinion is enhanced by the recognition of a more general common interest by the world's two leading powers in preventing the proliferation of nuclear weapons.

It is indeed true that joint interests exist despite the continued seriousness of the Soviet-American conflict; this fact was dramatized as recently as two years ago by the partial test ban agreement and the bitter Chinese attacks on it. Since the Chinese nuclear test explosions, however, the issues of nonproliferation and slowing down the growth of Chinese power have become entirely separate problems; the latter remains topical while the prospects

for preventing further nuclear proliferation following the Frenc\
and Chinese achievements appear increasingly poor.

There is one area where a common American and Soviet interest in opposing China is clearly apparent: fostering the growth
of India's economy and defensive strength. (As Russia's aid to
China has dwindled, its aid to India has assumed massive proportions and become a major issue in the Sino-Soviet conflict.) Of
course, parallel Western and Soviet aid to India is taking place
in a framework of competition for influence, not cooperation.
Still, the rivalry is limited by the fact that to Russia, the need
to make India a viable counterweight to Chinese expansion is
more important than the attempt to make her go Communist.
Similarly, to the West it is more important to keep India stable
than to make her join the Western system of alliances.

Such parallel interests help explain why, during the . . . fighting between India and Pakistan, the Chinese were issuing belligerent threats while the United States and Russia acted the role
of conciliators.

The chances of the United States and Russia extending such
a parallel policy to Southeast Asia are far more doubtful. One
major obstacle, of course, is the war in Vietnam. In Moscow's
view, the Communists are the only solid political force in Vietnam; hence the only hope of limiting Chinese influence in the
Indochinese peninsula lies in giving the local Communists a
chance to unify the country without prolonging the war, ending
their one-sided dependence on Chinese support. I must admit
that, in this case, the Soviet analysis seems to me more realistic
than the American commitment to the independence of South
Vietnam.

Yet beyond these specific obstacles to United States-Soviet cooperation, a more general problem arises. Does the emergence of
certain parallel interests mean that China has now become the
principal opponent of the United States? Would Washington be
justified in diverting its main attention and resources from Europe to Asia? Should America possibly offer to reward Russia in
Europe for cooperating with the United States in the Far East?

In the light of the present relative importance of the conflicts, my answer to all these questions is an emphatic No!

It is only in Europe—not Southeast Asia—that American world leadership could be lost, now and for a considerable time to come. The conflict with China is more bitterly acute and is at present partially responsible for the loss of American lives (I say partially because there is no evidence that China could have started the Vietnamese guerrilla war at will). But it is only the conflict with Russia that could lead to a major threat to American security in this decade, as it did three years ago during the missile crisis. "Asia first" one day may seem a correct assessment of United States concern in world affairs, but once again, that day is not yet.

In fact, it can be argued that the growth of Chinese power in Asia is of more immediate concern to Russian than to American security. The fewer the chances of an all-out United States military effort in the area, the more the Russians are likely to be forced to divert their resources eastward. Nor will we have to pay them with concessions for taking precautions against a danger of which they are fully aware.

As I suggested before, those European armchair strategists who would like to strengthen China so that Russia should be forced to withdraw from Central Europe may well be right in their long-term expectations, though not in their short-term prescriptions. The stronger China gets, the stronger the pull of Russia's Eastern frontier on her resources becomes, the less the Soviets will be able to afford their military commitment in the heart of Europe and the tension it creates between them and the West. Only when they become ready to recognize this will our major conflicts with the Soviets become capable of solution; only then can the main emphasis of our relations with the Kremlin be shifted toward cooperation.

Based on the foregoing analysis what should American foreign policy be in practice? First, it should recognize that since the present threat from China is not purely military but primarily revolutionary, the primary task is to strengthen the internal stability of China's neighbors. Even the military protection of such a constructive effort cannot be the exclusive task of the United States, but must largely depend on the major non-Communist powers of Asia, balancing the Chinese pressure with ultimate American backing. Instead of clinging to the shell of the SEATO alliance with weak and wavering governments, the United States should recognize that its interests—and the future of such governments—will be better served if they seek internal stability in neutrality, rather than struggle to keep a paper commitment to the West. At the same time, the United States should encourage Japan and India to play their natural geographic roles in containing Chinese expansion.

Second, the United States should continue its effort to maintain communication with the Soviets during acute international crises, such as the war in Vietnam, in order to keep the risk of escalation under control. At the same time, Washington's policy planners should think in terms of giving the Russians and the pro-Russian wing among the Hanoi leaders stronger arguments for entering negotiations to end the war. This may require the United States to stop the bombing of North Vietnam and to make an unambiguous declaration of its willingness to accept the Vietcong as a negotiating partner.

Third, the United States should stop its overanxious search for just any agreement with Moscow, no matter how meaningless. In particular, Washington should take a hard new look at the notion of stopping the spread of nuclear weapons by a United States-Soviet agreement.

Proliferation does not threaten from the Soviets, who are determined not to give the bomb to their allies. Nor can it be stopped by signing an agreement with the Soviets, since proliferation is proceeding independently as more and more countries set out to develop nuclear weapons.

It is therefore absurd for the Russians to demand concessions from the United States before signing such an agreement. They put a stiff price on a treaty, but cannot deliver the goods. We, on the other hand, have shelved plans for some kind of NATO nuclear force while talks continue with the Soviets over a ban on nuclear proliferation.

The order of priorities should be reversed: It is more urgent to restore some degree of cohesion inside NATO—with or without de Gaulle—than to exchange empty gestures with the Soviets....

The future may indeed hold bright opportunities, but if we lose hold of the present while pursuing the vision, the future may never materialize. That Soviet Russia will more and more become a European power, ready to cooperate with the West in the stabilization of world peace, is perhaps the best hope of mankind. But that happy day will arrive only when the Soviets no longer insist on holding down other European nations. For this policy is the root of the present conflict with the West, and it will be Moscow's choice, not ours, to end it.

BIBLIOGRAPHY

An asterisk (*) preceding a reference indicates that the article or a part of it has been reprinted in this book.

Books, Pamphlets, and Documents

Barnett, A. D. Communist China and Asia: challenge to American policy. Harper. New York. '60.

Barnett, A. D. Communist China in perspective. Praeger. New York. '62.

Barnett, A. D. ed. Communist strategies in Asia: a comparative analysis of governments and parties. Praeger. New York. '63.

Boyd, R. G. Communist China's foreign policy. Praeger. New York. '62.

Bromke, Adam, ed. Communist states at the crossroads; between Moscow and Peking. Praeger. New York. '65.

Brzezinski, Z. K. Soviet bloc: unity and conflict. Praeger. New York. '61.

Buchan, Alastair, ed. China and the peace of Asia. Praeger. New York. '65.

Chang, Hsin-hai. America and China; a new approach to Asia. Simon and Schuster. New York. '65.

Cheng, Chu-yuan. Economic relations between Peking and Moscow: 1949-63. Praeger. New York. '64.

Clubb, O. E. 20th century China. Columbia University Press. New York. '64.

Cohen, A. A. Communism of Mao Tse-tung. University of Chicago Press. Chicago. '64.

Conquest, Robert. Russia after Khrushchev. Praeger. New York. '65.

Cooley, J. K. East wind over Africa; Red China's African offensive. Walker. New York. '65.

Council on Foreign Relations. Moscow-Peking axis: strengths and strains, by H. L. Boorman and others. Harper. New York. '57.

Crankshaw, Edward. New cold war: Moscow v. Pekin. Penguin. Baltimore, Md. '63.

Doolin, D. J. Territorial claims in the Sino-Soviet conflict: documents & analysis. (Studies: 7) Stanford University. Hoover Institution on War, Revolution and Peace. Stanford, Calif. 94305. '65.

Fisher, M. W. and others. Himalayan battleground: Sino-Indian rivalry in Ladakh. Praeger. New York. '63.

*Floyd, David. Mao against Khrushchev: a short history of the Sino-Soviet conflict. Praeger. New York. '64.
    Reprinted in this book: Long live Leninism. p 270 *(originally published in* Red Flag. Ap. 16, '60).

*Foreign Policy Association. Great decisions 1963. The Association. 345 E. 46th St. New York 10017. '63.
    Reprinted in this book: Fact Sheet no 2. Red China and the U.S.S.R.—how firm an alliance? p 2-5.

*Foreign Policy Association. Great decisions 1965. The Association. 345 E. 46th St. New York 10017. '65.
    Reprinted in this book: Fact Sheet no 1. Red China—menace or paper tiger? p 6-9, 13-14.

*Foreign Policy Association. Great decisions 1966. The Association. 345 E. 46th St. New York 10017. '66.
    Reprinted in this book: Fact Sheet no 5. Russia after Khrushchev—does co-existence have a future? p 53-6.

Greene, Felix. China: the country Americans are not allowed to know. Ballantine. New York. '61.

Griffith, W. E. Albania and the Sino-Soviet rift. M.I.T. Press. Cambridge, Mass. '63.

Griffith, W. E. Communism in Europe; v. 1, continuity, change, and the Sino-Soviet dispute. M.I.T. Press. Cambridge, Mass. '64.

Griffith, W. E. Sino-Soviet rift. M.I.T. Press. Cambridge Mass. '64.

*Griffith, W. E. World communism divided. (Headline Series no 166) Foreign Policy Association. 345 E. 46th St. New York 10017. Ag. '64.
    Reprinted in this book: Current issues. p 6-9; Background. p 10-16; Point of no return. p 17-29; Impact on world communism. p 30-4. American policy. p 35-41; Excerpts from a report by M. A. Suslov on February 14, 1964. p 44-6.

Halperin, M. H. China and the bomb. Praeger. New York. '65.

Halpern, A. M., ed. Policies toward China: views from six continents. McGraw-Hill. New York. '65.

Honey, P. J. Communism in North Vietnam; its role in the Sino-Soviet dispute. M.I.T. Press. Cambridge, Mass. '63.

Hudson, G. F. and others, eds. Sino-Soviet dispute. Praeger. New York. '61.

Judy, Richard. Communist agriculture: crisis and change. (Headline Series no 162) Foreign Policy Association. 345 E. 46th St. New York 10017. N. '63.

Kennan, G. F. On dealing with the Communist world. Harper. New York. '64.

Klochko, M. A. Soviet scientist in Red China. Praeger. New York. '64.

Labedz, Leopold, ed. International communism after Khrushchev. M.I.T. Press. Cambridge, Mass. '65.

Laqueur, Walter and Labedz, Leopold, eds. Polycentrism: the new factor in international communism. Praeger. New York. '62.

London, Kurt, ed. Unity and contradiction: major aspects of Sino-Soviet relations. Praeger. New York. '62.

Lowenthal, Richard. World communism, the disintegration of a secular faith. Oxford. New York. '64.

MacFarquhar, Roderick, ed. Hundred flowers campaign, and the Chinese intellectuals. Praeger. New York. '60.

Mehnert, Klaus. Peking and Moscow. Putnam. New York. '63.

Mosely, P. E. Kremlin and world politics: studies in Soviet policy and action. Vintage. New York. '60.

Mosely, P. E. Soviet Union since Khrushchev. (Headline Series no 175) Foreign Policy Association. 345 E. 46th St. New York 10017. F. '66.

Patterson, G. N. Peking versus Delhi. Praeger. New York. '64.

Pentony, D. E. ed. Red world in tumult: Communist foreign policies. Chandler. San Francisco. '62.

Ronchey, Alberto. Two Red giants: an analysis of Sino-Soviet relations; tr. by Raymond Rosenthal. Norton. New York. '65.

Salisbury, H. E. Russia: an introduction to Russia, from czars to commissars, with emphasis on the factors that suggest the future. Atheneum. New York. '65.

Schwartz, Harry. China: an introduction to China, its role in the modern world and its importance for the future. Atheneum. New York. '65.

Schwartz, Harry. Soviet economy since Stalin. Lippincott. New York. '65.

Schwartz, Harry. Tsars, mandarins, and commissars; a history of Chinese-Russian relations. Lippincott. New York. '64.

Snow, Edgar. Other side of the river: Red China today. Random House. New York. '62.

Steele, A. T. The American people and China. McGraw-Hill. New York. '66.

Van der Post, Laurens. View of all the Russians. Morrow. New York. '64.

Whiting, A. S. Soviet policies in China, 1917-1924. Columbia University Press. New York. '54.

Zagoria, D. S. Sino-Soviet conflict, 1956-1961. Princeton University Press. Princeton, N.J. '62.

PERIODICALS

Academy of Political Science. Proceedings. 28:101-16. Ap. '65. Sino-Soviet conflict [with discussion]. W. A. Harriman.

Africa Report. 10:19-21. Ja. '65. Peking's strategic priorities. Colin Legum.

African Affairs. 64:91-102. Ap. '65. Communism and African independence. A. M. Crawley.

America. 104:689-90. F. 25, '61. When comrades clash; Khrushchev and Mao Tse-tung.

America. 106:850. Mr. 31, '62. Meaning of the Peking-Moscow feud. E. T. Folliard.

America. 111:651-2. N. 21, '64. Moscow-Peking unity.

America. 112:894. Je. 26, '65. Busy bees of Peiping.

*Annals of the American Academy of Political and Social Science. 349:1-162. S. '63. Communist China and the Soviet bloc; symposium, ed. by D. S. Zagoria.
  Reprinted in this book: Factors of unity and factors of conflict. Richard Lowenthal. p 106-16.

Annals of the American Academy of Political and Social Science. 351: 1-14. Ja. '64. Sino-Soviet conflict in perspective. R. A. Scalapino.

Annals of the American Academy of Political and Social Science. 351: 40-9. Ja. '64. Sino-Soviet balance sheet in the underdeveloped areas. C. P. Fitzgerald.

Asian Survey. 4:1123-34. N. '64. Communist China's Latin American policy. J. J. Lee.

Asian Survey. 5:321-32. Jl. '65. Sino-African relations: a survey. G. T. Yu.

Asian Survey. 5:408-16. Ag. '65. Racial issues and the Sino-Soviet dispute. Michael Freeberne.

Atlantic. 211:60-5. My. '63. Split between Russia and China. Edward Crankshaw.

*Atlantic. 215:69-75. Ap. '65. China goes it alone. Roderick MacFarquhar.

Atlantic. 215:76-83. Ap. '65. Kremlin's difficult choice; ideology vs. national interests. Richard Lowenthal.

Atlantic. 215:65-70. My. '65. Decline of communism in Latin America. Ernst Halperin.

*Atlantic. 215:71-5. My. '65. Containing communism East and West. W. E. Griffith.

Atlantic. 216:6+. N. '65. Atlantic report on the world today [American policy toward Communist China].

Atlas. 9:208-11. Ap. '65. China or Russia? Pablo Piacentini.

Atlas. 9:307-8. My. '65. U.S.S.R. and America: enemies in alliance. Heiner Gautschy.

Atlas. 10:13-16. Jl. '65. China's wedge in Africa. J. F. Chauvel.

Atlas. 10:161-2. S. '65. Peking and the world balance of power. C. G. Ströhm.

Atlas. 10:278-85. N. '65. China's confident propagandists.

Bulletin of the Atomic Scientists. 21:16-21. Ja. '65. Sino-Soviet nuclear dialogue: 1963. A. L. Hsieh.

Bulletin of the Atomic Scientists. 21:19-21. F. '65. Chinese bombshell. D. R. Inglis.

Bulletin of the Atomic Scientists. 21:21-4. F. '65. Political effects of the Chinese bomb. A. S. Lall.

Bulletin of the Atomic Scientists. 21:24-5. F. '65. Ten years of secrecy. Robert Guillain.

*Bulletin of the Atomic Scientists. 21:14-17. O. '65. Military aspects of the Sino-Soviet dispute. Malcolm Mackintosh.

Bulletin of the Atomic Scientists. 22:12-15. Ja. '66. Nuclear weapons development in China. L. A. Frank.

Business Week. p 24-5. Jl. 13, '63. Soviet-Chinese split looks permanent; red record: a forty year feud.

Business Week. p 28-9. Jl. 20, '63. Why Red China can defy Russia now.

Business Week. p 31. Ap. 11, '64. Toward two Red worlds? split in Communist camp.

China Quarterly. no 16:75-85. O.-D. '63. Mongolia in the Sino-Soviet dispute. R. A. Rupen.

Christian Science Monitor. p 1. Mr. 25, '66. Red split gets wider. D. K. Willis.

Commentary. 31:379-94. My. '61. Sino-Soviet dispute. Richard Lowenthal.

Commentary. 39:62-6. Mr. '65. China, Russia & the experts. George Lichtheim.

Commentary. 39:56-9. My. '65. Vietnam and China. George Lichtheim.

*Commentary. 40:61-6. N. '65. China's strategy—a critique. D. S. Zagoria.

Commonweal. 75:480. F. 2, '62. Cracks in the monolith.

Commonweal. 77:654. Mr. 22, '63. Battle of the giants. James O'Gara.

Commonweal. 79:91-4. O. 18, '63. Peculiar partnership. H. C. Hinton.

Commonweal. 81:684. F. 26, '65. Communist division.

Commonweal. 81:759-61. Mr. 12, '65. Mao vs. Moscow. Seymour Slessinger.

Commonweal. 82:70. Ap. 9, '65. Enemies fall out; Russian-Chinese split. James O'Gara.

Contemporary Review. 205:571-6. N. '64. Latin America: the Chinese drive. Daniel Tretiak.

Contemporary Review. 207:8-11. Jl. '65. Fundamentals of China's foreign policy. E. H. Rawlings.

Current History. 41:129-70. S. '61. Communist China: new world power; symposium.

Current History. 43:136-41+. S. '62. Red China's aims in south Asia. B. B. Fall.

Current History. 43:218-23+. O. '62. Russia and the uncommitted nations. A. Z. Rubinstein.

Current History. 45:129-35. S. '63. Sino-Soviet dialogue. Milton Kovner.

Current History. 45:223-9. O. '63. Sino-Soviet tensions; excerpts from Sino-Soviet relations: retrospect and prospect. P. S. H. Tang.

Current History. 47:129-35+. S. '64. Sino-Soviet dispute: communism at the crossroads. Milton Kovner.

Current History. 49:129-75. S. '65. Communist China, 1965; symposium.

Current History. 49:193-234+. O. '65. U.S.S.R.: the new regime; symposium.

Department of State Bulletin. 52:449-53. Mr. 29, '65. Communist China as a problem in U.S. policymaking; address. Marshall Green.

*East Europe. 14:2-14. Ag. '65. Yugoslavia: has Tito gone bourgeois? R. V. Burks.

Economist. 208:343-4. Jl. 27, '63. Clashing shades of red.

Economist. 211:115-16. Ap. 11, '64. Great rift; the divide between Moscow and Peking now yawns wide as well as deep.

Economist. 214:415-16. Ja. 30, '65. Russia and China; warning shots.

Economist. 215:1369-70. Je. 19, '65. Moscow's fateful choice.

Economist. 217:130-1. O. 9, '65. Chinese poker.

Economist. 217:360-1. O. 23, '65. Seeing China straight.

Encounter. 21:3-10. O. '63. World scene transformed. Richard Lowenthal.

Encounter. 24:3-18. Ja., 16-26. F. '65. Has the Revolution a future? Richard Lowenthal.

Encounter 24:49-53. F. '65. Soviet dream of Africa. L. B. Schapiro.

Far Eastern Economic Review. 47:330+. F. 25, '65. Accent on under-development: Peking's policies towards the newly-emerging forces. Peter Van Ness.

Foreign Affairs. 37:561-72. Jl. '59. Mao, Marx, and Moscow. G. F. Hudson.

Foreign Affairs. 39:430-43. Ap. '61. Challenge of change in the Soviet bloc. Z. K. Brzezinski.

Foreign Affairs. 40:360-73. Ap. '62. End of the monolith. W. Z. Laqueur.

Foreign Affairs. 41:152-70. O. '62. Communist ideology and Soviet for-eign policy. B. D. Wolfe.

Foreign Affairs. 41:171-90. O. '62. Sino-Soviet conflict and the West. D. S. Zagoria.

Foreign Affairs. 41:323-43. Ja. '63. Moscow, Peking and the Communist parties of Asia. R. A. Scalapino.

Foreign Affairs. 41:513-25. Ap. '63. Threat and opportunity in the Communist schism. Z. K. Brzezinski.

Foreign Affairs. 42:11-24. O. '63. Chinese-Soviet rift: origins and por-tents. P. E. Mosely.

Foreign Affairs. 42:171-83. Ja. '64. Polycentrism and Western policy. George Kennan.

*Foreign Affairs. 42:640-54. Jl. '64. Sino-Soviet competition in Africa. R. A. Scalapino.

Foreign Affairs. 43:217-36. Ja. '65. Communist China's capacity to make war. S. B. Griffith, II.

Foreign Affairs. 43:616-25. Jl. '65. China's bomb: exploitation and re-actions. R. L. Powell.

Harper's Magazine. 220:52-8. Ja. '60. Many faces of communism. Arthur Schlesinger, Jr.

Institute for the Study of the U.S.S.R. Bulletin. 11:21-5. My. '64. Mos-cow-Peking cold war flares up. Nikolai Galay.

Institute for the Study of the U.S.S.R. Bulletin. 11:21-33. Ag. '64. Afro-Asian solidarity and the Sino-Soviet dispute. G. A. von Stackelberg.

Institute for the Study of the U.S.S.R. Bulletin. 12:27-34. S. '65. Sino-Soviet quarrel: a balance sheet since Khrushchev. J. S. Prybyla.

International Affairs. 40:647-58. O. '64. Sino-Soviet dispute—its eco-nomic impact on China. Jean Polaris.

International Affairs. 41:204-22. Ap. '65. Sino-Soviet dispute—dogma and dialectics on disarmament. W. C. Clemens, Jr.

International Conciliation. 533:389-454. My. '61. Communist China in the world community. H. A. Steiner.

Look. 27:49-50. N. 19, '63. How can we profit from the Chinese-Soviet break? Victor Zorza.

Look. 29:81-3. My. 18, '65. How Russia has changed and what it means to us. J. P. Davies, Jr.

Look. 29:29-46. N. 2, '65. Red China. G. Zimmerman.

Modern Age. 9:343-53. Fall '65. Ideological diversities and crises within the Communist area. P. E. Mosely.

Nation. 194:332-3+. Ap. 14, '62. Moscow vs. Peking: reasons for the rift. Alexandre Metaxas.

Nation. 197:43-6. Jl. 27, '63. Recriminations in Moscow: Sino-Soviet loggerheads. Alexander Werth.

Nation. 199:294. N. 2, '64. New Russo-Chinese equation. Frederick Kuh.

*Nation. 201:3-4. Jl. 5, '65. Russia vs. China; clash over Vietnam. Isaac Deutscher.

Nation. 201:180-4. O. 4, '65. Image and reality: China from within. Charles Taylor.

Nation. 201:437-9+. D. 6, '65. Management, distribution, planning: new Russian revolution. Margaret Miller.

National Review. 14:16. Ja. 15, '63. Sino-Soviet sense and nonsense. James Burnham.

National Review. 14:447-9. Je. 4, '63. What about the Sino-Soviet split? Jules Monnerot.
  Discussion. 14:541. Jl. 2, '63.

National Review. 16:230. Mr. 24, '64. How blows the East wind? James Burnham.

National Review. 17:274. Ap. 6, '65. Dialectic of the split. James Burnham.

National Review. 17:1076-8. N. 30, '65. Principles and heresies; a crystallization of ten years. F. S. Meyer.

New Republic. 145:13-17. D. 18, '61. Communist disunity and the West. Z. K. Brzezinski.

New Republic. 146:13-16. Mr. 26, '62. Policy of peaceful engagement; how we can profit from Communist disunity. Z. K. Brzezinski.

New Republic. 147:14. N. 10, '62. Bear and the dragon. G. W. Johnson.

New Republic. 149:8. O. 12, '63. Two touchy borders; Sinkiang and Manchuria.

New Republic. 150:16-18. Je. 13, '64. Report from Russia. Philip Ben.

New Republic. 152:13-15. F. 13, '65. Russia's stake in Vietnam. Roger Morris.

New Republic. 152:12-13. My. 1, '65. Russia, the US and Vietnam. H. J. Morgenthau.
    Discussion. 152:34-5. My. 15, '65.

New Republic. 153:7-8. S. 18, '65. "People's wars."

New Republic. 153:9-10. O. 2, '65. China's presence at the UN. Philip Ben.

New Statesman. 67:509. Ap. 3, '64. Risks of Sino-Soviet conflict.

New York Times. p 2. My. 2, '64. Marxist disunity. Max Frankel.

New York Times. p E3. My. 10, '64. China challenges Russia's right to a role in Asia. Seymour Topping.

New York Times. p E3. My. 10, '64. Moscow and Peking on key foreign policy disputes.

*New York Times. p 9. N. 7, '64. Excerpts from Peking denunciation.

New York Times. p E3. F. 14, '65. China and the U.S.—a continuing struggle for Asia. Max Frankel.

*New York Times. p E5. Mr. 14, '65. Communist split: as both sides see it. Harry Schwartz.

*New York Times. p 2. S. 4, '65. Excerpts from Peking declaration urging 'people's war' to destroy U.S.

New York Times. p E3. O. 31, '65. China bids for West's trade. Seymour Topping.

New York Times. p E3. N. 7, '65. Moscow takes firmer line toward Peking. Peter Grose.

New York Times. p 1+. F. 6, '66. New phase of China-Soviet rift centers on U.S. encirclement. Seymour Topping.

New York Times. p 1+. Mr. 24, '66. Red bloc moving closer to break. Peter Grose.

New York Times. p 17. Mr. 24, '66. Moscow-Peking dispute: a decade of bitterness. Harry Schwartz.

New York Times Magazine. p 11-13+. Je. 12, '60. Haunting enigma of Red China. H. E. Salisbury.

New York Times Magazine. p 9+. F. 25, '62. Cracks in the Communist monolith. Richard Lowenthal.

New York Times Magazine. p 9+. Ap. 1, '62. Duel of communism's big two. Richard Hughes.

New York Times Magazine. p 25+. My. 26, '63. Cold war of the communisms. Edward Crankshaw.

New York Times Magazine. p 5+. Jl. 21, '63. Two dogmas shake the Communist world; Mao's challenge to the supremacy of Moscow. Edward Crankshaw.

New York Times Magazine. p 10+. F. 2, '64. Mao, at seventy, tries a big leap in the world. Richard Hughes.

New York Times Magazine. p 17+. Je. 7, '64. Mao: nationalist first, Communist second. Richard Hughes.

New York Times Magazine. p 5-7+. Ag. 2, '64. China: what we know and don't know. Max Frankel.

New York Times Magazine. p 40-1+. O. 18, '64. Communist China is a paper dragon. D. S. Zagoria.

New York Times Magazine. p 8-9+. Jl. 11, '65. It doesn't matter who succeeds Mao. Jacques Marcuse.

New York Times Magazine. p 46-7+. O. 24, '65. To Mao we are the prime enemy. Mark Gayn.

*New York Times Magazine. p 34-5+. N. 21, '65. Can we make common cause with Russia? Richard Lowenthal.

New York Times Magazine. p 10-11+. D. 19, '65. Muffled voice of Russian liberalism. Deming Brown.

New York Times Magazine. p 12-13+. Ja. 16, '66. Southeast Asia isn't scared of the Chinese dragon. Seymour Topping.

New York Times Magazine. p 28-9+. Mr. 13, '66. China (is, is not) an aggressive power [debate]. F. N. Trager and H. J. Morgenthau.

New Yorker. 41:41-2+. F. 12, '66. China watchers. Robert Shaplen.

Newsweek. 58:35-6. Jl. 17, '61. Moscow and Peking: how deep the rift?

Newsweek. 59:32-4+. Mr. 26, '62. Moscow and Peking: how wide the split?

Newsweek. 60:52+. O. 15, '62. Big schism.

Newsweek. 61:51-2+. Je. 24, '63. Communism's great debate; Sino-Soviet quarrel.

Newsweek. 63:43-4. F. 17, '64. China: the East wind gains force.

Newsweek. 65:30+. Mr. 22, '65. Deepening split.

Newsweek. 66:45. S. 13, '65. On the line; Sino-Soviet border. R. J. Korengold.

Newsweek. 66:29. N. 8, '65. Light at the end of the tunnel: Red China's expansion failures. Walter Lippmann.

Orbis. 8:790-815. Winter '65. Sino-Soviet schism. D. S. Carlisle.

*Orbis. 9:426-36. Summer '65. Sino-Soviet dispute and Vietnam. T. S. An.

Pacific Affairs. 37:426-35. Winter '64-'65. Communist party of Canada and the Sino-Soviet dispute. Ivan Avakumovic.

Political Quarterly. 35:241-350. Jl. '64. Special number on Communist China.

Political Quarterly. 36:92-104. Ja. '65. Policy of Russia towards Sino-Indian conflict. Hemen Ray.

*Problems of Communism. 13:1-107. Mr.-Ap. '64. Special issue: International communism and the Sino-Soviet conflict.

> Reprinted in this book:
> Article from Chinese publications *Jen-min Jih-pao* and *Hung Ch'i.* p 15.
> World in disarray. Wolfgang Leonhard. p 16-26.
> Rivalry in underdeveloped areas. Herbert Dinerstein. p 64-72.
> Letter sent by the Communist party of China to the Communist party of the Soviet Union, June 14, 1963. p 68 (*originally published in* Peking Review. Je. 21, '63).
> Open letter by the Communist party of the Soviet Union. p 68 (*originally published in* Pravda. Jl. 14, '63).
> Polemics seen by a non-polemicist. Benjamin Schwartz. p 102-6.

Problems of Communism. 14:22-31. Ja.-F. '65. Moscow and the third world. Uri Ra'anan.

Problems of Communism. 14:1-13. Jl.-Ag. '65. Maoism at home and abroad. Tang Tsou and M. H. Halperin.

Reader's Digest. 83:129-30. O. '63. How Red China shook the Kremlin. Joseph Alsop.

Reporter. 25:29-30. N. 23, '61. Pawn on the Adriatic. I. R. Levine.

Reporter. 26:23-5. Ja. 18, '62. Red rivalry in the black continent. Gordon Brook-Shepherd.

Reporter. 28:38-40. Ap. 25, '63. Widening gulf between Mao and Khrushchev. D. S. Zagoria.

Reporter. 29:32-4+. Ag. 15, '63. Sino-Soviet rift: an old, old story. J. P. Davies, Jr.

Reporter. 30:36-9. Je. 18, '64. Sinkiang: Soviet rustlers in China's Wild West. Stanley Karnow.

Reporter. 32:16-20. Ja. 14, '65. China fans the fires. Denis Warner.

Reporter. 33:22-3. Jl. 1, '65. Kremlin dilemma over Vietnam. Marvin Kalb.

Reporter. 33:24. S. 23, '65. China's new leap forward. Max Ascoli.

Reporter. 33:25-7. S. 23, '65. Peking-Djakarta axis. Denis Warner.

Russian Review. 23:215-22. Jl. '64. Quarrel of the Communist giants. W. H. Chamberlin.

Russian Review. 23:341-51. O. '64. Challenge to the Soviets in Asia and Africa. G. C. Guins.

Saturday Evening Post. 236:30+. Ap. 13, '63. Russian-Chinese struggle over who will bury us? [with editorial comment]. Max Frankel.

> *Same abridged with title:* Bitter feud that splits the Communist world. Reader's Digest. 83:138-44. Ag. '63.

Saturday Evening Post. 238:10+. Jl. 17, '65. Speaking out; we must woo Red China. A. J. Toynbee.

Saturday Review. 45:29-30. Je. 2, '62. Parting the veils over Red rifts. R. A. Burton.

Saturday Review. 46:38-9+. N. 23, '63. When a dragon and a bear disagree. P. E. Mosely.

Saturday Review. 47:6+. Ag. 1, '64. Communist schism. Henry Brandon.

Senior Scholastic. 80:18-20. Mr. 14, '62. Many shades of communism.

Senior Scholastic. 81:8-13. N. 14, '62. Behind the Sino-Soviet ideological conflict.

Senior Scholastic. 83:20-2+. S. 13, '63. Behind the big Red rift.

Senior Scholastic. 86:6-9. F. 11, '65. New scramble for Africa; Soviets and Red Chinese race for influence.

Slavic Review. 23:688-700. D. '64. Russia's special position in China during the early Ch'ing period. I. C. Y. Hsü.

*Soviet Documents. 2:10-17. Je. 1, '64. What the Chinese leaders are foisting upon the Communist movement in the guise of Marxism-Leninism.

Time. 81:25. Ja. 18, '63. Reading the Reds; plain words in Mao Tse-tung's *Red Flag* and *People's Daily* and retort in Khrushchev's *Pravda.*

Time. 83:31-2. Ap. 10, '64. Goulash, Mr. Mao? revolution, Mr. K.

Time. 84:40-1. S. 18, '64. Search for lebensraum? struggle between Russia and Red China.

Time. 84:44-6. N. 13, '64. Era of many Romes.

Time. 85:23-6+. F. 12, '65. Borrowing from the capitalists; economic change in Communist bloc.
     Same abridged with title: Russia tests the profits system. Reader's Digest. 86:107-11. My. '65.

Time. 86:26-7. Ag. 6, '65. Communism today: a refresher course; Time essay.

U.S. News & World Report. 52:43-6. Ja. 22, '62. Big split among Reds; its meaning; with analysis. F. B. Stevens.

U.S. News & World Report. 53:37-40. D. 31, '62. Why Russia is so worried about Red China.

U.S. News & World Report. 54:44-7. Mr. 18, '63. Russia-China split: how real?

U.S. News & World Report. 57:59. N. 23, '64. Russia, China, the U.S. today. F. B. Stevens.

U.S. News & World Report. 59:44-7. D. 6, '65. Where danger grows on a 4,500-mile border. R. P. Martin.

U.S. News & World Report. 60:34-7. Ja. 3, '66. Communism—facing a clouded future.

U.S. News & World Report. 60:60-5. Mr. 28, '66. Latest from inside Russia.

U.S. News & World Report. 60:29-31. Ap. 4, '66. How dangerous is Red China? the emerging answers.

Virginia Quarterly Review. 41:18-39. Winter '65. Polycentrism and the appeal of communism. George Urban.

Virginia Quarterly Review. 41:510-24. Autumn '65. Unsettled issues in the Sino-Soviet dispute. J. S. Prybyla.

Vital Speeches of the Day. 30:516-20. Je. 15, '64. Split between Peiping and Moscow; address, May 6, 1964. T. F. Tsiang.

Vital Speeches of the Day. 30:591-4. Jl. 15, '64. Crisis in Soviet-Chinese relations; address, June 14, 1964. C. B. Luce.

Vital Speeches of the Day. 31:527-34. Je. 15, '65. United States and Red China; address, April 29, 1965. R. L. Walker.

*Wall Street Journal. p 1+. O. 29, '65. Peking loses face: The U.S. could benefit as Red China suffers setbacks around the globe. Robert Keatley.

World Today. 20:457-61. N. '64. China and Africa. David Morison.

World Today. 20:509-16. D. '64. Changes in the Communist world. J. T. Degras.

Yale Review. 54:550-66. Je. '65. Peking's strategy in Indochina. King Chen.